Copyright *and* Cultural Institutions

Copyright *and* Cultural Institutions

Guidelines for Digitization for U.S. Libraries, Archives, and Museums

PETER B. HIRTLE,
EMILY HUDSON,
& ANDREW T. KENYON

CORNELL UNIVERSITY LIBRARY
ITHACA, NEW YORK

Published by
Cornell University Library
Ithaca, New York 14853

ISBN-13: 978-0-935995-10-7

Design and composition by India Amos

CONTENTS

Contents

Contents

PREFACE

THIS MANUAL IS based on *Copyright and Cultural Institutions: Guidelines for Digitisation* by Emily Hudson and Andrew T. Kenyon. The *Guidelines for Digitisation* were one of the products of a research project conducted by the Centre for Media and Communications Law and the Intellectual Property Research Institute of the Australia, both located at the University of Melbourne. The project examined the impact of copyright law on the digitization practices of public museums, galleries, libraries, and archives in Australia. The Australian *Guidelines for Digitisation* are available at http://ssrn.com/abstract=881699; updated Australian guidelines are due for release in 2010 and will be available via http://www.law.unimelb.edu.au/cmcl.

While reading the guidelines, Peter Hirtle realized that a similar document, drawing on American law and practice, would be of great benefit to administrators and curators in American cultural institutions, including libraries, archives, and museums. Digitization continues to be of great importance and interest to the cultural institution sector as a means of facilitating the public interest missions of access, research, preservation, and education. Yet there is also great uncertainty associated with the copyright implications of digitization initiatives.

One reason for institutional concern about copyright is the difficulty in *understanding and interpreting* the law: identifying the relevant legal principles; analyzing the relevant provisions of copyright legislation; and coming to grips with case law, little of which specifically addresses issues surrounding digitization by nonprofit institutions. Drafting and implementing copyright procedures often reveals the uncertainties in the law and demonstrates how difficult it can be to apply abstract legal principles to specific circumstances.

Another reason for institutional concern is the practical difficulty of *complying* with the law: the administrative costs associated with locating and contacting copyright owners; the frequent long delays in seeking permission; the cost of licenses; and, particularly for smaller institutions, the lack of specialist lawyers or copyright officers to assist in complying with copyright law.

Hudson and Kenyon's *Guidelines* were developed to inform Australian cultural institutions and assist them with the legal and practical aspects of copyright compliance. With their permission and assistance, Hirtle has prepared this manual to assist American cultural institutions in the same way. The manual is intended to provide some basic information on copyright law and offer a structure for considering copyright issues in digitization projects. Beginning with the question of when an item is protected by copyright, it moves on to explore strategies for dealing with copyright issues, including licensing and the legal exemptions that may allow digitization *without* obtaining permission. Two case studies are presented at the end of the manual that apply the preceding analysis to (1) interviews and oral histories and (2) student dissertations, theses, and papers. These were selected because they embody many of the principles and problems identified in the earlier chapters and are topics on which Hirtle frequently is questioned.

Note that this manual is for informational use only and does not constitute nor should be construed as legal opinion or advice. Furthermore, the law is in a constant state of evolution. Every effort has been made to ensure that the information presented is accurate, but the law is subject to change after publication. Cultural institutions should obtain the advice of a lawyer in relation to any specific questions regarding their copyright policies and practices.

A NOTE ON COPYRIGHT OWNERSHIP OF THIS MANUAL

The intricacies of copyright ownership are discussed in some detail in Chapter 2. This manual serves as a good example of some of the principles discussed in that chapter.

Copyright in the original *Guidelines for Digitisation* belongs jointly to Emily Hudson and Andrew Kenyon: it is a joint work. Hudson and Kenyon published the guidelines with a Creative Commons Attribution-NonCommercial-NoDerivatives 2.1 Australian Licence (see Chapter 7 for a discussion of Creative Commons licenses). Under this license, users are allowed to make noncommercial use of the original *Guidelines* so long as no changes are made to the work ("no derivatives") and Hudson and Kenyon receive credit as the authors ("attribution").

This manual is derived from Hudson and Kenyon's work, and so their permission was needed for its preparation. It is a joint work coauthored by Hirtle, Hudson, and Kenyon, and so each owns a share of its copyright. This manual is also licensed under a Creative Commons license: the Creative Commons Attribution-Noncommercial-No Derivatives Works 3.0 United States License. In addition, Hudson and Kenyon have granted Hirtle a nonexclusive license to use the original Guidelines in any subsequent noncommercial editions or works that are derived from this manual.

Many of the images used throughout the manual are in the public domain, and are so indicated. Others are used under the terms of a Creative Commons license. Still others are from ARTstor, and are used under its "Images for Academic Publishing" program http://www.artstor.org/what-is-artstor/w-html/services-publishing.shtml. A few are used under an assertion of fair use. Copyright and licensing information is provided with each image.

This manual is licensed under the Creative Commons Attribution-Noncommercial-No Derivative Works 3.0 United States License. To view a copy of this license, visit http://creativecommons.org/licenses/by-nc-nd/3.0/us/ or send a letter to Creative Commons, 171 Second Street, Suite 300, San Francisco, California, 94105, USA.

Bound copies of the guidelines are available for purchase through Amazon.com.

The law discussed in this manual is current to May 2009.

PETER HIRTLE
Ithaca, N.Y., U.S.A.

EMILY HUDSON AND ANDREW KENYON
Melbourne, Australia

1 *Introduction*

THE DEVELOPMENT OF new digital technologies has led to fundamental changes in the ways that copyright works are created, accessed, and distributed.

These developments have enhanced the ability of libraries, archives, museums, historical societies, and other cultural institutions to fulfill their public interest missions of access, preservation, research, and education. For instance, many institutions are developing publicly accessible Web sites in which users can visit online exhibitions, search collection databases, access images of collection items, and—in some cases—create their own digital content. Many internal activities are also facilitated by digital technologies, including collection management, preservation activities, exhibition planning, and record keeping for incoming and outgoing loans.

The increased use of digital technologies also raises many logistical issues, including those related to copyright. Institutions are aware that digitization raises the possibility of copyright infringement and are implementing systems to facilitate copyright compliance, such as centralized copyright management offices; copyright instruction programs to ensure that staff knowledge of copyright is current; and the use of new licensing models, including requesting broader rather than purpose-specific licenses and investigating new open licensing models.

These guidelines are intended to assist understanding and compliance with copyright law. They aim to assist staff and volunteers of cultural institutions determine the following:

▶ Whether an item is protected by copyright
▶ Whether that copyright is current and who owns the copyright
▶ What—if any—permission is required in order to digitize the item

The guidelines are broken down into the following chapters:

▶ Chapter 2: Copyright Fundamentals (including the types of works protected by copyright and the requirements for copyright protection)
▶ Chapter 3: Duration and Ownership of Copyright
▶ Chapter 4: Exclusive Rights and Infringement (that is, the acts that only

the owner of copyright may perform, and the circumstances in which a third party will infringe those rights)
- ▶ Chapter 5: Fair Use and Other Exemptions
- ▶ Chapter 6: The Libraries and Archives Exemptions
- ▶ Chapter 7: Copyright Permissions and Licenses
- ▶ Chapter 8: Locating Copyright Owners
- ▶ Chapter 9: Other Types of Intellectual Property, Contracts, and Jurisdictional Issues
- ▶ Chapter 10: Risk Management: How to Digitize Safely
- ▶ Case studies on the digitization of oral histories and dissertations and theses

In the United States, copyright is governed by the Copyright Act of 1976 as amended and incorporated in the United States Code as Title 17. The Copyright Act is a lengthy and complex piece of legislation, and it can be difficult to know where to start in determining whether a collection item is protected by copyright and, if so, whether digitization will infringe that copyright.

In order to help readers navigate through these guidelines—and, indeed, the Copyright Act—we have produced a flowchart that sets out a series of questions that will help identify whether digitization raises a copyright issue (see Flowchart 1). Sometimes, these questions will be difficult to answer, so we have included references to chapters in which each question is discussed in detail.

This chapter also includes a brief overview of copyright law.

1.1 What is copyright?

The basis for copyright in the United States is found in Article I, Section 8 of the U.S. Constitution, which authorizes Congress to enact laws "To promote the Progress of Science and useful Arts, by securing for limited Times to Authors and Inventors the exclusive Right to their respective Writings and Discoveries." (The phrase "Science and useful Arts" should be read broadly; to the authors of the Constitution, "science" meant all learning and "useful arts" included all the inventions and practical devices now protected by patents.) The underlying purpose of copyright in the United States is therefore to encourage progress and the development of knowledge.

◆ **FLOWCHART 1**
◆

Overview of copyright issues for digitization projects.

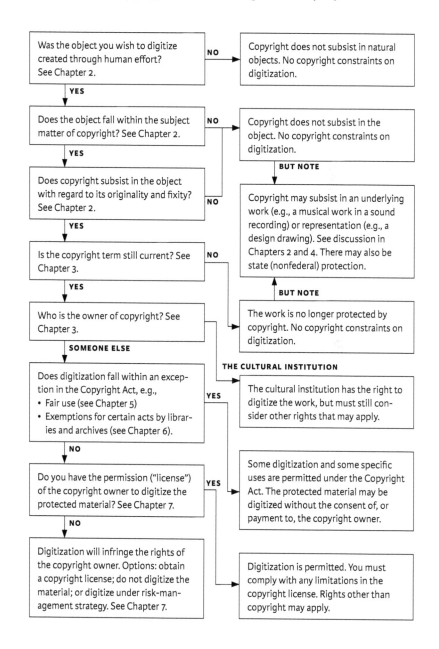

Was the object you wish to digitize created through human effort? See Chapter 2.	**NO** → Copyright does not subsist in natural objects. No copyright constraints on digitization.

YES ↓

Does the object fall within the subject matter of copyright? See Chapter 2.	**NO** → Copyright does not subsist in the object. No copyright constraints on digitization.

YES ↓

BUT NOTE ↓

Does copyright subsist in the object with regard to its originality and fixity? See Chapter 2.	**NO** → Copyright may subsist in an underlying work (e.g., a musical work in a sound recording) or representation (e.g., a design drawing). See discussion in Chapters 2 and 4. There may also be state (nonfederal) protection.

YES ↓

Is the copyright term still current? See Chapter 3.	**NO** →

BUT NOTE ↓

Who is the owner of copyright? See Chapter 3.	The work is no longer protected by copyright. No copyright constraints on digitization.

SOMEONE ELSE ↓

THE CULTURAL INSTITUTION

Does digitization fall within an exception in the Copyright Act, e.g., • Fair use (see Chapter 5) • Exemptions for certain acts by libraries and archives (see Chapter 6).	**YES** → The cultural institution has the right to digitize the work, but must still consider other rights that may apply.

NO ↓

Do you have the permission ("license") of the copyright owner to digitize the protected material? See Chapter 7.	**YES** → Some digitization and some specific uses are permitted under the Copyright Act. The protected material may be digitized without the consent of, or payment to, the copyright owner.

NO ↓

Digitization will infringe the rights of the copyright owner. Options: obtain a copyright license; do not digitize the material; or digitize under risk-management strategy. See Chapter 7.	Digitization is permitted. You must comply with any limitations in the copyright license. Rights other than copyright may apply.

The Founders chose to advance knowledge by striking a deal with creators (i.e., "Authors"). To encourage the creation and distribution of new works, copyright law grants to creators a set of exclusive rights for a limited period of time, after which the work becomes free for everyone to use (i.e., it enters the "public domain"). By enabling them to benefit economically from their creations, copyright provides authors with an incentive to create, publish, and disseminate creative and original works. As the Supreme Court has explained:

> The economic philosophy behind the clause empowering Congress to grant patents and copyrights is the conviction that encouragement of individual effort by personal gain is the best way to advance the public welfare through the talents of authors and inventors in "Science and useful Arts."[1]

Put another way, "the monopoly created by copyright thus rewards the individual author in order to benefit the public."[2]

Thus, although private interests are essential to the operation of the copyright system, public interests (and not private profits) remain at the heart of copyright. As the Supreme Court has noted:

> The limited scope of the copyright holder's statutory monopoly, like the limited copyright duration required by the Constitution, reflects a balance of competing claims upon the public interest: creative work is to be encouraged and rewarded, but private motivation must ultimately serve the cause of promoting broad public availability of literature, music, and the other arts. The immediate effect of our copyright law is to secure a fair return for an "author's" creative labor. But the ultimate aim is, by this incentive, to stimulate artistic creativity for the general public good. "The sole interest of the United States and the primary object in conferring the monopoly," this Court has said, "lie in the general benefits derived by the public from the labors of authors."[3]

Copyright law therefore creates a legal framework for the use and management of a broad range of creative and intellectual works found in cultural institutions, including books, manuscripts, plays, computer programs, works of art, maps, architectural plans, musical scores, sound recordings, and films.

It does this by granting the owner of copyright in 17 U.S.C. § 106 the exclusive right to perform certain acts in relation to the protected work, including the right:

▶ to "reproduce the copyrighted work in copies or phonorecords" (which includes digitizing the work)
▶ to "distribute copies or phonorecords of the copyrighted work to the public by sale or other transfer of ownership, or by rental, lease, or lending" (which includes making a copy of the work available online)
▶ for literary, musical, dramatic, and choreographic works, pantomimes, and pictorial, graphic, and sculptural works, to "display the copyrighted work publicly" (which includes displaying the work on a computer screen)

Rights in copyright are separate from ownership of the underlying physical work. For instance, the purchaser of a book or CD does not become the owner of the copyright in his or her purchase. Instead, copyright is retained by one or more of the composer, music publisher, performer, and record company that produces and distributes the recording.

Copyright is relevant to cultural institutions because they commonly do not own copyright in collection items. Cultural institutions must therefore

Image: Bristol Museum and Art Gallery, Bristol, England

Photographer: Adrian Pingstone

License: Public domain, through gift of author

Source: http://commons. wikimedia.org/wiki/ File:Bristol_art.gallery. interior.arp.jpg

consider copyright law when they are digitizing works or putting digital content on the Internet.

■ **QUESTION**

Are there other rationales for copyright law?

In the United States, the primary justification for copyright is utilitarian: copyright law provides the incentives that some creators are thought to need in order to produce and distribute works. Without these incentives, many authors and creators would keep their works to themselves. By limiting the ways in which users can deal with copyrighted works, copyright law is thought to benefit not only creators but also society generally, through facilitating access to these works.

In many other countries, however, there are primarily noneconomic justifications for copyright law. For instance, many people argue that creators have a "natural right" to enjoy and profit from the "fruits of their labor," including preventing others from "reaping where they have not sowed." Copyright is also supported by moral rights arguments: that because copyrighted works represent the personality of the creator, the creator therefore should be able to control uses by other people.

The different justifications for copyright present real challenges to ongoing efforts to harmonize international copyright laws. They can also create problems for cultural institutions when dealing with works created by authors from outside the United States who may have a very different conception of the extent of their copyright rights.

1.2 The framework of copyright law

There are certain requirements that must be met in order for a work to be protected by copyright:

▶ The work or subject matter must fall within a category of material protected by the Copyright Act (see Chapter 2)
▶ Copyright must subsist in that particular work or subject matter, having regard to its originality, authorship, and fixity (see Chapter 2)
▶ Copyright must not have expired (see Chapter 3)

QUESTION

Do I need to register copyright?

No. Since 1 March 1989 there is no requirement in U.S. law to register copyright with the Copyright Office. Nor is it necessary to include the copyright notice on a work (© Author Name 2009) to obtain copyright protection. Copyright exists in an original work from the moment it is fixed in some tangible medium.

The Copyright Act contains a default rule that the "author" of protected material is the owner of copyright. However, there are exceptions—for instance, for works created by employees. It is also possible for the owner to transfer their rights to another person. The rules regarding ownership are discussed in Chapter 3.

The owner of copyright has the exclusive right to perform certain acts in relation to the protected material. For instance, the owner of copyright in a manuscript, play, or musical score has the exclusive right to reproduce, distribute, publicly perform, and adapt it for new media, venues, and uses. The nature of these exclusive acts is considered in Chapter 4.

Third parties who perform any of these exclusive acts risk infringing copyright in the work. Copyright in a work is infringed when:

▶ a person who is not the owner of copyright
▶ performs any of the exclusive acts (or authorizes or enables someone else to perform one of these acts)
▶ without the permission (i.e., "license") of the copyright owner.

This suggests that a cultural institution will infringe copyright if it digitizes a collection item for which it is not the copyright owner: see Chapter 4. However, there will be no infringement when any of the following apply:

▶ Any copyright has expired
▶ The institution has permission from the copyright owner(s)
▶ The act falls under an express exemption in the Copyright Act or is allowed under a statutory license

■ **KEY POINT**

The exclusive rights of the copyright owner include digitization and online distribution of works. If a cultural institution performs either of these acts in relation to a copyrighted work for which it does not own copyright, in many instances, it will have infringed copyright.

Two sets of exemptions are particularly relevant for cultural institutions: fair use and the "libraries and archives" provisions. Both of these allow cultural institutions and their users to perform otherwise infringing acts without the permission of the copyright owner. Fair use is discussed in Chapter 5, and the libraries and archives provisions are outlined in Chapter 6.

■ **KEY POINT**

It is not an infringement of copyright to perform an exclusive act of copyright with the permission ("license") of the copyright owner. Nor is it an infringement if the act is authorized by one of the exemptions found in the Copyright Act, such as fair use or the libraries and archives provisions.

As noted above, there will be no infringement of copyright if the cultural institution has the permission of the copyright owner. Permission and licenses are considered in detail in Chapter 7. Locating copyright owners in order to seek permission is discussed in Chapter 8.

All digitization involves some level of risk. For example, works that are in the public domain in the United States may still be protected in other countries; presumed copyright owners who grant permission for digitization may not actually have the authority to grant permission; overlapping levels of copyright in any particular work may make it hard to identify all potential copyright claimants; and many copyright owners are impossible to locate, even after extensive searches. Furthermore, the easy accessibility of the Web (and hence the potential for locating and identifying possible infringements) increases the likelihood that technical infringements will become known. Lastly, the belief of many individuals that Web publication is an economic goldmine increases the likelihood that some will charge infringement and seek compensation even when they have no reasonable grounds for doing so.

A cultural institution that undertakes a digitization project, therefore, is going to assume some risk. Chapter 10 discusses strategies for managing the risks associated with every digitization project.

> **KEY POINT**
>
> All digitization involves some risk. These guidelines are designed to educate you about the potential risks and help you assess the threat that they pose to your institution. Each institution must decide on its own how much and what type of risks it is willing to assume. The answer will vary from institution to institution.

Finally, although these guidelines are primarily about copyright, there are other laws that can impinge on digitization efforts. Chief among these are rights of privacy, publicity, and trademark. Contractual agreements can also limit digitization, as can concerns over whose laws apply when digitizing foreign works. All these topics are discussed briefly in Chapter 9.

1.3 Principles of copyright law

Before the substantive discussion of copyright in later chapters, it is useful to explore four of its underlying principles: the copyright/property distinction, the "public domain", the "idea/expression dichotomy," and the causal connections that are required under the Copyright Act.

COPYRIGHT/PROPERTY DISTINCTION

Copyright is separate from ownership of the physical object in which copyright is embodied [17 U.S.C. § 202]. Consider a typical contract of sale for a painting (one that transfers ownership of the physical work from the seller to the purchaser). Since at least 1978, such a contract results in the purchaser obtaining ownership of the painting, but not any copyright, which remains with the artist or copyright owner.[4] If the purchaser wants to obtain an assignment of copyright (which transfers copyright to the purchaser) or a license (which permits certain uses under the license terms), this must be specifically negotiated for and (for assignments) agreed to in writing. (Note that it is not essential for a license to be in writing to be legally binding, but it is strongly encouraged: see Chapter 7.)

TIP

When negotiating copyright licenses or assignments, it is important to remember that the donor, seller, or depositor of an object may have no rights in relation to copyright. In that case, any purported license or assignment will be ineffective at law. The institution will need to identify the copyright owner and enter into separate discussions with him or her if it wishes to obtain a license or assignment.

THE PUBLIC DOMAIN

A second important principle is that copyright is a limited right of fixed duration. Once copyright expires, works enter the public domain and may be dealt with without obtaining any copyright permissions.

Some cultural institutions have targeted their digitization projects on objects in the public domain, thereby avoiding the legal and practical difficulties of copyright compliance. The main copyright issue in those instances is whether there is a new copyright in the digitized form of the item (see Chapter 2). In addition, there may be jurisdictional disputes over material in the public domain in the United States but not abroad (see Chapter 9).

IDEA/EXPRESSION DICHOTOMY

A third principle is that copyright protects the expression of ideas, rather than the ideas themselves. As detailed in the Copyright Act,

> In no case does copyright protection for an original work of authorship extend to any idea, procedure, process, system, method of operation, concept, principle, or discovery, regardless of the form in which it is described, explained, illustrated, or embodied in such work [17 U.S.C. § 102(b)].

The level of protection that is given to a work depends on its nature and subject matter. The simpler the expression of an idea, the more likely that a variation of that expression will not infringe copyright. For instance, copyright can exist in a basic sketch of a commonplace item, such as a spoon. However, copyright will only protect that particular version of the commonplace idea of spoon drawing—and not the general idea of drawing a picture of a spoon. This means that the owner of copyright may be given a remedy only in relation to literal copying of the sketch, because otherwise he or she would effectively enjoy a monopoly in relation to spoon drawing.

INDEPENDENT CREATION

A plaintiff who brings an action alleging copyright infringement must demonstrate that the allegedly infringing work was copied or derived from his or her own work. This is normally done by demonstrating that the alleged infringer had access to the plaintiff's work and that there is a "striking similarity" between the two works. There is no infringement when a person independently creates his or her work without reference to the plaintiff's work.

1.4 Common law copyright

In the United States, there are two layers of copyright protection. The largest and most important is federal copyright protection, which is secured under the provisions of the Copyright Act. If a work is eligible for protection under the Copyright Act, then only the federal law applies; any state laws are preempted by the federal law.

Certain types of work are not eligible for federal copyright protection. They include works that are never fixed (such as a conversation between two friends) and sound recordings made before 1972. Works that are not protected by federal copyright laws may still be protected by what is often called "common law copyright." Common law copyright is a mishmash of state-based law deriving in some cases from formal state copyright statutes, in other cases from related laws (such as antibootlegging legislation), and from judicial decisions. It can vary from state to state.

We believe that most of the material (except for sound recordings) that cultural institutions are likely to wish to digitize will be protected by federal law, and hence federal law will be the focus of these guidelines.

1.5 Copyright timeline

In the United States, copyright is governed by the Copyright Act of 1976. This legislation came into force on 1 January 1978 and since that time has undergone regular amendment. There are times, however, when it is also necessary to consult the terms of the previous law, the Copyright Act of 1909. Most cultural institutions own or possess collection items that were created well before the entry into force of the Copyright Act in 1978. The copyright status, authorship, and ownership of these objects could be determined in part by the previous law.

TITLE 17

The Copyright Act of 1976 and the subsequent amendments are codified in Title 17 of the United States Code, a compilation of the general and permanent federal laws of the United States. References to relevant code sections are given in the body of this manual in standard legal format. For example, [17 U.S.C. § 107] refers to Section 107 (the Fair Use section) of Title 17 in the U.S. Code. In the narrative, this would be shortened just to "Section 107."

The timeline, Table 1.1, sets out important legislation and law reform reports in the development of copyright law.

TABLE 1.1

Copyright Timetable[5]

1709	The first copyright act, the "Statute of Anne," passes in England. It grants copyright protection to the authors of books.
1787	U.S. Constitution in Article 1, Section 8, authorizes Congress to pass copyright and patent legislation.
1790	First federal copyright statute passes. Protection is limited to maps, charts, and books. Duration is for 14 years, with the possibility of a 14-year renewal term if the author is still living.
1831	Term extends to 28 years with the possibility of a 14-year extension. Protection extends to published music, which is protected against reproduction (but not performance, until 1891).
1856	Copyright protection for dramatic public performances is added.
1865	Photographs and negatives become eligible for copyright protection.

1870 Protection for dramatic works, pantomimes, paintings, drawings, and sculpture is added to the Copyright Act.

1886 Formulation of the first major international treaty in relation to copyright, the *Berne Convention for the Protection of Literary and Artistic Works*. The treaty has been revised 5 times since then. Currently, over 150 countries are members of the Berne Convention, including the United States (which joined over a century later, in 1988).

1891 First U.S. copyright protection for foreign works. Prior to this, most major American publishers were "pirates," reprinting without permission the works of noted European authors such as Dickens and Dumas.

1909 Copyright law in the United States undergoes a major revision with the Copyright Act of 1909. It broadens the definition of works of authorship and extends terms to 28 years with the possibility of a 28-year renewal. Amendments later in the century would extend the renewal term to 67 years (for a total of 95 years of protection).

1912 Movies are afforded copyright protection.

1955 United States becomes a signatory to the Universal Copyright Convention (UCC), affording U.S. authors expanded protection abroad.

1972 Sound recordings receive federal copyright protection.

1976 Copyright Act of 1976, which went into effect in 1978, passes. It makes a number of major revisions to U.S. copyright, including: granting federal protection to unpublished items (which had been protected by state common law); calculating copyright duration based on life of the author plus 50 years (with no renewals) rather than on a fixed term with the possibility of renewal; codifying the judicial doctrine of fair use; and adding specific exemptions for libraries and archives in Section 108.

1988 The United States joins the Berne Convention. This leads to the eventual dismantling of all formal requirements (notice, registration, renewal) for copyright.

1990 Works of architecture receive federal copyright protection.

1992 Copyright renewal is made automatic. All works published from 1964 to 1978 are given an automatic 75-year term.

1994 Conference on Fair Use (CONFU) is convened to develop guidelines on acceptable fair use of material (including digital use) in interlibrary loan, electronic reserves, digital images, distance education, and multimedia. No consensus could be reached in the final report in 1998.

1996	Provisions of the Uruguay Round Agreements Act (URAA), which implemented the General Agreement on Tariffs and Trade (GATT), go into effect. Copyright in hundreds of thousands of foreign works in the public domain is restored.
1998	Sonny Bono Copyright Extension Act extends almost all copyrights by another 20 years, so works of authorship now have a term of the life of the author plus 70 years.
1998	Digital Millennium Copyright Act gives online service providers some important safe harbors from copyright-infringement suits, but also adds criminal sanctions to anyone bypassing certain technological protection measures on digital content.
2002	Technology Education and Copyright Harmonization Act (TEACH Act) authorizes the use of some digital resources in distance education settings.
2005	The Copyright Office begins studying the "orphan works" problem and issues a final report early in 2006.
2005	Section 108 Study Group is convened to examine the exemptions available to libraries and archives. Its report is issued in 2008.

2 *Copyright Fundamentals*

2.1 Introduction

This chapter helps you answer two questions:

▸ What types of work are protected by copyright?
▸ What are the prerequisites for a work to be protected by copyright?

By answering these two questions, you will be able to identify the collection items in which copyright "subsists" (the term used in Title 17 to identify works protected by copyright). Once you have identified these works, you will need to consider, for each item, when copyright is due to expire and who owns copyright. These questions will be considered in Chapter 3 of these guidelines.

Federal copyright protection does not apply to objects that do not meet the requirements set out in the Copyright Act, regardless of how deserving of protection those objects are. Thus, categorizing an object as within or outside the scope of material protected by the Copyright Act is extremely important. However, as discussed in this chapter, the requirements for protection are frequently easy to satisfy.

> **TIP**
> This chapter describes the step-by-step process for determining whether an item is protected by copyright. However, in most cases, it will be obvious that an item is copyrighted, and the appropriate course of action is to ascertain whether copyright has expired and—if it has not—implement a strategy for dealing with potential infringement (e.g., identify the copyright owner(s), obtain a permission, rely on a statutory exemption, etc).

2.2 Types of work protected by copyright

There is no exhaustive list of the types of works that can receive protection. The Copyright Act [17 U.S.C. § 102] offers these illustrative examples:

- ▶ Literary works
- ▶ Musical works, including any accompanying words
- ▶ Dramatic works, including any accompanying music
- ▶ Pantomimes and choreographic works
- ▶ Pictorial, graphic, and sculptural works
- ▶ Motion pictures and other audiovisual works
- ▶ Sound recordings
- ▶ Architectural works

These categories should be viewed broadly. For example, computer programs may be protected as "literary works," and maps and architectural plans may be protected as "pictorial, graphic, and sculptural works."

The following section examines in more detail each category of work and subject matter identified as copyrightable in the Copyright Act. As noted above, this is not a closed list; other subject matter can also be protected. However, the list in the Copyright Act covers a large body of material.

LITERARY WORKS

The phrase "literary works" sounds highbrow, but it is not. It covers non-dramatic textual works, both with and without illustrations. The defining feature of a literary work is that it presents information using words, numbers, or other verbal or numerical symbols (as opposed to purely through images). The format of the media on which those words and numbers are stored does not matter. Literary works can exist as books, disks, tape, or cards. Note that dramatic textual works, although seemingly "literary," are treated separately.

Examples of literary works frequently found in cultural collections include:

- ▶ Fiction
- ▶ Nonfiction
- ▶ Manuscripts
- ▶ Poetry
- ▶ Periodicals and journals
- ▶ Dissertations and theses
- ▶ Reports

◆ **FLOWCHART 2**
◇
Subsistence of copyright

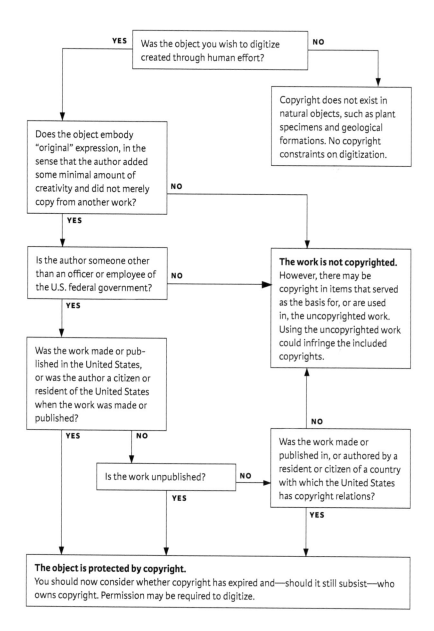

YES ← Was the object you wish to digitize created through human effort? → **NO**

Copyright does not exist in natural objects, such as plant specimens and geological formations. No copyright constraints on digitization.

Does the object embody "original" expression, in the sense that the author added some minimal amount of creativity and did not merely copy from another work? — **NO** →

YES

Is the author someone other than an officer or employee of the U.S. federal government? — **NO** →

YES

The work is not copyrighted. However, there may be copyright in items that served as the basis for, or are used in, the uncopyrighted work. Using the uncopyrighted work could infringe the included copyrights.

Was the work made or published in the United States, or was the author a citizen or resident of the United States when the work was made or published?

YES   **NO**

NO

Was the work made or published in, or authored by a resident or citizen of a country with which the United States has copyright relations?

Is the work unpublished? — **NO** →

YES   **YES**

The object is protected by copyright.
You should now consider whether copyright has expired and—should it still subsist—who owns copyright. Permission may be required to digitize.

17

- ▶ Speeches
- ▶ Bound or loose-leaf volumes
- ▶ Pamphlets and brochures
- ▶ Textbooks
- ▶ Reference works
- ▶ Directories
- ▶ Catalogs
- ▶ Advertising copy
- ▶ Games
- ▶ Automated databases
- ▶ Computer programs
- ▶ E-mail messages
- ▶ Web sites and other online works

There is no requirement that a literary work have literary or aesthetic merit. Indeed, courts have concluded that a broad range of highly mundane items are encompassed in literary works for the purposes of copyright law, including circus posters, descriptions of refrigeration supplies, and sunglass display cards. The only requirement is that the literary work needs to have some amount, however small, of "original" textual or numeric expression. (The requirement of originality is discussed later in this chapter.)

MUSICAL WORKS, INCLUDING ANY ACCOMPANYING WORDS

There is no explicit definition of "musical work" in the Copyright Act, but the intended meaning is clear. It encompasses original compositions as well as new arrangements of earlier compositions to which new copyrightable authorship has been added. The term musical work can encapsulate a variety of styles, from classical music through to contemporary popular forms.

Copyright in a musical work is distinguished from copyright in the sound recording of that work (discussed below). The owner of the copyright in the musical work has an important right: the right to make or authorize the first recording of that work. Once recorded and distributed to the public, subsequent recordings of nondramatic musical works can be made under the terms of a compulsory license [17 U.S.C. § 115].

Interesting questions arise as to the boundaries of musical works. John Cage, for example, registered his composition 4'33" as a textual work—even though the composition consists of 4½ minutes of silence. And his estate has actively sought to enforce its copyright against other composers of silence.

Image: America's pinch hit march [sheet music]
Composer: Bertha Stanfield Dempsey
Published: McMillan, 1919
Source: Library of Congress, Music Division, http://lcweb2.loc.gov/diglib/ihas/loc.natlib.ihas.200033287/
License: In the public domain because copyright has expired.

DRAMATIC WORKS, INCLUDING ANY ACCOMPANYING MUSIC

Dramatic works are also not explicitly defined in the Copyright Act, but they include such things as published and unpublished plays and scripts for radio, television, and cinema: works, in other words, that are meant to be performed. Dramatic works normally consist of spoken text, plot, and directions for action.

As with musical works, a separate copyright can exist for a recording of a performance of the dramatic work. If the dramatic work is derived from a literary work, a separate copyright may exist for the original literary work. Cultural institutions wishing to digitize a filmed performance of a play will have to evaluate at a minimum the copyright status of the play itself, any literary work on which that play was based, and the recording of the play.

PANTOMIMES AND CHOREOGRAPHIC WORKS

Choreography and pantomimes are also copyrightable dramatic works. Choreography is the composition and arrangement of dance movements and patterns usually intended to be accompanied by music. It can be differentiated from social dance steps and simple routines, which cannot be protected by copyright. Pantomime is the art of imitating or acting out situations, characters, or other events.

To be protected by copyright, pantomimes and choreography need not tell a story or be presented before an audience. Each work, however, must be fixed in a tangible medium of expression from which the work can be performed, such as dance notation. (The general requirement for fixation is discussed in more detail below.)

PICTORIAL, GRAPHIC, AND SCULPTURAL WORKS

The Copyright Act [17 U.S.C. § 101] defines "pictorial, graphic, and sculptural works" to include two-dimensional and three-dimensional representations of the following types of objects:

▶ Works of fine, graphic, and applied art
▶ Photographs
▶ Prints and art reproductions
▶ Maps, charts, globes, and other cartographic works
▶ Diagrams, models, and technical drawings
▶ Architectural plans

Vincent van Gogh, Dutch, 1853–1890
La Berceuse (Woman Rocking a Cradle; Augustine-Alix Pellicot Roulin, 1851–1930), 1889
The Metropolitan Museum of Art
Source of file: ArtStor
"Image © The Metropolitan Museum of Art"
License: Images for Academic Publishing Initiative

Many items are eligible for copyright protection under this provision. According to the Copyright Office,[1] the range of works eligible for copyright protection under this provision includes:

- ▶ Advertisements, commercial prints, labels
- ▶ Artificial flowers and plants
- ▶ Artwork applied to clothing or to other useful articles
- ▶ Bumper stickers, decals, stickers
- ▶ Cartographic works, such as maps, globes, relief models
- ▶ Cartoons, comic strips
- ▶ Collages
- ▶ Dolls, toys
- ▶ Drawings, paintings, murals
- ▶ Enamel works
- ▶ Fabric, floor, and wall-covering designs
- ▶ Games, puzzles
- ▶ Greeting cards, postcards, stationery
- ▶ Holograms, computer and laser artwork
- ▶ Jewelry designs
- ▶ Models
- ▶ Mosaics
- ▶ Needlework and craft kits
- ▶ Original prints, such as engravings, etchings, serigraphs, silk screen prints, woodblock prints
- ▶ Patterns for sewing, knitting, crochet, needlework
- ▶ Photographs, photomontages
- ▶ Posters
- ▶ Record jacket artwork or photography
- ▶ Relief and intaglio prints
- ▶ Reproductions, such as lithographs, collotypes
- ▶ Sculpture, such as carvings, ceramics, figurines, maquettes, molds, relief sculptures
- ▶ Stained glass designs
- ▶ Stencils, cut-outs
- ▶ Technical drawings, architectural drawings or plans, blueprints, diagrams, mechanical drawings
- ▶ Weaving designs, lace designs, tapestries

As will be seen in the next section, there are, however, some limitations on the scope of protection given to applied art and useful articles.

It is important to bear in mind that, as with literary works, items protected under the rubric of "pictorial, graphic, or sculptural works" do not require any artistic merit. As the legislative history notes, "there is no implied criterion of artistic taste, aesthetic value, or intrinsic quality."[2] Thus, although works of fine art are granted some extra protections, as is discussed in Chapter 4, any work of art will be afforded copyright protection, so long as it is original and fixed.

KEY POINT

Originality, not aesthetic merit, is the basis for copyright protection. Even banal images and writings are eligible for copyright protection, so long as they meet the threshold requirements.

"USEFUL ARTICLES" AND "APPLIED ART"

Eligibility for copyright protection becomes complicated when an object is both utilitarian in function and sculptural or decorative in execution. This is because of concern that protecting the sculptural or decorative components of such items may, inadvertently, also give rights to utilitarian aspects (which would be inconsistent with the idea/expression dichotomy, discussed in Chapter 1). Thus, copyright protection does not exist for the intrinsic mechanical or utilitarian aspects of "useful articles" such as clothing, furniture, machinery, dinnerware, and lighting fixtures. (Such aspects may, however, be protected by patents.) Nor does copyright protection automatically exist for the shape or design of a utilitarian object, even if it is aesthetically pleasing.

Copyright can only protect pictorial, graphic, or sculptural elements in useful objects when those elements can be identified separately from the utilitarian aspects of the object. Unless the shape of an automobile, airplane, dress, food processor, television set, or any other industrial product contains some element that, physically or conceptually, can be identified as separable from the utilitarian aspects of that article, the design cannot be protected by copyright. If the aesthetic element can be separated from the useful item, then that separate element can be protected. For example, even though the design of a chair may not be eligible for copyright protection, a carving on

Fulper Pottery Company, 1814–1935
Table Lamp, 1910–15
The Metropolitan Museum of Art
Image © The Metropolitan Museum of Art
Image source: ARTstor
License: Images for Academic Publishing (AIP) initiative

the back of that chair could be protected by copyright. The general design of a lamp may not be protected by copyright, but a sculpture incorporated into a lamp could be protected by copyright (since in theory, it would be possible to still have a lamp without necessarily including the sculpture). The protection, however, applies only to the separated item, and not to the underlying object as a whole.

Unfortunately, one can only determine on a fact-specific, case-by-case basis whether pictorial, graphic, or (especially) sculptural features can be separated from the design of the useful object and hence be eligible for copyright protection. There are few general principles to guide us. Courts have found that figures of humans can be artistic and copyrightable (as in a sculpture), or primarily useful (and hence uncopyrightable) when expressed as a mannequin. The body of a fish, however, when used in taxidermy, may be copyrightable. (Apparently there is a difference between draping clothing on a mannequin and attaching fish skin on an underlying form.) Sometimes clothing and jewelry that incorporate sculptural elements have been found to be protected by copyright; at other times the reverse has been held. Similarly, flowers and floral arrangements at times have been protected by copyright, and at other times have not. And in one case (*Brandir v. Cascade*), a bicycle rack derived from a copyrighted sculpture was found to be unprotected by copyright.

Here are other examples of works that have been found to be sculptures and hence copyrightable—although some may not consider the works to be sculptures in any ordinary sense of the word:

▶ A lamp base consisting of male and female figures dancing (*Mazer v. Stein*)

▶ Miniature hockey players in a hockey game (*Innovative Concepts in Entertainment, Inc. v. Entertainment Enterprises, Ltd.*)

▶ A doll of Zippy the chimpanzee (*Rushton v. Vitale*)

▶ Western belt buckles (*Kieselstein-Cord v. Accessories by Pearl, Inc.*)

▶ Artificial Christmas trees (*B. Wilmsen, Inc. v. Consolidated Novelty Co.*)

Thus, the functional or utilitarian nature of an item does not automatically preclude it from being a sculpture. What is important is that the item expresses the ideas of the sculptor in a three-dimensional form and that the sculptor's conception can be separated from the utilitarian object.

What about a depiction of a noncopyrightable useful article? Does creating a copyrightable representation of a useful article give one any rights regarding the design of that article? The short answer is no [17 U.S.C. § 113(b)]. For example, a drawing or photograph of an automobile or a dress design may be copyrighted, but that does not give the artist or photographer the exclusive right to make automobiles or dresses of the same design.

MOTION PICTURES AND OTHER AUDIOVISUAL WORKS

The Copyright Act defines audiovisual works as "works that consist of a series of related images which are intrinsically intended to be shown by the use of machines, or devices such as projectors, viewers, or electronic equipment, together with accompanying sounds, if any, regardless of the nature of the material objects, such as films or tapes, in which the works are embodied" [17 U.S.C. § 101]. Audiovisual works include filmstrips, slide sets, and sets of transparencies. The key defining feature is that they are a series of related images and that machines are needed to show them. In the Copyright Act, showing images in any sequence is a performance; hence, by definition, audiovisual works are performed.

Motion pictures are a specific type of audiovisual work. They are "audiovisual works consisting of a series of related images which, when shown in succession, impart an impression of motion" [17 U.S.C. § 101]. There is no requirement of dramatic content in a "motion picture," and the term therefore extends beyond feature films to cover things like commercials, documentaries, raw footage, television programs, home movies, and multimedia works such as computer games. If images have accompanying sound, that sound also becomes part of the motion picture.

In addition to the motion picture or audiovisual copyright, there may also be a separate copyright in any literary, dramatic, or musical work that is the basis for the audiovisual work (such as a script or original story). Separate copyrights may also exist in different contributions to a motion picture, such as the music used in the sound track. The copyright protection available to motion pictures and other audiovisual works relates only to the visual images embodied in the film and any soundtrack created specifically for the film.

SOUND RECORDINGS

Since 15 February 1972, sound recordings have received federal copyright protection [17 U.S.C. § 301(c)]. State laws and common law copyright govern sound recordings created in the United States prior to this date.[3]

Sound recordings are defined in the Copyright Act as "works that result from the fixation of a series of musical, spoken, or other sounds . . . regardless of the nature of the material objects, such as disks, tapes, or other phonorecords, in which they are embodied" [17 U.S.C. § 101]. It is important to note that sound recording copyright is separate from the media on which it is stored (even though the word "recording" might make us think of tape or CD). Just as the copyright in a text is separate from the physical manifestation in which it is found (such as a book), so, too, is the sound recording copyright separate from the medium on which it is recorded.

The copyright in a sound recording protects the particular sounds embodied in that recording. How the sounds get on a record often requires judgment and originality; the Copyright Act seeks to protect these elements.

As with motion pictures, in addition to the sound recording copyright, there may also be a separate copyright in any literary, dramatic, or musical work that is recorded. Furthermore, as discussed in Chapter 4, the rights of the owner of copyright in a sound recording revolve around copying and communicating *that recording*, and it will not be an infringement of copyright for another person to make a "soundalike" recording. However, such a recording may infringe copyright in any underlying literary, dramatic, or musical works.

Note that one special type of sound recording is excluded from the

Image: Thomas Edison and his early phonograph, circa 1877. Cropped from Library of Congress copy. Edited Version. Dust removed by Arad.

Photographer: Levin C. Hardy

License: Public domain

Source: http://commons.wikimedia.org/wiki/File:Edison_and_phonograph_edit2.jpg

definition of sound recordings found in the Copyright Act: namely "the sounds accompanying a motion picture or other audiovisual work" [17 U.S.C. § 101]. These recordings are protected under the provisions for motion pictures and other audiovisual works. This has implications for some of the exemptions available in the Copyright Act. For example, one exemption allows a library or archives to make a copy of a portion of a spoken sound recording (such as an oral history) at the request of a patron [17 U.S.C. § 108(d)]. That library or archives would not be able to make a copy for a patron of the same portion of the interview if it had been videotaped because the interview was initially made as an audiovisual and audiovisuals are excluded from this particular exemption [17 U.S.C. 108(h)]. This is discussed further in Chapter 6.

■ **KEY POINT**

The copyright in a sound recording or film exists independently of any literary, dramatic, or musical work that it embodies. This means that multiple copyrights may subsist in relation to one object. For instance, a sound recording of a song may embody the following separate copyrighted works:

▶ A literary work (assuming the lyrics were composed separately)
▶ A musical work (the musical score)
▶ A sound recording (the capture of a specific performance)

This can result in special issues when obtaining copyright licenses in relation to audiovisual items, some of which are addressed in Chapter 7.

ARCHITECTURAL WORKS

In 1990, Congress afforded copyright protection to architectural works. Prior to that date, architectural plans could be protected as "pictorial, graphic, or sculptural works," but the buildings constructed according to those plans had no separate protection. Thus, if you liked the look of a building, you could have your own architect reproduce it for you—just so long as she did not consult or copy the original copyrighted plans, but only worked from the building as constructed.

By adding a new category—architectural works—to the Copyright Act, buildings themselves became copyrighted. An architectural work is defined as:

> ... the design of a building as embodied in any tangible medium of expression, including a building, architectural plans, or drawings. The work includes the overall form as well as the arrangement and composition of spaces and elements in the design, but does not include individual standard features [17 U.S.C. § 101].

Two important limitations were included when architectural works were afforded copyright protection. First, the protection is not retroactive; it only applies to buildings created on or after 1 December 1990 or built before 31 December 2002 from unpublished plans created prior to 1990. Second, as is discussed in more detail in Chapter 5, the copyright in a built architectural work does not include the right to prevent anyone from making or distributing photographs or other depictions of the building if the building can be seen from a public place [17 U.S.C. § 120].

■ **TRICKY AREA**

Government Works

One class of works expressly *excluded* from copyright protection, even though exemplars of them are likely to fall in one of the categories listed above, are "works of the United States Government." These are defined as works "prepared by an officer or employee of the United States Government as part of that person's official duties" [17 U.S.C. § 105].

On its face, this would seem to mean that works published by the Government Printing Office (GPO) or by a specific federal agency are in the public domain and can be used freely. There are, however, several important caveats to this generalization, and it should not be assumed that all works emanating from the U.S. government necessarily fall within this exclusion. For example:

▶ Works prepared by non-government employees working under contract to the federal government would not be considered to be a work of the federal government.

▶ Not all staff working for government agencies are necessarily "officers or employees" of the U.S. government. The Smithsonian Institution, for example, hires many employees with non-government-supplied funds. Copyright in a photograph taken by one of those employees as part of his or her official duties would belong to the Smithsonian Institution (and government agencies are allowed to own copyrights created by others).

▶ As with any publisher, GPO or an agency might license the use of a copyrighted item for inclusion in a government publication. Publication by the government does not place that item in the public domain, and replicating that publication could potentially infringe the copyrights of the licensor.

▶ This provision only applies to works of the Federal government; publications by other governmental bodies at the state or local level are likely to be copyrighted. That said, edicts of government, such as judicial opinions, administrative rulings, legislative enactments, public ordinances, and similar official legal documents, are normally not copyrightable for reasons of public policy, regardless of the level of government that created them. Furthermore, state law may stipulate that other state publica-tions are in the public domain, but this would vary on a state-by-state basis.

▶ U.S. government publications are protected by copyright abroad; they are only in the public domain in the United States.

For more information on copyright of government works, see CENDI's "Frequently Asked Questions About Copyright: Issues Affecting the U.S. Government" at http://www.cendi.gov/publications/04–8copyright.html.

2.3 What are the prerequisites for an item to be protected by copyright?

In addition to being a type of work that copyright protects (for instance, because it falls within the nonexhaustive list of recognized works and subject matter in the Copyright Act), an item must meet four additional conditions in order to be afforded copyright protections. To be protected, works must:

- ▶ exist in a tangible form
- ▶ be a work of authorship
- ▶ be original, and
- ▶ meet the requirements regarding the nationality of the author.

These conditions may seem onerous, but they are not difficult to satisfy. For instance, the requirement of originality does not require that the work contain novel ideas, but merely that it meets a minimal level of creativity and was not copied.

▪ KEY POINT

It is not necessary that material be published in order to gain copyright protection.

TANGIBLE FORM

It would appear to go without saying that when a cultural institution wishes to digitize an item from its collection, that item will already exist in a "tangible form." However, for completeness, the requirement of tangibility is discussed briefly.

Federal copyright protection only arises when a work is fixed in a tangible medium of expression. It is not necessary for the work to be humanly perceptible, merely that it can be perceived, reproduced, or otherwise communicated. This can be done either directly or with the aid of a machine or device [17 U.S.C. § 102]. A book printed on paper, a photograph captured on film, and a manuscript saved in a computer's memory are all fixed and copyrighted from the moment of creation.

The requirement that a work must exist in a tangible form can mean that meritorious subject matter—such as improvised music and dance, extemporaneous speeches, oral stories, and so forth—are ineligible for federal copyright protection because they have never been committed to material form. In many cases, however, state common law copyright protections may be able to protect unfixed expressions.[4] For further discussion, see Case Study 1, which relates to oral histories.

TRICKY AREA

Publication

When determining copyright status, duration of copyright, and the applicability of various exemptions, it is often necessary to know whether a work has been published. According to the Copyright Act [17 U.S.C. § 101], works are "published" when the copyright owner authorizes the distribution of copies of a work to the public. The distribution can be by sale, rental, lease, or lending. Even just offering to distribute copies can constitute publication. A public performance or display of a work, however, does not of itself constitute publication. For this reason most television programs—at least until the advent of VHS and DVD sale copies—were considered to be unpublished. They were performed when first broadcast, but not sold, rented, or leased.

Subsequent case law suggests that the distribution offer must be made to the general public. If circulation is restricted to a particular group of people, only "limited" publication has occurred. For instance, some courts have concluded that Dr. Martin Luther King Jr.'s famous "I have a dream" speech, delivered before more than 200,000 civil rights supporters at the Lincoln Memorial in Washington, D.C., in 1963, was initially unpublished. The performance itself, of course, did not constitute publication, but copies of the speech were distributed to the press for its use. One court ruled that this was only a limited, not general, publication, and that the speech in effect remained unpublished (*Estate of Martin Luther King, Jr., Inc. v. CBS, Inc.*). A month later Dr. King registered his copyright with the Copyright Office, and his estate continues to enforce its copyright.

QUESTION

Does donating material to a cultural heritage institution constitute publication?

At first glance, one might answer "how could donation constitute publication?" Donation of a work to a repository does not seem to have anything to do with what we normally think of as publication. But remember the definition of copyright in the law: the "distribution of copies . . . of a work to the public by sale or other transfer of ownership, or by rental, lease, or lending." "Copies" in the copyright law refers not only to reproductions that are made of a work but also to the original work itself. One could, therefore, argue that if a copyright owner puts unpublished works into an archival repository where those works can be consulted, this would constitute an offer to lend a copy to the public and thus be (in copyright terms) publication.

This argument is found in Ralph Shaw's *Literary Property in the United States*.[5] More recent commentators have also suggested it may have relevance.[6] If true, it would surprise copyright owners and archivists alike. For much of the twentieth century, publication without adherence to copyright formalities injected a work into the public domain. By depositing unpublished works with an archival repository, a copyright owner theoretically could have "published" those works—and relinquished all copyright in them.

A court case finally tested this theory in 1990. The district court opinion in *Wright v. Warner Books* flatly rejected it, stating that "an unpublished work's presence in an academic library, on its own, is not the same thing as publication."[7] Assuming other courts elect to follow this decision, the likelihood that deposit of unpublished materials in a repository constitutes publication would seem small.

AUTHORSHIP

Copyright can only exist in original works of authorship, which implies that they must have an author. The Copyright Office has long required, and some case law has supported the idea, that the author of a work must be human. Works created by natural forces, computer programs, or supernatural beings are not eligible for copyright protection—though the editing or compilation of works supposedly authored by supernatural beings usually has been found to be copyrightable!

> **KEY POINT**
> The common element of protected works is that they have been created through human effort. There are no copyright issues when digitizing items from natural collections, such as fossils, plant or animal specimens, and geological formations. There may, however, be copyright in photographs, recordings, or other depictions of natural objects.

ORIGINALITY

The Copyright Act specifies that copyright only exists in "original works of authorship" [17 U.S.C. § 102(a)]. The term "original" is not defined in the law. However, case law provides some guidance as to its meaning.

In the United States, there is a very low threshold for when a work will be considered original: it must only be the result of some minimal level of creativity. As the Supreme Court has noted, "the requisite level of creativity is extremely low; even a slight amount will suffice. The vast majority of works make the grade quite easily, as they possess some creative spark, 'no matter how crude, humble or obvious' it might be."[8] Nor does originality require novelty. So long as the similarity between two works is fortuitous, and not the product of copying, copyright can exist.

Nevertheless, some creativity is a prerequisite for originality. Works that are merely a product of labor (what is sometimes called "sweat of the brow") are not eligible for copyright protection. In the leading court case on the subject, a telephone book was found to be unprotected by copyright because, although it took real effort to compile it, the arrangement of information in the book was unoriginal: merely a listing by last name. In other cases, only the original items such as headnotes or summaries in legal databases have been found to be protected by copyright; the bulk of the factual data in the database remains in the public domain.[9] American practice stands in sharp contrast with other countries, many of which recognize a "sweat of the brow" copyright, and some of which have also created special database protection rights that afford limited protection to collections of facts.

TRICKY AREA

Databases and Compilations

Databases are compilations, often of vast amounts of information, stored in electronic format. Databases can be extremely valuable, both in terms of their commercial value and their capacity to facilitate public access to information. In cultural institutions, subscriptions to individual, hard-copy periodicals increasingly are being replaced by licenses to large commercial databases. Some cultural institutions are also involved in generating their own databases, including large databases of digitized images.

Databases can be protected under the Copyright Act as compilations. Compilations are works "formed by the collection and assembling of pre-existing materials or of data that are selected, coordinated, or arranged in such a way that the resulting work as a whole constitutes an original work of authorship" [17 U.S.C. § 101]. Copyright in the compilation can only exist if the selection or arrangement meets the standards for originality discussed above.

The copyright in the compilation extends only to the selection, coordination, and arrangement of the component parts, but not to the underlying data. Copyright can prevent the wholesale duplication of a database, but if the component parts are in the public domain, it cannot stop anyone from extracting and using that public domain material. To regulate such behavior, most database providers have turned to licenses.

Issues in relation to negotiating licenses to access databases are discussed in Chapter 7.

Case law suggests that the more commonplace a particular type of work is, and the more it draws from preexisting materials, the greater the burden on the person claiming copyright in the item to prove that original copyrightable elements exist in it, should this be put in issue in court. Nevertheless, it may not stop the producers of resources built on public domain or factual material, be they transcribers of cemetery inscriptions or publishers of microfilmed sets of public domain material, from asserting a copyright claim and threatening a digitizer with legal action.

■

QUESTION

Are Copies of Public Domain Items Original?

We often say that anyone is free to use an object in the public domain, but what is the copyright status of a photograph or other copy of a public domain item? Can the copy have enough originality to warrant its own separate copyright protection, or does it, like the original object depicted in the copy, reside in the public domain?

The answer to this question has major implications for cultural institutions. On one hand, if reproductions of public domain items are themselves in the public domain, then libraries, archives, and museums might be free to digitize commercially produced microfilm sets of public domain documents or slides and transparencies found in an art library. On the other hand, cultural institutions would not be able to use the Copyright Act to stop third parties from making unauthorized use of the institution's own digital reproductions of public domain works.

Bridgeman Art Library v. Corel offers some indication of how a court might rule on these questions.[10] Bridgeman Art Library is a British commercial stock photo agency that markets reproductions of public domain works of art. It brought a copyright action against Corel in which it alleged that Corel, a CD publisher, had marketed CD-ROMs containing unauthorized copies of Bridgeman's reproductions of public domain artworks. In order to succeed in its action, Bridgeman needed to demonstrate that its reproductions were original and thus copyrightable.

The judge considered the application of the different tests for originality used in both the United States and the United Kingdom and held that the relevant works failed to satisfy either of them. He noted that in copying two-dimensional works of art, Bridgeman sought to replicate as closely as possible the original paintings. Labor and skill may be necessary to produce what the judge called "slavish copies," but no distinguishable variation that would go beyond differences in technical skill is required. Nor does changing the medium (from painting to transparencies or digital photographs) by itself generate the originality needed for copyright protection.

The ruling may have been different if the issue concerned

photographs of three-dimensional public domain works. Reproductions of three-dimensional objects require that many creative decisions be made on the composition, lighting, angle of filming, and so on. The result is that an original representation of the public domain work is often created, one that is likely to be protected by copyright.[11]

The decision in *Bridgeman* has been criticized on a number of grounds, especially abroad. Some have argued that the American judge misconstrued the test of originality that is preferred in the UK.[12] Others have argued that fine art reproduction is not a mere skill, but meets the low level of creativity required by copyright.[13] Defenders of *Bridgeman* note that it reflects perfectly the American requirement for originality in copyright and is consistent with previous court decisions. For now, *Bridgeman* stands as an important bulwark for any cultural institution interested in digitizing reproductions of two-dimensional works in the public domain.

(It should be noted that where a photograph is taken of an artistic work that is not in the public domain but is still protected by copyright, that photograph may infringe copyright in the artistic work. The issue is considered in Chapter 4.)

NATIONALITY

A further prerequisite for copyright protection relates to nationality: some factor that connects the authorship or publication of the work to the United States (or, as will be seen, other countries with whom the United States has reciprocal arrangements under treaty).

In relation to unpublished works, the rule is that *all* such works are provided federal copyright protection, regardless of the nationality of the author [17 U.S.C. § 104(a)].

Published works will be afforded copyright protection if *one* of the following is true:

▶ The author is a citizen of or living in the United States
▶ The work is first published in the United States or a country that is a signatory to one of several different copyright treaties, e.g., the Berne Convention, the Universal Copyright Convention, or the WTO Agreement on Trade-Related Aspects of Intellectual Property Rights (TRIPS

Agreement). See the definition of "international agreement" in section 101, and further below.

▶ The author is citizen of one of those treaty countries [17 U.S.C. § 104(b)]

Foreign works that meet one of the above conditions are treated as if they were published in the United States. This means that it is not always necessary to master the copyright laws of foreign countries. So long as you are limiting your use to the United States, you can treat a book published in France or Australia according to U.S. copyright law.

A different approach may be necessary when your proposed use is international, as will be the case with many online projects. This is because courts may apply the law of the country in which a work on the Internet was *accessed*, rather than the laws of the country from which it is *served*. International jurisdictional issues are discussed further in Chapter 9.

KEY POINT

Copyright can exist in foreign works. If your use of the copyrighted material occurs in the United State, U.S. law applies regardless of the nationality of the author or place of publication of the original work.

The most important treaty for copyright purposes is the Berne Convention for the Protection of Literary and Artistic Works, an international treaty dealing with copyright law. The Berne Convention requires that member states afford citizens of a foreign country the same protection they offer to their own citizens. Consequently, copyright in works authored, made, or first published overseas is recognized in the United States, and vice versa. Currently, over 150 countries are members of the Berne Convention. The United States also provides reciprocal protection to signatories of the Universal Copyright Convention (UCC); the World Trade Organization (WTO) agreements; and the World Intellectual Property Organization (WIPO) Copyright Treaty (WCT), and through direct bilateral treaties with other countries.[14]

2.4 Works made prior to 1978

The United States' current copyright legislation, the Copyright Act of 1976, came into force on 1 January 1978 (see Copyright Timeline in Chapter 1). It replaced the existing copyright legislation in force in the United States, the Copyright Act of 1909.

The 1976 Act contained many important differences from the 1909 Act. The 1976 Act, for example, for the first time provided federal copyright protection for unpublished works. Duration of copyright (which is discussed in Chapter 3) changed from a fixed term with one possible renewal to a single term based generally on the life of the author. Subsequent amendments have provided protection for new subject matter (architectural works) and eliminated the need for copyright notices or renewals. An important question, therefore, is how the 1976 Act and subsequent amendments treat material that pre-dates their entry into force.

Most provisions of the 1976 Act apply equally to all subject matter, regardless of their date of creation or publication. Fair use [17 U.S.C. § 107] is one such example: it applies to all copyrighted material, regardless of when they came into existence. The same is true for the other exemptions in copyright as well as the statutory provisions regarding infringement and remedies.

In other areas, a distinction is made between works created before and after entry into force of the 1976 Act (in 1978). Two are of particular importance to digitization projects. First, the rules regarding duration of copyright differ depending upon the date of creation. The copyright term for published works created before 1978, for example, differs from the term for works created after 1978. Sound recordings made before 1978 also have a different duration than current recordings. Rules regarding copyright term are discussed in Chapter 3. Second, authorship, and hence initial copyright ownership, of works is determined by the law in effect at the time of the work's creation. Authorship of a work created before 1978 may be different than for similar works created since 1977 due to the possible differing definitions of "work made for hire" in pre- and post-1978 copyright law, as is discussed further in Chapter 3.

Some of the changes to copyright law since 1976 have only been partially retroactive. For example, although some changes have extended the duration of protection for copyrighted works, they generally have not revived copyright in a work for which copyright has already expired. Works that entered the public domain under the 1909 Act, for instance, because of failure to comply with copyright formalities (as is explained in Chapter 3), remain in the public domain even though the need for formalities has been abolished. (The one major exception to this has been the restoration of copyright in foreign works that had earlier entered the public domain.)

It is important, then, for cultural institutions to understand some of the basic features of the 1909 Act, especially its insistence on formalities to secure copyright protection, so that they can identify current copyright owners and accurately assess the copyright status of collection items. The elements of particular importance to contemporary cultural heritage digitization projects are the former requirements for copyright notice, registration, and renewal.

▪ KEY POINT

Copyright rules and procedures have changed over time. It is often necessary to know the law at the time of creation of a work as well as the current law.

NOTICE

Most people are familiar with the copyright notice: the word "Copyright," the abbreviation "Copr.," or the copyright symbol "©," followed by the date and the name of the copyright owner, placed prominently on the work. Until 1 March 1989, use of the notice was mandatory on most textual works; failure to include a copyright notice on a published work normally led to the introduction of the work into the public domain. Including the notice on a published work gave the copyright owner an automatic 28-year copyright term.

REGISTRATION AND RENEWAL

Registration of the copyright with the Copyright Office has never been required to secure copyright protection. Under the current law, as soon as an original work is fixed in a tangible medium of expression, it is copyrighted. Under the 1909 Act, publication with notice secured federal copyright protection. Registration, however, has always and continues to secure to the copyright owner the fullest protections of the law, and prior to 1976, it was a prerequisite for renewal.

Copyright renewal granted the copyright owner a second term of copyright. Initially set at 28 years, it was gradually extended by Congress to a period of 67 years. When combined with the initial copyright term of 28 years, it creates a theoretical copyright term for works published before 1978 of 95 years. Failure to renew a copyright in the year prior to the 28th anniversary of publication injected the work into the public domain.

3 *Duration and Ownership of Copyright*

3.1 Introduction

This chapter deals with two important issues:

- What is the duration of copyright?
- Who is the owner of copyright?

Any analysis of ownership and duration must be performed on a case-by-case basis for each work.

If a work is not protected by copyright (i.e., all copyrights have expired, leaving the work in the public domain), then there are no copyright constraints on digitization—although other laws may be relevant (see Chapter 9 with regard to non-copyright issues). If a work is still protected by copyright and someone other than the cultural institution owns that copyright, then the institution risks infringing copyright if it digitizes the material unless it has the permission of the copyright owner or is protected by an exemption in the Copyright Act. Infringement and exemptions are discussed in Chapters 4, 5, and 6 of the guidelines; permission is discussed in Chapter 7.

Deciding whether a work is still copyrighted and who owns that copyright requires information regarding the work, including:

- What type of work it is
- When it was created
- Who was the author of the work
- Whether and where it was first published or offered for sale
- Whether any required copyright formalities were complied with
- The circumstances under which it was created
- Whether copyright has been transferred (for instance, by written assignment or as a bequest under a will)

Many institutions obtain information about the copyright status of items as part of the acquisition process. If possible, this should include:

▶ The current owner of copyright (not necessarily the person donating the item)

▶ If the item is unpublished, when it was made and the circumstances of creation

▶ If the item has been published, when and where it was first published

Obviously, it is not always possible to obtain complete copyright information even at the time of donation. For instance, the work may be anonymous or the person donating the item may have no information as to its maker or the copyright owner. This is discussed further in Chapter 7 in the section on orphan works and copyright risk management.

The questions addressed in this chapter are summarized in Flowchart 3.1.

◆ **FLOWCHART 3.1**

Ownership and Duration of Copyright

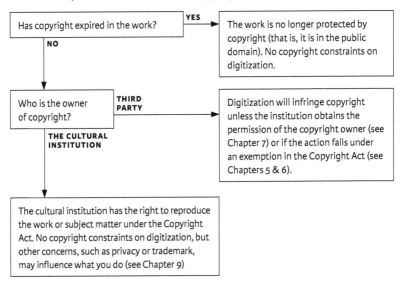

3.2 What is the duration of copyright?

The duration of copyright varies according to factors including the type of work, its publication status, and the place of first publication. There are five main classes of works that we will consider:

- ▸ Unpublished works
- ▸ Works first published in the United States
- ▸ Works first published abroad
- ▸ Sound recordings
- ▸ Architectural works

Within each category of work, the date of creation and/or publication, the circumstances of creation (including authorship), and the work's compliance with copyright formalities may all affect how long copyright endures.

The end result is that it is often very difficult to remember all of the different permutations that govern whether a work is still protected by copyright. Peter Hirtle has prepared a chart,[1] based on earlier work by Laura Gasaway,[2] as a guide to the various rules. The following discussion builds on the information found in the chart to discuss each of the five major categories of work.

3.2.1 *Unpublished Works*

Table 3.2.1 sets out the copyright term for works that, as of 1 January 1978, had neither been published with the authority of the copyright owner nor registered for copyright with the Copyright Office. (Note that unpublished works registered with the Copyright Office are treated as if they were published on the date of registration.)

The rules for unpublished works are simpler than for published works. They apply to *all* unpublished works that will be used in the United States, regardless of the nationality of the owner or place of creation [17 U.S.C. § 104(a)].

KEY POINT

When determining whether a collection item has been published, it is very important not to simply rely on that item's format or physical appearance, as it exists in the collection. For example, a manuscript letter may have been printed with the authority of the copyright owner, thus creating a statutory copyright. From the date of publication, its copyright term is calculated as a published work— even though the copy in the repository physically still looks like a manuscript item. This means that a manuscript letter from 1775 could still theoretically be protected by copyright if it was published prior to 2003 (see below). For more on the meaning of publication, see the text boxes in Chapter 2.

TABLE 3.2.1

Never Published, Never Registered, Works

Type of Work	Copyright Term	What was in the public domain in the United States as of 1 January 2009
Unpublished works	Life of the author +70 years	Works from authors who died before 1939
Unpublished anonymous and pseudonymous works, and works made for hire (corporate authorship)	120 years from date of creation	Works created before 1889
Unpublished works created before 1978 that were published after 1977 but before 2003	Life of the author +70 years or 31 December 2047, whichever is greater	Nothing. The soonest the works can enter the public domain is 1 January 2048
Unpublished works created before 1978 that were published after 31 December 2002	Life of the author +70 years	Works of authors who died before 1939
Unpublished works when the death date of the author is not known	120 years from date of creation	Works created before 1889

The basic rule for unpublished works is that copyright endures for life of the author plus 70 years [17 U.S.C. § 302(a), 303(b)]. All terms of copyright run through the end of the calendar year in which they would otherwise expire [17 U.S.C. § 305]. That means that for an author who died on 15 March 1940, copyright has to last until at least 16 March 2010, but because terms run through the calendar year, copyright will not expire until 1 January 2011.

A special rule applies for unpublished anonymous and pseudonymous works, and for "works made for hire" (which is discussed later in this chapter, but is most commonly found when someone creates a work as part of his or her employment). Copyright in these works expires 120 years from the date of creation [17 U.S.C. § 302(c)].

> **TIP**
>
> All works created more than 120 years ago (currently, before 1888) that have *never* been published with the authority of the copyright owner have entered the public domain and can be used without copyright restriction in the United States. They may still be protected, however, in other countries.

DURATION OF PUBLISHED MANUSCRIPTS

The copyright term for unpublished works, once they are published, is normally the same as for other published works.

Thus for works created and published *prior* to 1 January 1978, the copyright term is calculated by reference to the applicable rule for published works of that era, as discussed in the next sessions. For example, an unpublished work written in 1850 by an author who died in 1880 and first published in 1970 would receive up to a 95-year copyright term from publication date (assuming it met all of the requirements regarding authorization, notice, etc.).

In contrast, if that same unpublished 1850 work were published today, it would receive no copyright protection because its copyright would have expired under the current "life +70 years" term [17 U.S.C. §§ 302(a), 303(a)]. That is, if copyright has already expired in a work, publication will not cause it to "revive."

The position is different for unpublished works that were created *before* 1978 and first published after 1 January 1978 but on or before 31 December, 2002. The Copyright Act stipulates that for those works, copyright shall not expire before 31 December 2047 [17 U.S.C. § 303(a)]. That is, the copyright term extends to 31 December 2047 *or* the life of the author plus 70 years—whichever results in the longer term.

The source for this exception was the extension of federal copyright protection to unpublished works with the Copyright Act of 1976. Prior to the 1976 Act, unpublished works were afforded perpetual copyright protection. When unpublished works were published, they lost their common law perpetual protection and became subject to the federal rules for published works. With the advent of copyright terms based on the life of the author in 1978, the owners of copyright in unpublished works lost their exclusive perpetual right to first publication; unpublished works became subject to the same copyright term as published works (i.e., life of the author plus 50 years). Without further amendment, this would have placed many unpublished items in the public domain (i.e., the works of authors who had died more than 50 years before the entry into force of this provision). To protect the interests of copyright owners and to encourage the publication of unpublished works, Congress created a 25-year window, from 1978 to 2003, during which first publication of any work would ensure copyright protection at least until 2047.

■ DID YOU KNOW?

Mark Twain may have died in 1910, but his copyrights live on. The Mark Twain Papers & Project at the Bancroft Library at the University of California, Berkeley, has been collecting copies of Twain's correspondence, which they have been editing and publishing in scholarly volumes. In 2001, with the permission of the Mark Twain Foundation, which owns all of the copyrights in Mark Twain's writings, they offered for sale a microfilm edition of all of the letters in their possession that had not yet been published in letterpress. There is no evidence that anyone bought a set—but by merely offering it for sale, the project extended the copyright in the letters until 2048, or almost 140 years after Twain's death.

The copyright protection would not extend to incoming correspondence (since neither the Project nor the Foundation owned the copyright in those letters), nor would it apply to any Mark Twain letters discovered since the publication of the microfilm edition. Those works would have entered the public domain.

Image: *Mark Twain, America's best humorist*
J. Keppler; Mayer, Merkel & Ottman, lith. 1885.
License: Public domain because of copyright expiration.
Source: Prints and Photographs Division, Library of Congress.
http://hdl.loc.gov/loc.pnp/cph.3g04294

3.2.2 *Works first published in the United States*

▮▮ **TABLE 3.2.2**

Works first published in the United States

Date of Publication	Conditions	Copyright Term
Before 1923	None	None: in the public domain due to copyright expiration[3]
1923 through 1977	Published without a copyright notice	None: in the public domain due to failure to comply with required formalities
1978 to 1 March 1989	Published without notice, and without subsequent registration	None: in the public domain due to failure to comply with required formalities
1978 to 1 March 1989	Published without notice, but with subsequent registration	70 years after the death of author, or if work of corporate authorship, 95 years from publication
1923 through 1963	Published with notice but copyright was not renewed	None: in the public domain due to failure to comply with required formalities
1923 through 1963	Published with notice and the copyright was renewed	95 years after publication date
1964 through 1977	Published with notice	95 years after publication date
1978 to 1 March 1989	Published with notice	70 years after death of author, or if work of corporate authorship, 95 years from publication
After 1 March 1989	None	70 years after death of author, or if work of corporate authorship, 95 years from publication

For works first published in the United States, there are in effect three eras of copyright duration that are of concern. The first and last are relatively simple, but the middle one will require some explanation.

The first era for copyright duration is for works published before 1923. Prior to the passage of the 1976 Copyright Act, works published in the

United States had a fixed term of copyright. Under the 1909 Copyright Act, this was 28 years with the possibility of a 28-year renewal term. Extensions by Congress lengthened the renewal period to 47 years, meaning that published works could have at most a 75-year copyright term. In 1998, with the Sonny Bono Copyright Term Extension Act, all copyright terms were increased by another 20 years, including the term for preexisting copyrighted works. Those works, however, whose 75-year term had expired before 1998 remained in the public domain. That means that all works published before 1923 in the United States are freely available for use; they have no copyright protection.

The last era for copyright protection is similarly simple. With the passage of the Berne Convention Implementation Act of 1988, the last of the formalities in American law became optional. Works created since 1 March 1989 are copyrighted as soon as they are fixed; there is no need for notice, registration, or other action on the part of the copyright owner. Copyright endures for either the life of the author plus 70 years or, in the case of a work made for hire, 95 years from publication [17 U.S.C. § 302].

The period between 1923 and 1989 is, however, fraught with difficulties when trying to determine copyright status and applicable duration. Whether a work entered the public domain or remained protected by copyright depends on the subtle interaction of changing notice requirements and the date of publication. We can consider each briefly in turn.

COPYRIGHT NOTICE

From 1923 to 1 March 1989, a constant in copyright was the requirement that the volume contain a copyright notice. (See Chapter 2 for more on copyright notice.) A work first published in the United States without a copyright notice during this period usually automatically entered the public domain.

RENEWAL

Assuming it was published with notice, there was a further requirement (until 1964) that the work had to have its copyright renewed. If a book published during this period had its copyright renewed, then it is protected for a total copyright term of 95 years.

Why 1964? The Copyright Renewal Act of 1992 made renewal optional for any work in its first term of copyright (i.e., published less than 28 years before passage of the Act). Works published after 1963, therefore, automatically have a 95-year copyright term. Those published before 1963 will only have the 95-year term if their copyright was renewed. If not, they are in the public domain.

TIP

Investigating copyright renewals

Copyright renewal is very important for works published between 1922 and 1964. But how can you tell if copyright in a work published during this time period was renewed? There are three options:

▶ **Use the records at the Copyright Office**
You can lookup items in the records yourself, or pay the Copyright Office to investigate the status of the work.

▶ **Use the *Catalog of Copyright Entries (CCE)***
These volumes, published by the Copyright Office, contain abbreviated records of registrations and renewals.

▶ **Use online databases**
  ▽ *Works published after 1951:* The Copyright Office has an online searchable file of records since 1978, which includes renewal records for works published since 1951, and some records for works from 1950. See http://www.copyright.gov.
  ▽ *Works published before 1951:* Volunteer efforts have digitized and proofread the CCE volumes and placed them online. See http://collections.stanford.edu/copyrightrenewals/. Note that this is for books only; for other formats, you need to turn to the other options. Note, too, that although apparently accurate, it is an unofficial resource. Discovering a title in the database is likely evidence that copyright was renewed and the work is protected. The absence of a title, however, is not necessarily proof that the book is in the public domain. Depending on how risk averse you are, further research in other sources may be warranted.

DATE OF PUBLICATION

Let's assume that the work you are investigating was published with notice and renewed. The duration of the copyright will depend on the date of publication:

▶ **Prior to 1978**
Copyrighted works published prior to 1978 are protected for 95 years from publication.

▶ **Since 1978**
Copyrighted works published since 1978 are protected for a period of life of the author plus 70 years or, if a work made for hire, 95 years from publication.

Flowchart 3.2 represents one method for investigating the copyright status of works published between 1923 and 1989.

◆ **FLOWCHART 3.2**

Copyright status of U.S. works published between 1923 and 1989

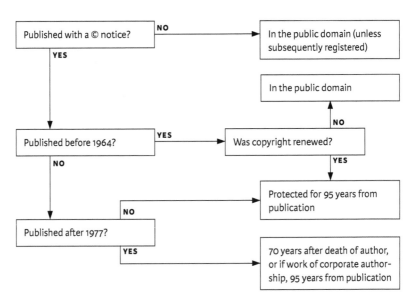

3.2.3 *Published foreign works*

Published foreign works include a variety of works:

▶ Works by non-U.S. citizens published only outside the United States
▶ Works by non-U.S. citizens published both inside and outside the United States. Note that to fall within this category, U.S. publication must have occurred more than 30 days after foreign publication, and there could not be a subsequent registration in the United States. (If publication occurred within 30 days, or if there was subsequent U.S. registration and renewal, the work is treated as if it was an American work.)
▶ Works by U.S. citizens living outside the United States, published only outside the United States

The rules on copyright duration for foreign works are simpler than for U.S. works. Close examination of Table 3.3 will reveal that almost all foreign works published since 1923 are protected by copyright.

▪ ▪ TABLE 3.3

Works First Published Outside the United States by Foreign Nationals or U.S. Citizens Living Abroad

Date of Publication	Conditions	Copyright Term in the United States
Before 1923	None	In the public domain
Works Published Abroad Before 1978		
1923 through 1977	Published in compliance with all U.S. formalities (i.e., notice, renewal)	95 years after publication date
1923 through 1977	Published without compliance with U.S. formalities, and in the public domain in its home country as of 1 January 1996	In the public domain
1923 through 1977	Solely published abroad, without compliance with U.S. formalities or republication in the United States, and not in the public domain in its home country as of 1 January 1996.	95 years after publication date

Date of Publication	Conditions	Copyright Term in the United States
1923 through 1977	Published in the United States less than 30 days after publication abroad	Use the U.S. publication chart to determine duration
1923 through 1977	Published in the United States more than 30 days after publication abroad, without compliance with U.S. formalities, and not in the public domain in its home country as of 1 January 1996.	95 years after publication date

Works Published Abroad After 1 January 1978

After 1 January 1978	Published without copyright notice, and in the public domain in its home country as of 1 January 1996	In the public domain
After 1 January 1978	Published either with or without copyright notice, and not in the public domain in its home country as of 1 January 1996	70 years after death of author, or if work of corporate authorship, 95 years from publication

Special Cases

1 July 1909 through 1978	In Alaska, Arizona, California, Hawaii, Idaho, Montana, Nevada, Oregon, Washington, Guam, and the Northern Mariana Islands ONLY. Published in a language other than English, and without subsequent republication with a copyright notice.	The same as for an unpublished work
Anytime	Created by a resident of Afghanistan, Eritrea, Ethiopia, Iran, Iraq, San Marino, and possibly Yemen, and published in one of these countries	Not protected by U.S. copyright law because they are not party to international copyright agreements
Anytime	Works whose copyright was once owned or administered by the Alien Property Custodian, and whose copyright, if restored, would as of January 1, 1996, be owned by a government	Not protected by U.S. copyright law

Date of Publication	Conditions	Copyright Term in the United States
Anytime	Countries that joined Berne or signed a copyright treaty after 1 Jan. 1996.	Date for determining public-domain status is the date of adherence to a treaty, not 1 Jan. 1996

Until 1955, to receive protection in the United States, foreign works had to comply with United States requirements for notice, manufacture, obligatory deposit, and renewal. In 1955 the Universal Copyright Convention (U.C.C.) dropped the requirements for U.S. manufacture and deposit of copies of foreign books, and the copyright notice requirement could be met by the more lenient U.C.C. standard. Copyright renewal in the United States was still required to achieve the maximum term of copyright protection, however.

In 1994, the Uruguay Round Agreements Act (URAA) removed the requirement that foreign works had to comply with United States formalities. Furthermore, its provisions were retroactive. Works that had never been protected in the United States suddenly received protection, and works by foreign authors that had fallen into the public domain in the United States (because the copyright had originally been registered but not renewed) had their copyright restored. For the first time in U.S. history, works that had been in the public domain fell back under copyright protection.

TIP

It can often be difficult to determine if a work was first published in the United States or abroad. Many works published in the United States by American publishers had actually first appeared overseas—and there is no indication in the book to indicate this. Digitizing this book, even if its American copyright has expired, could be an infringement of its foreign copyright.[4]

WATCH THIS SPACE

The constitutionality of restoration of copyright in foreign works is currently being challenged in a suit entitled *Golan v. Holder*. In 2009, the U.S. District Court for the District of Colorado ruled that the restoration provisions are unconstitutional under the First Amendment, at least as far as they impact "reliance parties" (people who were exploiting public domain works prior to copyright restoration). An appeal is likely. Institutions that own foreign works should follow this case closely; see http://cyberlaw.stanford.edu/case/golan-v-gonzales for updates.

Duration for most works first published abroad is very simple. They receive the copyright term they would have had if they had followed all U.S. formalities at the time of publication. For works published before 1978, that means 95 years from publication. For works published since 1978, it is life of the author plus 70 years or 95 years for an anonymous and pseudonymous works and works made for hire.

■ **KEY POINT**

United States and foreign countries may have different terms for the same work

The copyright terms for foreign works in the United States are set by U.S. law. However, the copyright term in a work's country of origin may differ from the protection that the United States affords. For example, Australian photographs made before 1955 are in the public domain in Australia,[5] but would still be protected by copyright in the United States.

The Naxos record label found this out when they tried to reissue in the United States sound recordings made in England. The recordings had entered the public domain in England before 1 January 1996 because those recordings had a 50-year copyright term. A New York court, however, concluded that the recordings were still protected in the United States because of the differing laws in the United States regarding sound recordings *(Capitol Records v. Naxos)*. In order to distribute the recordings in New York, Naxos needed the permission of Capitol Records, the owner of the American rights in the recordings.

■ **TRICKY AREA**

Foreign works in western states

The discussion about the copyright status of foreign works in the United States is accurate for most of the country, but a special situation prevails in states governed by the 9th Judicial Circuit (Alaska,

Arizona, California, Hawaii, Idaho, Montana, Nevada, Oregon, Washington, and Guam and the Northern Mariana Islands). In the 1966 case of *Twin Books v. Walt Disney Co.*, the 9th Circuit Court of Appeals concluded that different rules applied to works published outside the United States in a foreign language and without a copyright notice. The court concluded, "publication without a copyright notice in a foreign country did not put the work in the public domain in the United States." These foreign-language publications were instead in effect "unpublished" in the United States, and hence had the same copyright term as unpublished works. For example, in a 2006 decision in Arizona, the court found that sculptures by Jean Renoir published in France in 1917 were still protected by copyright in the United States (even though we normally assume that works published before 1923 are in the public domain) (*Société Civile Succession Richard Guino v. Beseder*).

The 9th Circuit decision has been harshly criticized in *Nimmer on Copyright*, a leading treatise on copyright, as being incompatible with previous decisions and the intent of Congress when it restored foreign copyrights.[6] The Copyright Office also ignores the *Twin Books* decision in its circular on restored copyrights.[7] It is possible that in subsequent cases, the 9th Circuit will reverse its opinion. Nevertheless, any cultural institution in one of the states governed by this court needs to be aware that they may end up in court if they digitize non-English foreign publications. It will have to determine if it is willing to run the risk.

3.2.4 *Sound recordings*

The duration of sound recording copyright is both simple and complex. The bottom line is that almost all sound recordings, regardless of when they were made, are protected to some extent.

Published and unpublished U.S. sound recordings and unpublished foreign sound recordings made before 15 February 1972 are protected by state common law copyright. At least one state (California) has a law that specifies that sound recordings will begin to enter the public domain in the state in 2047. Most states, however, have a combination of antipiracy and antibootlegging legislation that, in addition to case law, serves as the basis of protection for the recording. These protections run at least until 2067, when all pre-1972 recordings will enter the public domain.

Recordings made between 1972 and 1989 were subject to the same copyright formalities as published works. American published recordings that failed to include a copyright notice on the recording entered the public domain. Sound recordings published with notice received the same copyright term as any other published work: 95 years from publication for works before 1978, and life of the author plus 70 years for works made since 1978.[8]

Published foreign sound recordings have more federal protection than do American works. Sound recordings published abroad before 1972 receive federal copyright protection for a period of 95 years after publication. (Remember that U.S. recordings only receive state common law protection.) If the foreign work had entered the public domain in its home country by 1 January 1996, it is not eligible for federal copyright protection but can still be protected by state common law copyrights.

KEY POINT

Most sound recordings are copyrighted

The only sound recordings that have entered the public domain through expiration of copyright are U.S. recordings published between 1972 and 1989 without proper notice of copyright. All other sound recordings are protected.

3.2.5 *Architectural works*

It is unlikely that a cultural heritage institution would want to digitize a building as constructed, but for the sake of completeness it is worth noting that only buildings constructed since 1990 are protected by copyright. Duration is the same as for published works: life of the author plus 70 years or 95 years for works made for hire.

It is more likely that institutions might wish to digitize the plans or representations of buildings. The plans and drawings of pre-1990 buildings can be protected by copyright. The photographer of photographs of pre- and post-1990 buildings may also have a copyright in their photographs. For post-1990 buildings, the copyright owner of the building may also have a copyright interest in a photograph, but only if it was not taken from a public space (see Chapter 5).

3.3 Who is the owner of copyright?

The default rule contained in the Copyright Act is that the "author" of a work is the initial owner of copyright [17 U.S.C. § 201(a)]. As will be seen, the copyright understanding of authorship differs significantly from the way the term is normally used, and in one important concept—work for hire—there is a radical shift in definition. It is also possible for copyright ownership to be transferred by written agreement, bequest, or operation of law [17 U.S.C. § 201(d)].

The following sections consider these questions:

1. Who is the "author" or "maker" of a work?
2. What happens when there is more than one author?
3. Who owns copyright in material produced by employees, contractors, and volunteers?
4. How is copyright transferred to third parties?

TIP

Given that copyright can be transferred and inherited, it is possible that copyright has been transmitted—possibly multiple times—from the original owner. As such, when assessing who owns copyright, it should not be assumed that the author of the work retains ownership of copyright.

WHO IS THE "AUTHOR" OF A WORK?

In general, the author of a copyrighted work is the person who wrote or produced the relevant expression: "the person who translates an idea into a fixed, tangible expression entitled to copyright protection" (*CCNV v. Reid*).

Thus, where one person supplies the ideas (such as a celebrity) and another expresses those ideas in writing (such as a ghostwriter), it is the latter who is the author of the resulting literary work and would own its copyright, regardless of what the title page might say. (For this reason, ghostwriting contracts normally include a provision that all copyrights are to be transferred to the presumptive author and/or publisher.) But what happens when material dictated by someone else is transcribed? This will be considered in Case Study 1 on oral histories.

Authorship of sound recordings is slightly different than authorship of other materials. There are a number of possible "authors" of such items, namely the people making the sounds being recorded, as well as the people responsible for capturing those sounds. Ownership of copyright will depend on the relative contributions of these people. For instance, a, performer whose performance is captured in a recording is generally considered to be an author of the recording. The Beatles, for example, would be considered to be an author of a performance of "She Loves You." But the creation of a sound recording is also likely to involve authorship "on the part of the record producer responsible for setting up the recording session, capturing and electronically processing the sounds, and compiling and editing them to make the final sound recording."[9] George Martin, the producer of the Beatles recording of "Please Please Me," is likely therefore to share ownership with the Beatles of the sound recording copyright in that specific recording—at least in the United States. (For reasons discussed under the "work made for hire" section below, Martin's employer at that time, EMI, would actually own the copyright. He would not gain his ownership of part of the recording until he became an independent contractor.)

In some cases, the role of the recording engineer may be so minimal that the performance is the only copyrightable element in the work. Think, for example, of an oral history interview at which a tape recorder is placed between the participants and turned on. In other cases, such as with recordings of birdsongs, only the record producer's contribution is copyrightable. And in some cases, there may be no performers and the role of the record producer is minimal; think of a microphone turned on in the middle of a demonstration, with no subsequent editorial work on the recording. In such a case, where the sounds are fixed by some purely mechanical means without originality of any kind, there would be no sound recording copyright.

For discussion of the issues surrounding ownership of copyright in sound recordings, see Case Study 1.

JOINT AUTHORSHIP

Some works have more than one author. Works with more than one author under the Copyright Act can either be "joint works of authorship," compilations, or derivative works. The copyright ownership implications of each are quite different.

A joint work "is a work prepared by two or more authors with the intention that their contributions be merged into inseparable or interdependent parts of a unitary whole" [17 U.S.C. § 101]. The authors might have collaborated with each other, or they could have prepared their contributions separately, but with the intent that their contributions be merged into a single work. The key element in identifying a joint work is the intention, at the time the expression is fixed, "that the parts be absorbed or combined into an integrated unit, although the parts themselves may be either "inseparable" (as the case of a novel or painting) or "interdependent" (as in the case of a motion picture, opera, or the words and music of a song)."[10]

A joint work can be distinguished from a collective work, which is a specific kind of compilation. A collective work, such as a periodical issue, encyclopedia, or festschrift, consists of contributions from multiple authors. But the contributions to collective works are gathered; there is not the sense of merger or unity to them. For example, when two people cowrite a script, they will be joint authors of the script. But the inclusion of that script in a compilation of "the year's best plays" does not make the playwrights joint authors of the compilation. The playwrights are the authors and copyright owners of their original play, whereas the compiler of the anthology is the owner of the copyright in the selection.

When one copyrighted work serves as the basis for another work, the second work is identified not as a joint work but rather as a derivative work. The copyright in any new expression that the author of the derivative work creates belongs solely to that author. The author of the original work may not use the derivative work without the permission of the second author. At the same time, no use of the derivative work can be made without the permission of the original author, since any use might infringe on his or her original copyright. Imagine a book that is transformed (with permission) by a playwright into a play. A movie studio then seeks to make a film version of the play. It needs the permission of both the playwright, since it wants to use his or her copyrighted additions, and the original author.

The copyright in a work of joint authorship is co-owned by the authors of that work as tenants in common. Each author can exercise in full any of the rights granted to a copyright owner. He or she has no obligation to seek the consent of the other copyright owners. The only requirement is that the copyright owner must share with the other co-owners any profits derived from the use of the work.[11]

The principles of tenancy in common that govern copyright ownership of a joint work of copyright also apply when multiple heirs inherit a copyright. Consider the situation when four siblings inherit a copyright. Each sibling now owns one quarter of the copyright. Any sibling could grant permission for the institution to digitize the work; there is no need to seek permission from the others. Furthermore, if that sibling transferred his or her ownership share to a cultural institution, that institution would now be the owner of the quarter share. If the institution decided to sell reproductions of the copyrighted work, it would be required to account to the other siblings for any profits earned on the reproductions. It would not, however, need to seek the permission of the other co-owners to digitize the work. (For further discussion on permission, see Chapter 7.)

> **TIP**
> Any co-owner of copyright can grant nonexclusive permission for the reproduction, distribution, or performance of a work. It is not necessary to secure the permission of all of the co-owners.

WORK MADE FOR HIRE: MATERIAL PRODUCED BY EMPLOYEES, CONTRACTORS, AND VOLUNTEERS

We have said that the author is normally the initial owner of copyright and that the author is "the person who translates an idea into a fixed, tangible expression entitled to copyright protection" (*CCNV v. Reid*). If that person is an employee, however, and if the fixation is part of that person's employment duties, then the employer, not the person, is considered to be the author and, as such, owns the copyright in the work. The work itself is considered to be a "work made for hire" [17 U.S.C. § 201(b)]. When, for example, a staff member of a cultural institution writes that institution's annual report, the institution, and not the employee, is considered to be the author of the report—even if the report states that it is authored by that employee.

In certain fields, most notably academic institutions, employment contracts may alter the default position found in copyright law. For example, it is common for universities to allow faculty members to assert authorship and copyright ownership of scholarly books and articles that they produce, even though faculty are normally required to write as part of their employment contracts. The situation regarding authorship and ownership of course materials such as syllabi and lectures is much less clear.[12]

■ **KEY POINT**

When an employee produces a work as part of his or her duties, the employer, and not the person who created the work, is considered to be the author and copyright owner.

Determining whether a work was created independently or as part of employment is important for two reasons.[13] First, it determines who actually owns the copyright. Second, it determines how long that copyright lasts. If a work is created independently, copyright will endure for 70 years after the death of the author (assuming it was made after 1977) [17 U.S.C. § 302(a)]. If it was done as part of employment and the employer is the author, copyright will endure for 95 years from publication or 120 years from creation [17 U.S.C. § 302(c)].

■ **TIP**

When acquiring material from individuals, try to identify which works were produced in that person's individual capacity and which were produced as part of his or her employment. Remember that a copyright transfer agreement cannot apply to works for which the person does not hold the copyright. It may be necessary to secure a copyright transfer agreement from an employer as well.

Many assume that the "work made for hire" doctrine would also apply to works produced by independent contractors hired to produce them. The definition of work made for hire in Section 101 of the Copyright Act does include some very precise situations in which contracted work can be considered to be work made for hire. Works made for hire are specially ordered or commissioned works that are one of the following:

▶ A contribution to a collective work
▶ Part of a motion picture or other audiovisual work
▶ A translation
▶ A supplementary work (i.e., "a work prepared for publication as a secondary adjunct to a work by another author for the purpose of introducing, concluding, illustrating, explaining, revising, commenting upon, or assisting in the use of the other work, such as forewords, afterwords, pictorial illustrations, maps, charts, tables, editorial notes, musical

arrangements, answer material for tests, bibliographies, appendixes, and indexes" [17 U.S.C. § 101])

▶ A compilation
▶ An instructional text (i.e., "a literary, pictorial, or graphic work prepared for publication and with the purpose of use in systematic instructional activities" [17 U.S.C. § 101])
▶ A test or answer material for a test
▶ An atlas

In addition to falling into one of these categories, the parties must expressly agree in a written instrument signed by them that the work is a work made for hire [17 U.S.C. § 101]. If you hire someone to translate a work but do not agree in writing in advance that the work is to be considered to be a work made for hire, then the copyright in the translation would belong to the translator, not you.

Note that these categories are exceptionally limited. Motion pictures, for example, are normally produced as work made for hire, and the studio would own the copyright of any contractors working on the movie. Photographs taken by a contract photographer, however, hired to take stills on the movie set, most likely would not be work made for hire and so the copyright could belong to the photographer and not the studio. Similarly, copyright in photographs taken by employees of a cultural institution would belong to the institution, but copyright in photographs taken by independent contractors hired by the institution would belong to the photographer—unless the photographs were for a collective work or compilation, and unless there was an agreement in writing that they were to be considered to be work made for hire. If the work is not a work made for hire, then the contract with the photographer should state that he or she will transfer all copyrights in the photographs to the institution.

▪ KEY POINT

Except in certain very limited circumstances, copyright in the work of independent contractors belongs to the contractor, not to the agency that hired them. When hiring someone to do work, you should consider whether an assignment or license is required and, if appropriate, include in the contract terms a provision that assigns or licenses to you the rights you need.

What about volunteers? Volunteers are normally not considered to be employees, and unless their work falls under one of the precise categories for independent contractors listed above, their work would not normally be considered to be work made for hire. The courts, however, have tempered the exact language of the copyright law by introducing the concept of agency. Under agency law, an individual can be considered to be an employee by weighing a number of factors. The court in *Aymes v. Bonelli*, building on the Supreme Court's decision in *CCNV v. Reid*, articulated five that are almost always likely to be significant:

▶ The hiring party's right to control the manner and means of creation
▶ The skill required
▶ The provision of employee benefits
▶ The tax treatment of the hired party
▶ Whether the hiring party has the right to assign additional projects to the hired party

The closer a relationship comes to regular, salaried employment, the more likely it is that a work-made-for-hire situation exists. Using the principles of agency law, at least one court has found a volunteer to be an employee. In *Town of Clarkstown v. Reeder*, a volunteer member of the executive board of an organization was found not to be the copyright owner of a manual he largely wrote on behalf of the board.

TIP

Although it may be theoretically possible to view volunteers as employees, clearly the safest thing to do is to assume that work produced by volunteers is not work made for hire. You should consider whether an assignment or license is appropriate and require that all volunteers sign agreements that transfer or license the copyright in any work that they produce for you to your institution. There is no particular wording that must be used; just make sure that the language makes the intention of the parties clear.

PRE-1978 WORK MADE FOR HIRE

The preceding discussion of works made for hire is based on the 1976 Copyright Act and describes the doctrine as it exists today. Prior to 1978, a different definition of work made for hire prevailed. The operative presumption was that, in the absence of express contractual reservations to the contrary, copyright belonged to the person at whose initiative and expense the work was done. In other words, it was assumed that copyright in work produced by independent contractors belonged to the person or organization that hired them unless written agreements or professional norms said otherwise.

As a result of these differing interpretations, one must consider the date of creation when determining the initial copyright ownership of a work. (Remember, however, that the initial copyright owner can always transfer or license the copyright to others.) Consider the following different situations and see how the date of creation affects copyright ownership:

▶ Professional photographer makes a portrait photo at the request of a customer
▶ Pre-1978: copyright likely belongs to customer (*Lumiere v. Robertson-Cole*)
   Post-1978: copyright likely belongs to photographer (*Granse v. Brown Photo*)
▶ Professional photographer prepares portrait photograph at her initiative and expense
   Pre-1978: copyright likely belongs to photographer
   Post-1978: copyright belongs to photographer
▶ Artist commissioned to create artwork for a building
   Pre-1978: copyright belongs to builder (*Yardley v. Houghton Mifflin*)
   Post-1978: copyright belongs to sculptor (*CCNV v. Reid*)

■ **TRICKY POINT**
An agreement to the contrary can always trump the default presumptions of the works-made-for-hire doctrine. For example, copyright ownership of a portrait photo taken before 1978 would normally belong to the person who commissioned the work—unless there was a contract to the contrary. Many famous portrait photographers (including Bachrach and Karsh) routinely retained copyright in their work. Unfortunately, with older works, it is often difficult to determine whether there was a contract in effect that governed copyright ownership.

3.4 How is copyright transferred to others?

The Copyright Act provides that copyright can be transferred by the copyright owner. Transfer can be absolute (all copyright rights are transferred) or limited (individual rights are assigned, or only for a certain duration or territory). For example, it would be possible to transfer to another the right to reproduce a work in which you hold the copyright, but retain the right to make derivative works from that work.

Transfer can take place in a number of ways, including by assignment, will, and operation of law [17 U.S.C. § 201(d)]. For the purpose of these guidelines, it is worth discussing transfer by assignment and will. Transfer by operation of law includes transfer as a result of bankruptcy or court order, and is not discussed further. Copyright also can be licensed, which is discussed in Chapter 7.

TRANSFERS BY ASSIGNMENTS, MORTGAGES, AND EXCLUSIVE LICENSE

The Copyright Act allows the transfer of copyright by assignment: the designation that someone else will own the right. It also equates mortgages and exclusive licenses with transfer of ownership. When copyright is transferred, the recipient enjoys all relevant rights in copyright. The recipient can enforce these rights even to the exclusion of the former copyright owner. In essence, transfer results in a new owner of copyright.

In order to take effect, a transfer of ownership of copyright must be:

▶ in writing, and
▶ signed "by the owner of the rights conveyed or such owner's duly authorized agent" [17 U.S.C. § 204(a)]

Rights can be divided and assigned to different people. Hence, an owner of the copyright in a book could assign its rights of reproduction to one person and rights of adaptation to another. Similarly, assignment can be limited according to territory (such as U.S. rights) or limited according to time (such as an assignment for five years).

Courts have ruled that a person may also assign copyright in material that does not yet exist, although this is not explicitly mentioned in the Copyright Act,[14] This means an assignment may be obtained from a volunteer at the start of duties, or a commercial designer at the beginning of a contract, to cover material produced in the future.

TRANSFER OF COPYRIGHT BY WILL

When a person dies, any copyrights they own become part of their estate and are bequeathed just like any other personal property. The copyrights may be expressly mentioned in a will, or they may be assigned as part of the remainder of an estate. If there is no will, then the relevant state probate laws would govern the disposition of the intellectual property.

TRANSFER OF COPYRIGHT BY SALE

Section 202 of the 1976 Copyright Act states: "Transfer of ownership of any material object, including the copy or phonorecord in which the work is first fixed, does not of itself convey any rights in the copyrighted work embodied in the object." The addition of this section to the copyright law in 1976 was a conscious decision to reverse what had been known as the "Pushman presumption": a common law doctrine that authors or artists were presumed to have transferred common law literary property rights when they sold a work of art, unless those rights were specifically reserved.[15] The doctrine was named after *Pushman v. New York Graphic Society* in which the court concluded that the total and unconditional transfer of a work of art conveyed with it all copyrights.

In a subsequent case, *Grandma Moses v. This Week Magazine*, the court, building in part on *Pushman*, reaffirmed its belief that the unrestricted general sale of an unpublished painting constituted "publication" and, in the absence of the proper formalities, concluded the work had entered the public domain.

The Pushman presumption was overturned through legislation in many states, including New York in 1966, before the 1976 Act overturned it completely. Yet for a certain period, the unconditional sale of a painting by a copyright owner could either transfer ownership to the recipient or place the item in the public domain. Museums may wish to investigate and document the circumstances surrounding the acquisition of their holdings for they may, without realizing it, have acquired copyright ownership of many works of art prior to the repeal of the Pushman presumption.

3.5 Conclusion

As this chapter has made clear, the issues surrounding authorship, duration, and current ownership of copyright are complex and intertwined. Whether a work was created independently or as a product of employment can affect both the initial ownership and duration of the copyright. The complex issue of whether a work has been published will also determine whether it may have entered the public domain. And transfers in ownership may make it difficult to identify and locate current copyright owners in order to seek any needed permissions for digitization.

In spite of its difficulty, however, it is imperative that participants in digitization projects master the intricacies of copyright ownership and duration if they wish to minimize the risk of infringement. Many project managers assert that they will only digitize material in the public domain; it is only with a deep understanding of what the public domain is and how works enter the public domain that this risk-avoidance strategy can be properly implemented.

4 *Exclusive Rights and Infringement*

4.1 Introduction

The Copyright Act grants to the owner of a copyrighted work certain exclusive rights. Anyone who violates any of these exclusive rights is a potential infringer, and the owner of that right is allowed to bring suit against the infringer for the violation of that right. In addition, certain commercial dealings with infringing articles (such as importing bootleg CDs or DVDs) also constitute infringements of copyright [17 U.S.C. § 501].

There are several different types of infringement. Direct infringement, which is specified in the Copyright Act, occurs when someone's actions immediately violate one of the exclusive rights. For example, making an unauthorized reproduction of a copyrighted work would be a direct infringement of copyright. The courts have also identified two forms of indirect infringement: contributory infringement and vicarious liability. Put crudely, a person may indirectly infringe copyright where they encourage or assist a direct infringement undertaken by someone else. As will be seen, there are principles to determine the requisite level of participation for indirect liability to arise. Given that direct infringement is far more relevant to digitization projects than indirect infringement, it will be the main focus of this chapter.

In addition to the exclusive rights of the copyright owner specified in the Copyright Act, the Digital Millennium Copyright Act (DMCA) created a new, de facto right to control, through technological measures, access to, and some copying of, a work. Although they are not limited to copyright owners, its provisions form part of the Copyright Act.

This chapter deals with three questions:

▶ What are the exclusive rights of the copyright owner (including moral rights and DMCA protections)?
▶ In what circumstances will a person directly infringe those rights?
▶ What remedies can a court award in relation to that infringement?

The chapter presupposes that one of the exclusive rights has been infringed *beyond what is permitted by one of the exemptions to copyright* (see Chapters 5 and 6). An exempted activity, such as a fair-use reproduction of a work, is not an infringement of the copyright owner's exclusive right of reproduction.

4.2 Exclusive rights

The copyright owner is granted six main groups of exclusive rights in Section 106 of the Copyright Act. They are the rights to do, or authorize the doing of, any of the following acts:

▶ Reproduction
▶ Preparation of derivative works (such as adaptations)
▶ Distribution
▶ Public performance (for literary, musical, dramatic, and choreographic works, pantomimes, motion pictures, and other audiovisuals)
▶ Public display (for literary, musical, dramatic, and choreographic works, pantomimes, and pictorial, graphic, or sculptural works, including the individual images of a motion picture or other audiovisual work)
▶ Public performance of sound recordings via digital audio transmission

In addition, Section 106(a) establishes certain moral rights for works of visual art. They are discussed later in this chapter.

As seen from the list above, the exclusive rights of copyright differ for various types of work protected by the Copyright Act. The reproduction, public distribution, and derivative works rights apply to all copyrighted works. In contrast, the performance and display rights only apply to particular types of copyright subject matter. In the case of the public performance rights for sound recordings, that right is limited to digital transmission. It is not an infringement of the sound recording copyright to play such a work aloud or broadcast it via analog radio waves (although it may be an infringement of the rights of the copyright owner of the underlying musical work, if any).

The exclusive rights in Section 106 are said to be "subject to sections 107 through 122." These provisions identify activities that are deemed *not* to constitute an infringement of copyright (limitations on or exemptions to copyright infringement). Some of these limitations are unremunerated (e.g., fair use, the libraries and archives provisions), and others require payment of a fee (i.e., are "statutory" or "compulsory" licenses). Thus, where an activity falls within an exemption or limitation, it is not necessary to obtain a license or transfer of rights from the copyright owner. The content of limitations most relevant to cultural institutions is discussed in detail in Chapters 5 and 6.

■ **KEY POINT**

Many of the activities undertaken by cultural institutions, including digitization, may run afoul of one of the exclusive rights granted by copyright. For example:

▶ Digitizing an analog print-based or artistic work reproduces the work.

▶ Making digitized content available online, for instance on publicly accessible Web sites, may constitute distribution of the item.

▶ If the work presented in digital form is an audiovisual work, making it available online may infringe on the right to perform a work

Each of the exclusive rights is briefly discussed in the following section.

REPRODUCTION

Section 106(1) gives the owner of copyright the exclusive right to "reproduce the copyrighted work in copies or phonocopies."

The reproduction right should be construed broadly. For instance, a House Report prepared during passage of the 1976 Act explained that the right to reproduce a copyrighted work means "the right to produce a material object in which the work is duplicated, transcribed, imitated, or simulated in a fixed form from which it can be 'perceived, reproduced, or otherwise communicated, either directly or with the aid of a machine or device.'"[1] This form of words is reflected in the definitions of "copies" and "phonorecords" in Section 101.

Imagine the different ways that one could reprint a book: by setting new type of the text, photocopying the original, or digitizing the text to create a machine-readable version. All would infringe on the exclusive right of reproduction. Imitating the appearance of a painting could also infringe on that right, as could turning a photograph into a sculpture (*Rogers v. Koons*). As long as there is substantial similarity between the two works, copying is presumed to have taken place. The key issue with reproduction is that the author's "expression"—the author's original contribution to the work—has been taken.

The reproduction right for sound recordings is somewhat more limited than for other copyrighted materials. The owner of the sound recording copyright only has the exclusive right to reproduce the actual sounds fixed on that particular sound recording [17 U.S.C. § 114(b)]. But anyone else can record a "sound alike" performance intended to duplicate the sound on a sound recording without infringing on the rights of the copyright owner of that recording (though if there is a copyright owner of the underlying musical work, it may infringe on his or her rights. It could also infringe on publicity rights: see Chapter 9). This limitation on exclusive rights only exists for sound recordings, however, and not for audiovisual works.

DERIVATIVE WORKS

Section 106(2) grants the copyright owner the exclusive right "to prepare derivative works based upon the copyrighted work." Derivative works are therefore adaptations of the copyrighted work. The following are examples derivative works listed in Section 101 of the Copyright Act:

David Koller of the Institute for Advanced Technology in the Humanities makes a 3D scan of the Laocoon statue in the Vatican Museums. Though found on a government website (http://www.lbl.gov/cs/Archive/news122208b.html), which would suggest that the image is in the public domain, it is actually an uncredited photo by Chad Keller of IATH.

Photo Credit: Chad Keller and the Institute for Advanced Technology in the Humanities at the University of Virginia.

License: Used with permission.

- ▶ Translations
- ▶ Musical arrangements
- ▶ Dramatizations
- ▶ Fictionalizations
- ▶ Motion picture versions
- ▶ Sound recordings
- ▶ Art reproductions
- ▶ Abridgments
- ▶ Condensations
- ▶ Any other form in which a work may be recast, transformed, or adapted

TRICKY QUESTION

Does reformatting a work create a derivative work?

Many institutions want to convert items from one format to another for preservation or to increase access to the original. For example, an institution might want to convert a ¾" analog videotape to MPEG 4 format or convert e-mail in Microsoft Outlook's .pst mailboxes into a generic XML format. In some cases, the institution may hope to claim copyright protection in the new work. Is the reformatted item a derivative work?

The answer to this difficult question hinges on the amount of originality required to produce the derivative work. If the modifications are primarily mechanical, then the work would be primarily a reproduction, not a derivative work. If in creating the new work, however, the modifications are such that one could argue that original works of authorship have been added, then a derivative work has been created.

In many ways, the issue is moot. Regardless of whether it is a reproduction or a derivative work, a reformatted copy would infringe on the exclusive rights of the copyright owner—unless an exemption applies.

DISTRIBUTION

The right of distribution gives copyright owners the exclusive right to distribute copies of copyrighted works to the public "by sale or other transfer of ownership, or by rental, lease, or lending" [17 U.S.C. § 106(3)]. Distribution could therefore occur by publishing the copyrighted work and distributing the copies. It could also possibly occur by making the work available for downloading on a Web site or through a file-sharing program. In at least one case, distribution was said to have occurred merely by including records for illegal copies in the catalog of a library, with no evidence the items were ever borrowed (*Hotaling v. LDS*).

The courts have extended the right of distribution to encompass a general right of first publication. Under this concept, the copyright owner not only has the exclusive right to control how a work will be distributed but also the right to determine *whether* and *when* a particular work will be made available to the public. The copyright owner has, under ordinary circumstances, the right to control the first public appearance of his or her undisseminated expression (*Harper & Row v. Nation*). Digitizing unpublished manuscripts and making them publicly accessible via the Internet is likely to be an infringement of the copyright owner's distribution right.

The exclusive right of distribution is tempered by an important limitation on this right found in Section 109. The "first sale" doctrine stipulates that some of the copyright owner's rights over a specific copy of a work end once his or her ownership of that copy ends. The copyright owner cannot, for example, stop a library from lending a legally acquired copy of a work, nor can he or she stop someone from selling a legally acquired copy in a used-book store. Nor can the copyright owner prevent a purchaser from displaying the work in public, which allows museums and libraries to exhibit copies of their works.

DID YOU KNOW?

In 2004, the Irish National Library wanted to exhibit some of James Joyce's manuscripts in order to commemorate the centenary of Bloomsday, the day on which *Ulysses* is set. The copyright owner of the manuscripts, Joyce's grandson, objected to the display. Because Ireland does not have a law comparable to Section 109 that allows the display of legally acquired copies, the Irish Parliament had to rush through emergency legislation to allow the exhibition to go forward.[2]

PUBLIC PERFORMANCE

The public performance right in Section 106(4) applies to literary, musical, dramatic, and choreographic works, pantomimes, and motion pictures and other audiovisual works.

A public performance can include reading a work aloud, staging a play, singing or playing music, and dancing a ballet or other choreographic work. A public performance may have multiple iterations. For example, when a theater troupe stages a play, it is performing. When a network transmits that performance to its local affiliates, it is also performing the play, regardless of whether they are broadcasting live or on tape. When the local television affiliate broadcasts the play over the air and through cable systems, it is performing. Putting a digital copy of the performance on a server from which it can be viewed or downloaded would also constitute a performance. When an individual watches the performance by turning on the television or computer, that individual is performing (in copyright terms) the play.

Both the performance and display rights are limited to "public" expressions of the work. To perform or display a work publicly means to perform or display it anywhere that is open to the public or anywhere that a "substantial number of persons outside of a normal circle of a family and its social acquaintances is gathered" [17 U.S.C. § 101]. Semipublic places such as clubs, lodges, factories, summer camps, and schools are all considered "public" for purposes of copyright. Transmitting the performance or display to such a place also makes it public.

PUBLIC DISPLAY

Section 106(5) grants a right of public display to copyright owners of literary, musical, dramatic, and choreographic works, pantomimes, and pictorial, graphic, or sculptural works, including the individual images of a motion picture or other audiovisual work.

Public display applies to the showing of any copy of the work, including the original work itself. As written, the right would prohibit museums from displaying artwork or archives from exhibiting manuscripts without the permission of the copyright owner. Section 109(c), however, contains an important exemption that allows the owner of a particular copy (or someone authorized by the owner) to display that work publicly either directly or by projection at the place where the work is located. Thus, exhibiting a painting from a cultural institution's collection would not infringe the display right, but putting a reproduction on the institution's Web site might.

PUBLIC PERFORMANCE OF SOUND RECORDINGS

The copyright owner has the exclusive right to perform sound recordings via digital (but not analog) transmissions [17 U.S.C. § 106(6)]. Some digital public performances are subject to a compulsory license; others, because they are viewed as being of higher risk to the copyright owner, must be negotiated in advance. Most digitization projects of cultural heritage institutions would fall into this later grouping.

4.3 Moral rights

In addition to the exclusive rights described above, Section 106A of the Copyright Act provides for moral rights for certain works of art. Although they are included in the Berne Convention and common in European copyright law, moral rights in the United States have traditionally been protected outside copyright via laws regarding slander, libel, and misappropriation. This practice changed slightly in 1990 with the passage of the Visual Artist Rights Act (VARA), which added Section 106A to the Copyright Act. It granted some artists rights relating to *attribution* and the *integrity* of works.

The right of attribution is intended to ensure that authors are only identified with works that they have created. Specifically, the author has:

▶ The right to be identified as author of a work he or she has created
▶ The right not to be identified as the author of a work that he or she did not create
▶ The right not to be identified as the author of a work he or she has created when distortion, mutilation, or other modification of the work would be prejudicial to his or her reputation [17 U.S.C. § 106A(a)]

The right of integrity is intended to protect the work against treatment that would be prejudicial to the author's honor or reputation [17 U.S.C. § 106A(a)]. Thus, under VARA, the author of a visual work of art has the right to prevent any prejudicial distortions to or mutilations of his or her work, even after the work has been given or sold to a third party. In addition, if the work is of "recognized stature," its author can prevent its destruction.

It is unlikely that VARA will pose much of burden to cultural institutions interested in digitizing works from their collections. First, the moral rights created in VARA apply only to a very limited number of types of works: paintings, drawings, prints, sculptures, and still photographs. Section 101 specifies further restrictions on eligibility for each type:

Paintings, drawings, and prints must:
▶ exist in a single copy, *or*
▶ exist in a limited edition of 200 copies or fewer that are signed and consecutively numbered by the author.

Sculptures must:
▶ exist in a single copy, or
▶ exist in multiple cast, carved, or fabricated sculptures of 200 or fewer that are consecutively numbered by the author and bear the signature or other identifying mark of the author.

Still photographs must:
▶ be produced for exhibition purposes only, and
▶ exist in a single copy that is signed by the author, or
▶ exist in a limited edition of 200 copies or fewer that are signed and consecutively numbered by the photographer.

More importantly, moral rights do not apply to certain uses, including most reproductions. The purpose of VARA is to protect the rights of the author with regard to the original work of art and to protect that work; they do not extend to any reproduction, depiction, portrayal, or other use of a work in "any poster, map, globe, chart, technical drawing, diagram, model, applied art, motion picture or other audiovisual work, book, magazine, newspaper, periodical, data base, electronic information service, electronic publication, or similar publication," or "any merchandising item or advertising, promotional, descriptive, covering, or packaging material or container" [17 U.S.C. § 106A(c)(3) and § 101]. This exclusion should encompass most digitization activities of cultural institutions.

Cultural institutions that own works of fine art need to know about their obligations regarding attribution and the integrity of works. Moral-rights issues, however, need not impinge on their digitization initiatives.

4.4 The right to control access to digital works

With the passage of the Digital Millennium Copyright Act (DMCA) in 1998, a new kind of implicit right was created. One of the sections of this wide-ranging act creates civil and criminal penalties for bypassing technological methods used to control or limit access to certain works. In effect, it gives the publisher of the work a new exclusive right of access. This right belongs not to the author or copyright owner, but rather to anyone who publishes a work containing a technological protection measure.

The DMCA has provisions to control both the access to and copying of protected works. Regarding access, the law prohibits two things:

▶ The actual act of circumventing a technological measure that effectively controls access to a copyrighted work [17 U.S.C. § 1201(a)(1)(A)]
▶ The manufacture or distribution of hardware and software designed primarily to enable people to carry out the act of circumvention [17 U.S.C. § 1201(a)(2)]

In other words, the law prohibits both the act of circumventing an access control as well as the tools that would enable one to carry out such an act.

What is a technological measure that effectively controls access to a work? Passwords are one form of access control; encrypting (or scrambling) a file is another. A very common form of access control is the Content Scrambling System (CSS) encryption required by the DVD Manufacturers Association on commercial DVDs. One of the most remarkable things about the DMCA is that the prohibition against circumvention applies *even if the intended use is otherwise lawful and noninfringing.* Another is that manufacturers have argued that the anticircumvention provision applies to a wide variety of works not normally associated with copyright, including ink jet printer cartridges and garage door openers!

Recognizing that this provision might unduly affect the rights of users, Congress directed that every three years the Librarian of Congress should determine whether the implementation of access-control measures is diminishing the ability of individuals to use copyrighted works in ways that are otherwise lawful. The focus of the rulemaking is on whether there are specific classes of copyrighted works the use of which is, or in the next three years is likely to be, adversely affected by the prohibition against bypassing access-control mechanisms. For those classes of works, the Librarian can determine that bypassing the access-control mechanism would not be an infringement.

To date, the approved exceptions have been limited in number and scope. Two were identified in 2000; they grew to four in 2003; and the 2006 rulemaking had six. None of the provisions to date could be interpreted to allow a cultural institution to bypass an access-control mechanism in order to make a digital object widely accessible via the Internet. Nor is there any similar rulemaking regarding the tools used to bypass access controls. The assumption seems to be that an organization given the right to bypass an access control will also have to figure out how technically to do this on their own; they are forbidden from sharing their findings with others.[3]

The DMCA also addresses reproduction and the other exclusive rights of the copyright owner. Unlike the situation with access controls, the actual act of copying a protected work is not banned (though it may be prohibited by other sections of the Copyright Act). The manufacturing or importation of hardware and software to assist with such copying is prohibited, however [17 U.S.C. § 1201(b)]. A cultural institution can, therefore, bypass copy (as opposed to access) controls on a work protected by technological protection measures—but it has to figure out how technically to do this, and it cannot share its solution with other institutions.

The DMCA prohibitions present an immense stumbling block to cultural institutions that wish to preserve and make available information that has been encrypted or otherwise controlled. Currently it is primarily commercially produced works that have such protections on them. More and more desktop software, however, is incorporating password and other access controls. Many times access controls are imposed on documents unintentionally. It is quite easy, for example, to create a PDF document that has security settings that forbid copying or text extraction. New versions of Microsoft Office include access controls and settings that can cause a document to disappear after a certain amount of time. Because of the DMCA, libraries, archives, and museums that receive documents incorporating technological protection measures will be hard-pressed to preserve them over time.[4]

4.5 Infringement

DIRECT INFRINGEMENT

Third parties who perform any of the exclusive acts set out above risk directly infringing copyright. Copyright is directly infringed when:

▶ a person who is not the owner of copyright
▶ with access to the copyrighted work
▶ violates any of the exclusive rights
▶ in a material and substantial manner
▶ beyond what is permitted by the statutory exemptions
▶ without the permission of the copyright owner.

Each of these factors is considered in turn.

NOT THE OWNER OF COPYRIGHT

As noted in Chapter 1, copyright and physical property are separate; a cultural institution may own a collection item without owning the copyright that subsists in the item.

One option is for cultural institutions to obtain an assignment of copyright from the copyright owner. Such an assignment transfers ownership of copyright to the cultural institution. This approach has the benefit of giving the cultural institution maximum flexibility in dealing with copyrighted works (although it may still need to consider other issues, such as moral rights and privacy, trademark, and publicity rights as discussed in Chapter 9).

That said, many institutions only obtain copyright assignments sparingly. This may be because the plethora of copyright owners in a modern manuscript collection or compound work makes it impossible to secure a significant number of permissions. And it may be because of the concern that assignments divest creators of potential income streams. This is particularly true for people such as visual artists, authors, and filmmakers who make a living from the intellectual property that they create. Thus, in many cases, a nonexclusive license is preferable as it can grant reproduction and distribution rights to the cultural institution on terms acceptable to both parties, while leaving ownership of copyright with the creator.

WITH ACCESS TO THE COPYRIGHTED WORK

For a person to infringe copyright, he or she must have access to the copyrighted work. It is not an infringement of copyright to create a work that is very similar to someone else's copyright work independently, without any knowledge of or access to the other copyrighted work.

VIOLATES ANY OF THE EXCLUSIVE RIGHTS

The liability for direct infringement is strict. One can be guilty of copyright infringement regardless of whether one knows that the act constituted infringement or even that the work was copyrighted.

Liability for infringement is found when, in addition to proof that the alleged infringer had access to the work, a substantial similarity exists between the two works. Taken together, access and substantial similarity prove that a violation of one of the exclusive rights has occurred.

The requirements of objective similarity and causal connection will be met in most instances of digitization, such as:

▶ scanning some pages from a book or manuscript
▶ taking a photograph of a painting
▶ making a copy of a sound recording.

IN A MATERIAL AND SUBSTANTIAL MANNER

The infringement must be real; to date, contemplating copyright infringement without doing it has not been a crime.[5] And the infringement must be of some substantial amount rather than *de minimis*. In other words, some significant portion of the original copyrighted expression must be taken to warrant a finding of infringement. There is no hard-and-fast rule on how little one can take, however. Thumbnails of images, for example, are not automatically considered to be *de minimis* and hence acceptable.

In most cases, a cultural institution will wish to digitize an entire work. They will do this by creating a new, material reproduction. And even when only part of a work is digitized, that part is likely to be significant or representative of the entire work. Thus most digitization initiatives are likely to surpass the minimum requirements for prima facie violation of this factor.

KEY POINT

A cultural institution may infringe copyright even if it only digitizes part of a work.

BEYOND WHAT IS PERMITTED BY THE STATUTORY EXEMPTIONS

The statutory exemptions most relevant to cultural institutions are discussed in Chapters 5 and 6.

WITHOUT THE PERMISSION OF THE COPYRIGHT OWNER

Copyright is not infringed where the cultural institution has the copyright owner's permission to perform the relevant act. Permission is discussed in Chapter 7.

INDIRECT INFRINGEMENT

In addition to direct infringement, one can also indirectly infringe copyright. There are two types of indirect infringement: contributory infringement and vicarious liability. To be guilty of contributory infringement, an institution would have to know that direct infringement was taking place. (Note that this is different from direct infringement, which can occur regardless of whether the infringer knew a work was copyrighted). In addition, the contributory infringer must induce, cause, or materially contribute to the infringement. Creating software that enables people to download music illegally has been found to be a contributory infringement (*Metro-Goldwyn-Mayer v. Grokster*). Knowingly facilitating infringing digitization by a third party of copyrighted works in an institution's collection would also be contributory infringement. The third party may have done the actual infringement, but the facilitating institution would be just as liable.

Could a library be found liable for contributory infringement for patron use of photocopiers located in the library? Possibly. By providing the copiers on which the infringing acts occur, the library could be viewed as materially contributing to the infringement. If the library knew or should have known that patrons were copying more than was permitted under fair use, they could be found liable.

It is possible that the library could also be found liable under the second form of indirect infringement: vicarious liability. In order to find an institution vicariously liable for the actions of a direct infringer, the institution must have the right and ability to control the infringer's acts and receive direct financial benefit from the infringement. Unlike contributory infringement, knowledge is not an element of vicarious liability. If the library received a profit from the photocopying, or even if the act saved wear and tear on its volumes or obviated the need to purchase additional copies, the argument could be made that the library was receiving direct financial benefit from the acts of infringers that the library could theoretically control.

Fortunately Section 108, which is discussed in Chapter 6, contains an explicit exemption from liability for libraries and archives for any infringing acts performed by patrons on library-owned reproduction equipment. As long as the proper signage is included on the machines, the library or archives is immune from indirect copyright liability.

TIP

Many cultural institutions permit the unsupervised use by patrons of machines (including photocopiers, videotape and DVD players, and computers) that can be used to copy copyrighted works. A warning notice should be attached to each machine in order to gain the protection of Section 108 and remove any liability the institution has for patron use. The text of the notice is not specified in law, but the following should work:

> Notice: The copyright law of the United States (Title 17, U.S. Code) governs the making of photocopies or other reproductions of copyrighted material. The person using this equipment is liable for any infringement.

QUESTION

Am I liable for patrons' use of their cameras?

Some cultural institutions have reported patrons using personal copying equipment (such as digital cameras) to photograph or scan collection items. Assuming that patrons use that equipment in a way that infringes copyright, could the cultural institution also be liable for copyright infringement?

There are no judgments directly on point, so we cannot say for sure. We can, however, consider the factors that determine contributory and vicarious infringement:

▶ The copying equipment was not provided by the cultural institution (minimizing the degree to which the institution could be said to "materially contribute" to the infringement).

▶ Cultural institutions frequently have no significant relationship with their individual patrons. In general, institutions do not monitor or direct patrons' activity while on their premises. Thus, the cultural institution may not have the actual knowledge of infringement that is required for a finding of contributory infringement.

▶ Institutions may not have the ability to control infringing acts of patrons, which is required for a finding of vicarious copyright infringement. The more institutions exercise supervision of the copying done by patrons, the more liable they may be. For example, requiring patrons to request permission before copying any individual document could increase an institution's theoretical liability.

▶ Cultural institutions do not normally charge for reproductions made by patrons using their own equipment. The institutions therefore are probably not receiving the direct financial benefit required for a finding of vicarious copyright infringement.

Facilitating access to information has emerged as one of the primary functions of cultural institutions. This role may be compromised if they are required to adopt intrusive procedures to police copyright law. However, it would be reasonable to post warnings about copyright in reading rooms and on any forms given to patrons prior to allowing them to bring equipment into the library (mirroring the procedure followed with library-supplied equipment).

Title: *The British Museum Reading Room*
Photographer: David Iliff
License: Creative Commons Attribution 2.5
Source: http://commons.wikimedia.org/wiki/File:British_Museum_Reading_Room_Panorama_Feb_2006.jpg

There are good arguments that a cultural institution does not "induce, cause, or materially contribute" to copyright infringement when a patron uses personal copying equipment on the institution's premises. Much would depend on the particular circumstances of the library and patron use, however, and it is possible that in a specific fact situation, a court might form a different opinion.

4.6 Remedies for Infringement

This section discusses the remedies available to a copyright owner who brings a successful court action in relation to an infringement of copyright. The Copyright Act sets out the remedies that can be awarded to a copyright owner. These include any or all of the following:

▶ Grant of an injunction
▶ Impounding and/or destruction of infringing articles
▶ Award of damages and profits
▶ Award of costs and attorney's fees
▶ Criminal liability

Each of these will be considered in turn.

Injunction [17 U.S.C. § 502]: An injunction is an order directing a person to refrain from undertaking a particular act, or, less frequently, requiring them to perform a particular act. For example, a copyright owner may seek a temporary or permanent injunction restraining a cultural institution from including certain material on its Web site.

Impounding and disposition of offending articles [17 U.S.C. § 503]: The Copyright Act allows the court to order the impounding of all infringing copies as well as any article that is used to reproduce the copies. The court could, for example, order the seizure of the institution's Web server if it was found to be distributing infringing copies. As part of its final judgment, the court may also order the destruction of such articles.

Damages [17 U.S.C. § 504]: Another way to compensate the plaintiff is through requiring the defendant to make a payment of money—legally, this is known as an award of damages. Three types of damages can be awarded:

▶ Actual damages
▶ Profits, and
▶ Statutory damages

Actual damages are intended to compensate a copyright owner for losses they incurred as a result of the infringement. Profits are the amount that the infringer realized due to his or her infringement separate from any actual damages suffered by the copyright owner. The purpose of including profits is to make sure that infringers cannot benefit from the infringing act.

A copyright owner in some cases can elect to receive statutory damages instead of actual damages and profits. Statutory damages can range from a minimum of $750 per infringed work to a maximum of $30,000 per infringement. If the court finds that the infringement was willful, that amount can increase up to $150,000 per infringed work.

It should be stressed that these merely set the range; the precise calculation of damages is determined according to the circumstances of each case.

Costs and attorney's fees [17 U.S.C. § 505]: The court may also, at its discretion, award to the prevailing party the costs associated with a settlement and reasonable attorney's fees. Bringing a copyright action in a federal court is an expensive proposition, and an award of attorney's fees can easily dwarf the other damages. For example, in a successful fair-use defense of his use of Barbie dolls in a series of artworks entitled "Food Chain Barbie," Tom Forsythe was awarded $300,000 in costs and $1.8 million in attorney's fees (*Mattel Inc. v. Walking Mountain Productions*). And settling out of court may not protect you. In a recent decision, a judge ruled that even though a lawsuit against James Joyce's grandson was settled out of court, the academic who brought the suit was the prevailing party and was eligible to receive reimbursement for her attorney's fees (*Schloss v. Sweeney*).

Tom Forsythe, *Every Barbie For Herself.* Uncredited photograph from http://www.tomforsythe.com/Details.cfm?ProdID=124&category=0.

License: No © statement at site; fair use asserted for this use.

Criminal liability [17 U.S.C. § 506]: In addition to the civil penalties outlined above, willful copyright infringement can also be a criminal violation, punishable by jail time lasting up to ten years (for repeat offenders) and fines ranging to $250,000 for an individual or $500,000 for an organization [18 U.S.C. § 2319].

DMCA civil and criminal liability [17 U.S.C. § 1203 & 1204]: Courts have the broad authority to grant injunctive and monetary relief, order the impounding and destruction of the tools or products involved in the violation, and award actual damages, profits gained through infringement, costs, and attorney's fees. Criminal penalties that range up to ten years in jail and a fine of up to $1 million (for a repeat offense) are possible, but nonprofit libraries, archives, educational institutions, and public broadcasting entities are immune from criminal penalties.

LIMITATIONS ON REMEDIES

The penalties associated with copyright infringement can be severe. There are several factors, however, that can mitigate some of the worst effects. For example, although it is not relevant in determining direct copyright infringement whether a defendant knew they were infringing copyright, the "innocence" of the defendant can be considered when determining remedies. If the court believes that the infringer "was not aware and had no reason to believe that his or her acts constituted an infringement of copyright," the court may reduce the statutory damage amount to not less than $200 [17 U.S.C. § 504(c)(2)]. In addition, no statutory damages can be awarded if the infringer is an employee of a nonprofit educational institution, library, or archives and had reasonable grounds for believing (and hence believed) that his or her use was a fair use. This exemption only applies to infringement by reproduction, however; other infringements (for example, distributing a copyrighted work from a Web site) fall outside this provision. Both these limitations—to innocent infringers generally, and for nonprofit institutions—only apply to statutory damages. All other penalties, including actual damages, attorney's fees, and impoundment, could still be enforced.

In addition, in order to be eligible for an award of statutory damages and attorney's fees, a work must have been registered with the Copyright Office prior to commencement of the infringement [17 U.S.C. § 412]. No statutory damages or attorney's fees, for example, can be awarded for any infringement of an unpublished work prior to its registration with the Copyright Office. Once again, however, all other penalties, including actual damages and impoundment, could still be enforced.

The importance of the limitations on remedies is considered further in Chapter 8 on Risk Management.

4.7 Conclusion

As should be evident from this chapter, digitization of copyrighted materials has the potential to infringe the exclusive rights of the copyright owner. And many of the penalties associated with this behavior can be high (though there are some special rules that limit the damages that cultural heritage institutions face).

Fortunately there are exemptions to copyright law that either excuse actions that would be otherwise infringing or lower the risks associated with infringement such that an institution might wish to consider actions that would otherwise be technically infringing. These exemptions are discussed in the next two chapters.

5 *Fair Use and Other Exemptions*

5.1 Introduction

This chapter discusses statutory limitations on the exclusive rights of the copyright owner, in particular the fair-use exemption.

A statutory exemption allows individuals to exercise one of the exclusive rights of copyright

- ▶ without obtaining the permission of the copyright owner, and
- ▶ without the payment of any license fee.

In addition to the statutory exemptions, the Copyright Act also contains some compulsory licenses. Like the statutory exemptions, these allow individuals to exercise one of the exclusive rights of copyright without obtaining the permission of the copyright owner. The difference is that users must also comply with formalities and pay a prescribed fee. An example is the license that permits the mechanical reproduction of musical works. Compulsory licenses will be discussed in Chapter 7.

The exemptions and limitations on the exclusive right of the copyright owner lie at the very heart of the copyright system. They ensure that the monopoly granted to copyright owners is not so complete that individuals cannot use existing works nor are unduly hampered in creating new ones. In this way, exemptions advance the constitutional purpose of copyright: "the progress of science and useful arts."

Limitations on the exclusive rights of copyright owners are found primarily, but not exclusively, in Sections 107 to 122 of the Copyright Act. Table 5.1 sets out some of the major groups of exemptions in the Copyright Act. These exemptions cover a range of conduct, although many only operate in limited circumstances.

These guidelines focus on the exemptions of greatest importance to cultural institutions engaged in digitization. They are:

- ▶ Fair use (Chapter 5)
- ▶ Exemptions specific to libraries, archives, and nonprofit educational institutions (Chapter 6)
- ▶ Educational performances (Chapter 5)

Other exemptions and limitations are also referred to, where relevant.

■■ **TABLE 5.1**

Some major groups of exemptions in the Copyright Act

Exemption	Application	Section
Fair use	Activities that are "fair" (as assessed using factors in the Copyright Act), for purposes including criticism, comment, news reporting, teaching (including multiple copies for classroom use), scholarship, or research.	107
Distribution of a particular copy ("First Sale Doctrine")	Subsequent lending, public display, or resale of a legally acquired copy of a work.	109
Educational use of performances	Includes in-classroom use of any work and the limited performance of nondramatic literary and musical works in distance learning.	110(1) and 110(2)
Other performances and displays of literary, dramatic, and musical works	Certain noncommercial and nonprofit charitable performances; some uses in religious services; rebroadcast in certain businesses, restaurants, and bars; use in governmental or nonprofit agricultural fairs; the performance of certain musical works in retail outlets for the sole purpose of promoting retail sales; and the transmission of performances of certain works to disabled persons.	110
Acts involving architectural works	Pictorial representations (including photographs) of buildings visible from a public place.	120
Sound recordings	Examples: compulsory license for making nondramatic recordings; broadcasts of certain sound recordings; copying sound recordings for the purpose of broadcasting or simulcasting; negotiated licenses for jukeboxes; loans by nonprofit libraries and educational institutions; noncommercial consumer use.	114–116, 118, 109, 1008
Computer programs	Reproductions made during normal use; backup copies; adaptations made to run programs on new machines; copies made as part of maintenance and repair.	117

Exemption	Application	Section
Cable and satellite television broadcasts	Special permissions for secondary transmissions of television signals originally transmitted by someone else.	111, 119, 122
Public television broadcasts	Availability of compulsory license to cover non-commercial broadcast use.	118
Transitory reproductions	Reproductions made during the transmittal or routing of material through a network.	512

Although it is not technically an exemption, the doctrine of sovereign immunity can also be used to excuse copyright infringements; it is discussed at the end of this chapter.

5.2 Fair Use

The fair-use exemption is one of the most important doctrines in copyright law. It serves as the primary protection for free speech, which might otherwise be constrained if the monopoly rights given to copyright owners were absolute. It ensures that the balance between the interests of copyright owners and users can be maintained and that copyright law does not stifle the very creativity it is intended to foster. On a very practical level, it provides important protections to libraries, archives, and nonprofit educational institutions. When those organizations have a reasonable belief that their use of a copyrighted work is a fair use, many of the most stringent remedies in copyright law cannot be applied (see Chapter 4).

Unfortunately, fair use can also be a difficult to understand and apply. Fair use is open-ended, which means that it can function as a flexible component of copyright law, responding to changes in technology or institutional and creative norms. However, this very flexibility can make it difficult to predict how a court will apply the doctrine in any particular case. Commentators try to extrapolate from the specifics of a particular case to other cases, but the truth is that each fair-use case stands on its own specific facts and thus its own merits. That is, although it is possible to analyze existing case law and industry customs, ultimately, each fair-use case is judged on a case-by-case basis. Because the fair use of any particular case is determined by a judge applying an equitable rule of reason, the result is that only five individuals in the United States can say with certainty whether any particular use is fair: a majority of the Supreme Court!

Given the nature of the fair-use privilege, it is not surprising that it is often misunderstood. Many people, for example, assume that any educational use is automatically a fair use. Others mistakenly believe that fair use allows 10 percent of a copyrighted work or alternatively an excerpt of 300 words or less to be reproduced for any purpose. This is not the case; there are no set limits in the statute.

Yet in spite of the inherent uncertainty about what constitutes a fair use and misunderstandings about its boundaries, fair use remains of fundamental importance to all cultural heritage institutions. There are a number of examples of institutional digitization activity where the fair use arguments are strong and even (given institutional norms and the lack of reported disputes or case law) relatively uncontroversial (such as production of record photographs for internal staff use). Some types of use can reasonably be predicted to be fair use. Fair use is much more than some of its critics have charged: "the right to hire a lawyer."[1]

This section will consider four aspects of fair use:

▶ Its general statutory purposes (e.g., criticism, comment, news reporting, teaching, scholarship, and research)
▶ The four factors in fair use (purpose, nature, amount, and market impact)
▶ Fair-use guidelines
▶ The relevance of fair use for the digitization projects of cultural institutions

The starting point for all discussions of fair use is the language of the statute:

REFERENCE

The Fair Use Exemption, Section 107

Limitations on exclusive rights: Fair use
Notwithstanding the provisions of sections 106 and 106A, the fair use of a copyrighted work, including such use by reproduction in copies or phonorecords or by any other means specified in that section, for purposes such as criticism, comment, news reporting, teaching (including multiple copies for classroom use), scholarship, or research, is not an infringement of copyright. In determining whether the use

made of a work in any particular case is a fair use the factors to be considered shall include—

5. The purpose and character of the use, including whether such use is of a commercial nature or is for nonprofit educational purposes
6. The nature of the copyrighted work
7. The amount and substantiality of the portion used in relation to the copyrighted work as a whole, and
8. The effect of the use upon the potential market for or value of the copyrighted work.

The fact that a work is unpublished shall not itself bar a finding of fair use if such finding is made upon consideration of all the above factors.

We can make three important general observations about fair use based on a reading of the text of this section. First, although we normally think of fair use when making reproductions, it can also apply to all of the exclusive rights of the copyright owner. A performance, for example, or a distribution of a copyrighted work can also be a fair use.

Second, if one's action is a fair use, it is consequently *not* an infringement of copyright. This differs from some of the other exemptions in copyright law that recognize that someone did something wrong but remove all liability for the action. If your use is a fair use, you did nothing wrong; no copyright was infringed.

■
KEY POINT
Fair use is not an excuse or justification for infringement; a fair use is not an infringement of copyright to begin with.

Third, and most important, potentially any use can be found to be a fair use. Section 107 identifies certain uses that are often a fair use, including "criticism, comment, news reporting, teaching (including multiple copies for classroom use), scholarship, or research." This list is illustrative, however, and not exclusive. The courts have found other uses to constitute fair use. For example, the Supreme Court has determined that "time-shifting" broadcast television programs at home is a fair use—even though the purpose is for entertainment (*Sony Corp v. Universal City Studios*). In another case, it found that a commercial parody of song also constituted a fair use (*Campbell v. Acuff-Rose Music, Inc.*).

> ### KEY POINT
> Purposes such as criticism, comment, news reporting, teaching, scholarship, and research are explicitly identified in the law as possible fair uses, but other activities may also constitute a fair use.

5.3 The four factors

When determining whether a particular use is fair, the Copyright Act lists four factors that shall be considered. These are:

▶ The purpose and character of the use, including whether such use is of a commercial nature or is for nonprofit educational purposes
▶ The nature of the copyrighted work
▶ The amount and substantiality of the portion used in relation to the copyrighted work as a whole, and
▶ The effect of the use upon the potential market for or value of the copyrighted work [17 U.S.C. § 107]

The list is not comprehensive; other factors can, and have, been considered when determining whether a particular use is fair. In general, however, most cases involving fair use focus on these four factors.

The fair-use calculation is also not mechanical. The relative importance of each factor can vary according the specifics of a case. It is possible, for example, for a court to conclude that one factor is fair but that the other three are not fair, and still find that the overall use is fair.[2] In general, however, the more one can argue that one's use is fair under each of the four factors, the more likely it is that one's overall use is likely to be fair.

Analysis of the fair-use case law reveals the following observations about the content of each of the factors:

THE PURPOSE AND CHARACTER OF THE USE

Acts that have a commercial or "for-profit" basis are more likely to be unfair than educational or noncommercial acts. However, the commercial purpose of a use is not determinative; many commercial reproductions have been found to be fair (*Campbell v. Acuff-Rose Music*). Indeed, the very list of presumptive fair-use activities—such as criticism and news reporting—often take place in the context of profit-making enterprises. Nor is educational use similarly determinative. Just because a use is educational does not make it automatically fair.

Acts that have a "transformative" effect, in that they add value or create something different, are more likely to be fair than those that do not (*Blanch v. Koons*).[3] Yet purely reproductive uses are not automatically ruled out, as the statutory mention of multiple copies for classroom use makes clear. Productive or socially beneficial uses are more likely to be found to be fair.

NATURE OF THE WORK

The use of factual works and scholarly works is more likely to be fair than the use of highly creative or original works, since copyright protects original expression and not facts (*Harper & Row Publishers v. Nation Enterprises*). The use of published works (as opposed to unpublished works) is more likely to be fair (though an amendment to the Act in 1992 made it clear that that the unpublished nature of a work did not *automatically* exclude it from fair-use consideration). Some argue that the commercial availability of a work augurs against a finding of fair use, whereas its unavailability in the marketplace may argue for a finding of fair use.

AMOUNT AND SUBSTANTIALITY

The greater the amount taken, the less likely the use is fair. In addition, if the heart of the work is taken, even if it is a small amount, the use is unlikely to be fair (*Harper & Row Publishers v. Nation Enterprises*).

MARKET IMPACT

A use is less likely to be fair when it serves as substitute for the original or supplants the work's "traditional, reasonable, or likely to be developed markets." Offering a version of the work that can substitute for the purchase of the original is unlikely to be a fair use. An easy method of licensing the use of the work may weigh against a finding of fair use (*American Geophysical v. Texaco*).

To repeat, none of these factors is decisive. The four statutory factors should not "be treated in isolation, one from another. All are to be explored, and the results weighed together, in light of the purposes of copyright" (*Campbell v. Acuff*-Rose). Reproducing an entire work can be fair, depending on the nature of the work, the purpose of the use, and so forth. Commercial uses can be fair, and educational uses can be unfair. Reasonable people can certainly disagree on what constitutes fair use, as the presence of dissenting opinions in most Supreme Court decisions involving fair use attest.

> **DID YOU KNOW?**
> Judge Pierre Leval, one of the foremost theorists on the nature and role of fair use, and yet who has seen many of his own decisions subsequently overturned by higher courts, had this to say on fair use:
>
> > I will tell you that I have found it instructive and exhilarating to be involved at the cutting edge of the law even though my presence at the cutting edge was in the role of the salami.[4]

5.4 Fair-use examples

There have been few cases on fair use involving cultural heritage institutions, but some recent developments involving commercial users may be instructive.

VISUAL CATALOGS

Two recent cases have considered the status of search engines that present results as thumbnail images, rather than text. At issue was whether the creation of these thumbnails infringed the rights of the copyright owners of the underlying images. These cases may be instructional for institutions creating online databases, especially (although not exclusively) of visual works.

In *Kelly v. Arriba Soft*, the plaintiff (Kelly) was a professional photographer whose images were available on his own and other authorized Web sites. Arriba operated a search engine that crawled the Web looking for images, copied those images (at small scale) onto its server, and then made those thumbnails available as part of the results of a search. The search results linked back to the full-size images on the original Web sites, though framed within Arriba's Web page. Arriba argued that its actions were permitted as a fair use.

How did the fair-use factors regarding Arriba's use of thumbnail images play out in this case?

Purpose: Arriba's Web site was commercial (it generated revenue from advertisements), but its creation and use of the thumbnails was transformative. It was not using the images for the same purpose that Kelly created them (e.g., artistic expression), but rather for something new (a research tool). Furthermore, the construction of a visual index benefited society. This factor favored fair use.

Nature: The photographs were highly creative, but were also published and readily available on the Internet. This factor slightly favored Kelly.

Amount: Arriba copied the entire image, but that amount was necessary in order to meet the intended purpose—it was necessary to enable users to identify and select interesting images. The court said this factor was neutral.

Market impact: The thumbnails did not displace the market for Kelly's work, but rather led people to it. It therefore did not hurt the value of his work. This factor favored fair use.

The overall decision: Arriba's use of thumbnails in its visual search index was a fair use. Arriba's practice of linking to and displaying the full-size images within an Arriba frame was found not to be a fair use.

Many of the issues in this case were revisited in 2007 in *Perfect 10 v. Google*. Perfect 10 hosted a Web site that included a "members only" area containing photographs of naked models. Many individuals would copy Perfect 10 images without permission and publish them on Web sites. The images were subsequently indexed by the image search engines run by Google, Amazon, and others. As part of the indexing process, Google would create and store thumbnails of the images. A district court initially found that Google's use was infringing and granted a preliminary injunction against Google (*Perfect 10 v. Google*).

On appeal (*Perfect 10 v. Amazon*), the injunction was lifted, with the court concluding that Google's use was likely to be found fair. The reasoning followed that in *Arriba*, but with one major difference. Perfect 10 argued that the market impact in this case was much greater than in *Arriba* because it had begun to market thumbnails of its images for use on cell phones. The free availability of the thumbnails from Google could directly impact this emerging market. The court disagreed, suggesting that until there was some evidence of real market impact, the factor would continue slightly to favor Google. It stressed as well the tremendous public benefit derived from the existence of image search engines.

What can we learn from these cases? It would seem that it is possible to create image indexes that can qualify as a fair use. Relevant to *Kelly v. Arriba Soft* and *Perfect 10 v. Amazon.com* was the transformative nature of the defendants' purpose (in these cases, a tool to assist research and learning), the social benefits of such a use, the size of the images (which divested them of much of their aesthetic quality), and the lack of demonstrated market impact. As will be discussed further below, these arguments may be relevant to some of the image databases created by cultural institutions. We must emphasize, though, that as with all fair-use cases, the specific facts of a case will matter tremendously. For instance, the use of full-size or high-resolution images may sit less comfortably in a fair-use analysis than use of thumbnails.

■ TIP

Fair-use decisions are never fixed in stone. As circumstances and facts change, the fair-use analysis can also change. What is a fair use today may not be tomorrow—and vice versa. That means that one needs to monitor developments in this area even after the original analysis is made.

TEXTUAL INDEXES

The *Arriba* and *Perfect 10* cases addressed visual search engines. At one point it seemed that the legality of textual search engines would be debated in *Authors Guild v. Google*, which challenged whether Google's Library Book Search program is a fair use.[5] For the program Google scanned, without the permission of their copyright owners, copyrighted works found in libraries. It then used the scans to make an index of the content of the books. When users search these books, they were presented with a "snippet" of the original—a few lines around the search term—along with links to library catalogs and book dealers. Google maintained that its use of the books was fair.

A group of publishers and authors disagreed and filed suit against Google. The question that faced the court in this case was similar to the questions raised in *Arriba* and *Perfect 10*. Google's purpose was commercial, but it was also transformative in constructing an index. The scanned works are a combination of factual and creative works, but they are also all published. The entire work was reproduced, but that was necessary in order to construct the index, and only a tiny amount was displayed to users. The possible market harm to publishers was the loss of licensing revenues that they could have theoretically charged Google to conduct this indexing or by providing this sort of service in some other way. Weighing against this was the impossibility of Google ever being able to identify and locate all of the copyright owners of the works.

Late in 2008, before the court could consider the arguments, Google and the plaintiffs reached a settlement agreement.[6] Even though it maintained that its fair-use argument was strong, Google felt that a settlement offered it more benefits. Under the terms of the settlement, Google's indexing is permitted. In addition, it can deliver the full text of books rather than just snippets—something it could only do with the permission of the copyright owners. If the settlement is accepted by the court, we will never learn whether Google's initial digitization program constituted copyright infringement.

TRANSFORMATIVE USES

In *Bill Graham Archives v. Dorling Kindersley Limited*, the defendants published a book about the rock group the Grateful Dead. The book included seven small-scale images of concert posters and tickets, copyright in which was owned by the Archives. The publishers and Archives had been negotiating for a license but could not agree on an appropriate fee. The publishers nevertheless published the book with the images and the Archives instituted legal proceedings. The publishers sought a motion for summary judgment (on the basis of fair use), which was granted. The Archives appealed, but the Court of Appeals upheld the decision of the lower court.

Although the Court considered the four factors sequentially, there was much repetition of ideas—and the findings in one factor clearly influenced determinations in others.

Purpose: The Court held that the transformativeness of the work was crucial to the analysis of the first factor. This factor favored the publishers, due to the nature of the book (a biographical account of the history of the group), and the difference between this purpose and that of the original images (promotion and artistic expression).

Nature: This factor weighed slightly in favor of the copyright owners, given that the underlying works were creative. However, the Court also downplayed the importance of this factor, given the transformative use of the publishers.

Amount: Although the posters and tickets had been reproduced in their entirety, this was both necessary (given the publisher's purpose) and performed at low resolution (which meant that the images could not be used for their original, aesthetic purpose).

Market impact: Much of the argument on the fourth factor related to the market for images appearing in books. The Archives argued there was an established market for the licensing of such images. However, the Court distinguished between a traditional, reasonable market, and a transformative market, concluding that "a copyright holder cannot prevent others from entering fair use markets merely 'by developing or licensing a market for parody, news reporting, educational or other transformative uses of its own creative work.'"[7] Thus, this factor did not favor the Archives.

This case is significant for cultural institutions for a number of reasons. First, it illustrates the current fascination with the importance of transformativeness in the fair-use analysis. Although the statute cites exact reproduction as a possible fair use ("multiple copies for classroom use"), most recent court decisions have focused on transformative uses. The result is that it may be much harder to establish that the digitization program of a cultural institution that reproduces exactly works in its collection is a fair use.

On a more positive note, the decision demonstrates the significance of resolution or image size in assessing the amount taken; it is not merely a question the area of the work copied. Finally, the analysis of the fourth factor suggests that the mere presence of a licensing system is not determinative on whether fair use applies. Indeed, it was not fatal to the publisher's fair-use argument that it had originally requested a license.

5.5 Fair-use guidelines

In the absence of statutory certainty regarding the boundaries of fair use, a number of efforts to establish formal guidelines governing the application of fair use have been undertaken. Some have been developed by specific user communities and others by coalitions composed of representatives of copyright owners and users. None have the force of law, though three have been at least recognized by Congress:

▶ Classroom copying of books and periodicals[8]
▶ Educational uses of music[9]
▶ Off-Air Recording of Broadcast Programming for Educational Purposes[10]

In the 1990s, the Conference on Fair Use (CONFU) was convened to try to develop fair-use guidelines for the digital age. Draft guidelines were developed in a number of areas:

▶ Digital Images
▶ Electronic Reserves
▶ Distance Learning
▶ Multimedia Development

Final agreement on the guidelines could not be reached, however.[11] Only the multimedia guidelines, which had been begun prior to the start of CONFU, have found a life through the endorsement of the Consortium of College and University Media Centers (CCUMC).[12]

The failure of the CONFU process highlighted some of the inherent problems with formal guidelines.[13] First, although the guidelines are often supposed to represent a minimum standard for fair use—what everyone can agree is fair—they often end up becoming a de facto maximum stipulation; no one is willing to do more, even though doing more may still be fair. For example, the guidelines on classroom photocopying set numerical limits on the amount that can be photocopied:

> (a) Either a complete article, story, or essay of less than 2,500 words, or (b) an excerpt from any prose work of not more than 1,000 words or 10 percent of the work, whichever is less, but in any event a minimum of 500 words.
>
> [Each of the numerical limits stated in "a" and "b" above may be expanded to permit the completion of an unfinished line of a poem or of an unfinished prose paragraph.]

Many institutions have adopted these guidelines as the *maximum* that can be photocopied for classroom use, rather than as merely an amount that all would agree is clearly a fair use. Academic books normally run 400 to 600 words per page, meaning that you can copy entire articles or essays when they are 5–6 pages in length, or 2–3 pages from a longer work. (Some academic publishing runs as high as 1,000 words per page, which means that you could only copy complete articles that were 2½ pages long.) The inappropriateness of these limitations for classroom teaching is one reason that both the American Association of University Professors and the Association of American Law Schools strongly opposed the guidelines at the time they were promulgated. Many institutions, realizing that the recommended limits were not useful, settled on the 10 percent guideline, but without realizing that it only applies if the total amount copied was less than 1,000 words.

The second problem with guidelines is that they do not necessarily correspond to the use one wants to make. Many of the guidelines, for example, address situations involving classroom teaching. They cannot be used if one is hoping to digitize materials for general access via the Internet.

The newest attempts at fair-use guidelines have come from the communities themselves. Groups of documentary filmmakers, working under the auspices of the Center for Social Media at American University and without the involvement of commercial rights owners, developed the "Documentary Filmmakers' Statement of Best Practices in Fair Use."[14] The filmmakers thought about what uses others should be able to make of their films, as well as what uses they wanted to make of the work of others, and wrote their best-practices statement accordingly. The Center's "Code of Best Practices in Fair Use for Online Video" was developed by a panel of experts drawn from cultural scholarship, legal scholarship, and legal practice.[15] These guidelines may represent a new direction for the future development of guidelines, which seemed dead after the collapse of the CONFU process.

> **TIP**
>
> Guidelines may only define the minimum level of use that is fair, but they can still be helpful in at least three ways:
>
> ▶ If your proposed use falls within the guidelines, you can rest more easily that it is not an infringement of copyright.
> ▶ You can use the guidelines to identify, reassess, and confirm the reasonableness of your fair-use arguments when your proposed use exceeds what is found in them.
> ▶ In a risk assessment (see Chapter 10), any use that far exceeds the guidelines is more likely to anger copyright owners and hence increase your risk—even if you conclude that your proposed use is fair.

5.6   Fair use and cultural institutions

The fair-use exemption is extremely important to cultural institutions and their patrons. In spite of the seeming ambiguity in the law, libraries, archives, and museums use it every day to serve their clientele and fulfill their missions.

First, fair use is the basis on which much copying for patrons is done. As we will see in the next chapter, there are provisions that allow libraries and archives to copy textual work for users. Pictorial, graphic, and photographic works are excluded from those provisions, however. Thus, every time a repository copies a copyrighted photograph for a patron to support their study, scholarship, or research, that repository relies on fair use (even if it does not conduct a formal fair-use analysis).

In addition, fair use is the justification for much of the preservation activities in cultural heritage institutions. There is no general provision in copyright law that permits libraries and archives to reproduce and preserve published material. The House of Representatives, however, in response to the threat of loss posed by motion pictures on nitrate film stock, concluded that "the making of duplicate copies for purposes of archival preservation certainly falls within the scope of 'fair use.'"[16]

Fair use can also be used in the copyright management strategies developed for certain digitization projects by cultural heritage institutions. A visual catalog or textual index of material, for example, may be an acceptable fair use (see the discussion of the *Arriba Soft* and *Google* cases above). Supplanting the market for the original by making a full copy available may be a fair use if the copyright owner cannot be found (see the discussion in Chapter 8). Fair use can be an important part of the digitization program of any cultural heritage institution—but only if the program careful assesses each situation and is willing to assume the risk inherent in using fair use. More on minimizing risks is found in Chapter 9.

> **TIP**
>
> ## Document your fair-use analysis
>
> Any time you rely upon fair use as a justification for an action, it is important to document your analysis. How to do this, and the reasons for doing so, are discussed further in Chapter 9.

5.7 Educational performances

The Technology, Education, and Copyright Harmonization (TEACH) Act of 2002 expanded the ability of educators at nonprofit institutions and at government agencies to display and perform copyrighted digital works in their teaching. Specifically, the TEACH Act created new exemptions to copyright that allow educators and government agencies to digitize copyrighted works in certain narrow, carefully defined, circumstances.

Even prior to the passage of the TEACH Act, Section 110 of the Copyright Act contained an exemption that allowed educators to display and perform *any* copyrighted work during the course of face-to-face teaching in a classroom in a nonprofit educational institution. There was also a provision that would allow the synchronous transmission of instruction through cable or satellite television to another classroom.

The TEACH Act amended Section 110(2) of the Copyright Act to permit the use of digital technology for the transmission and to remove the requirement that the use of the material had to be concurrent with a classroom lecture. There are a number of requirements that institutions and government bodies that wish to utilize the TEACH Act exemption must meet. For example, use of the material is still restricted to mediated instructional activities. Schools must take measures to try to protect the material from downstream reproduction. They must limit access to the material to students enrolled in a class. And they must also have copyright education programs in place.[17]

Assuming that the basic requirements of the TEACH Act are met, educational institutions may make copyrighted work available in digital form. They may even digitize material that is not already available in digital form in a format free from technological protection measures [17 U.S.C. § 112(f)]. The type of works, the amount that can be digitized and delivered, and the amount of time that the institution may keep the work on its servers are all limited, however.

Works and uses in digital form that are permitted by Section 110(2) include:

▶ The *performance* of an entire nondramatic literary or musical work (such as reading a poem or playing a symphony)
▶ The *performance* of a limited and reasonable portion of any other work (such as a film or play)
▶ The *display* of any work in an amount comparable to what would be used during the course of a live classroom session.

Any copies made under the TEACH Act can only be retained and used by the institution or government body solely in support of instruction authorized by the TEACH Act. One cannot, for example, digitize material for use in a specific course and then later decide to make it generally available on a Web site. Certain uses, such as creating electronic reserves or course packets for a course, are not eligible for TEACH Act exemptions [17 U.S.C. § 110(11)]

■ **KEY POINT**

The exemptions to copyright found in the TEACH Act are not broad enough to support a general program of digitization. For those non-profit institutions and government bodies primarily interested in using digitization to support mediated instruction, however, the TEACH Act exemptions may be of great value and should be explored.

5.8 Other exemptions

Given the broad range of activities undertaken by cultural institutions, it is possible that many of the Copyright Act's other exemptions to and limitations on the exclusive rights of copyright owners may be of interest. A museum with a café, for example, might want to know about the exemptions for the performance of music in food establishments in Section 110. Another repository might be interested in using the exemption for mechanical reproductions of musical works to create its own CDs. It is not possible in these guidelines to cover all of the limitations. Two, however, are worthy of brief discussion.

PHOTOGRAPHS OF ARCHITECTURAL WORKS

Cesar Pelli, Reagan National Airport, Washington, D.C.

Photograph: D.B. King

License: Creative Commons Attribution 2.0 Generic for the photograph; no permission needed for the structure

Source: http://www.flickr.com/photos/ bootbearwdc/87386298/

With most copyrighted works, reproduction in photographs or other pictorial representations would be an infringement of copyright. With architectural works, however, it is not an infringement of copyright to photograph the work if it is visible from a public place [17 U.S.C. § 120]. A cultural heritage institution would be able, for example, to digitize a photograph of the Reagan National Airport terminal in Washington, D.C., designed by Cesar Pelli without worrying about whether doing so would infringe on the architect's copyrights. (They would, of course, still have to consider the photographer's copyright.)

TRICKY QUESTION

Do photographs of public works of sculpture infringe copyright?

The law is explicit that one can take photographs of architectural works when they can be viewed from public spaces, but what about works of sculpture? This issue was at the heart of a 2006 lawsuit, *Di Modica v. North Fork*. Sculptor Arturo Di Modica sued Wal-Mart, North Fork Bank, and eight other defendants for using pictures of the sculpture of a bull that he created. He placed the sculpture in Wall Street, where it has become the unofficial symbol of New York's financial prowess. The Copyright Act does not have an explicit limitation on the rights of copyright owners of public statues similar to the limitation on the rights of architects. Many commentators hoped the case might settle the issue of whether public sculpture was legally similar to public architecture,[18] but the case was voluntarily dismissed in 2008 before a decision was reached.

Arturo Di Modica, *Charging Bull*.
Photograph: David Prior
License: Creative Commons Attribution 2.0 Generic for the photograph. Fair use asserted for the reproduction of the sculpture.
Source: http://www.flickr.com/photos/davidprior/125263215/

FIRST SALE PROJECTION RIGHTS

The second limitation of possible utility is found in Section 109. This section, encompassing what is commonly referred to as the "first sale doctrine," is of fundamental importance. It makes clear that transferring a legally acquired copy of a work to another individual by sale or lending is not an infringement of the distribution rights of the copyright owner. Without Section 109, libraries could not lend books and individuals could not give a copy of a book to a friend because this would amount to distribution.

One little-used provision of the section allows the owner of the work to display or project the work one image at a time to viewers at the place where the item is located. "Projection" was used deliberately; Congress wanted to make sure that only the display, and not the reproduction right, was implicated. It was worried about the "the potentialities of the new communications media, notably television, cable and optical transmission devices, and information storage and retrieval devices, for replacing printed copies with visual images."[19] Nevertheless, it might be possible to develop a system that would mimic the right to display a single copy of a work at the place where it is located, and thus utilizing the protection found in Section 109(c).

5.9 Sovereign immunity

Most of the exemptions listed above limit the scope of the exclusive rights granted to copyright owners in such a way that the use of the exemption is not an infringement of copyright. The doctrine of sovereign immunity can also protect against the damages associated with copyright infringement, but via a different method.

Thanks to the Eleventh Amendment, the Supreme Court has ruled that state and tribal governments and their component units such as a state university are immune from intellectual property suits (*Marketing Information Masters Inc. v. The Board of Trustees of the California State University*). The issue of whether an actual infringement has occurred is moot; a state unit cannot be sued in Federal court for damages for infringement if it does not want to be sued.

Does this mean that state and tribal agencies and units can engage in rampant copyright infringement? We would recommend against it, both on ethical and legal grounds. State entities cannot be sued for monetary damages, but they are subject to injunctive relief. Furthermore, there is some case law that suggests that government employees *can* be sued in their private capacity for copyright infringement that they oversee or undertake in their official role, even when their employer is immune. Furthermore, most state liability regulations will not allow the state to defend an employee who engages in illegal acts. The whole weight of a copyright-infringement lawsuit could therefore rest on the personal shoulders of the employee who made the reproduction.

Sovereign immunity can be important in the assessment of risk (see Chapter 9). Before deciding to utilize its immunity from prosecution as a basis for a digitization program, employees of state-owned and operated cultural institutions would do well to consult with their legal advisers.

6 *The Libraries and Archives Exemptions*

6.1 Introduction

This chapter explores the operation of the explicit exemptions for libraries and archives found in the Copyright Act. Most of these exemptions are contained in Section 108: "Limitations on exclusive rights: Reproduction by libraries and archives." The Section 108 provisions allow libraries and archives to reproduce collection items in certain specific circumstances without payment to or without the permission of the copyright owner. The provisions also prescribe when these reproductions can be accessed by, or supplied to, members of the public, and remove any liability libraries and archives might have for certain acts by users.

Section 108 supplements the fair-use exemption found in Section 107 of the Copyright Act. It does so in two ways:

▶ It provides some "bright line" rules that exempt certain types of reproductions by libraries and archives from infringing copyright (as opposed to the uncertainty inherent in a fair-use analysis).

▶ In authorizing some reproductions that would likely be found to be infringing under a fair-use analysis, it goes beyond fair use.

Section 108 also includes explicit limits and requirements intended to protect the interests of authors and publishers.

As discussed in section 6.2, the definition of libraries and archives in Section 108 is broad and encompasses both nonprofit and for-profit institutions in some of its provisions. Most of the exemptions apply equally to libraries and to archives. However, some of the provisions, such as the exemption for interlibrary loan copying, are most likely to be of interest to libraries.

Although most of the exemptions applicable to libraries and archives are found in Section 108, there are other exemptions for them in other sections of the Copyright Act. These are discussed briefly at the end of this chapter. The law also includes exemptions that apply to specific institutions. For example, 2 U.S.C. § 170 allows the Library of Congress to reproduce certain television and radio programs, and 44 U.S.C. § 2117 exempts the National Archives and Records Administration from copyright infringement for the reproduction, display, or use of unregistered unpublished copyrighted works. These provisions are not discussed as part of these guidelines due to their limited relevance to other cultural institutions.

Table 6.1 summarizes the major exemptions available to libraries, archives, and nonprofit educational institutions.

■■ **TABLE 6.1**

Major specific exemptions for cultural institutions

Libraries and archives exemptions	User requests; interlibrary loans; certain uses of unpublished items; replacement copies; digitization during the last 20 years of copyright term. See Chapter 6.	108
Nonprofit libraries, archives, and educational institutions	Certain circumventions of access-control mechanisms	1201
Nonprofit libraries and educational institutions	Rental, lease, or lending of phonorecords	109(b)
Nonprofit libraries	Loan of computer programs	109(b)(2)
Nonprofit scholarly, educational, or religious organizations	Importation of one copy of an audio-visual work for archival purposes or up to five copies of other works for archival or lending purposes	602(a)(3)

The chapter starts by discussing eligibility for the libraries and archives exemptions. It then discusses in detail provisions of the Copyright Act relevant to:

▶ Preservation copying of unpublished works [17 U.S.C. § 108(b)]
▶ Replacement copying of published works [17 U.S.C. § 108(c)]
▶ Reproduction services for patrons [17 U.S.C. § 108(d) and (e)]
▶ Interlibrary loan [17 U.S.C. § 109 and 108(g)(2)]
▶ Acquisition and reproduction of television news programs [17 U.S.C. § 108(f)(3)]
▶ Reproduction equipment in libraries [17 U.S.C. § 108(f)(1)]

- ▶ Digitization of published works in their last 20 years of copyright [17 U.S.C. § 108(h)]
- ▶ Libraries and archives privileges found outside Section 108.

There is also a checklist at the end of this chapter to help readers identify whether digitization falls under an exemption in the libraries and archives provisions, and the extent to which the public can access digitized content.

■ WATCH THIS SPACE

In 2005, the Library of Congress convened the Section 108 Study Group. The group was charged with reexamining the exemptions and limitations applicable to libraries and archives under the Copyright Act in light of the changes wrought by digital media. It was also asked to make recommendations as to how the law might be changed to take account more appropriately of the interests of creators, copyright holders, libraries, and archives in a manner that best serves the national interest. Its final report, issued in 2008, contained recommendations for legislative change that could alter the shape of Section 108.[1]

This chapter will discuss the law as it exists in 2009, but occasional reference will be made to the recommendations in the report.

Flowchart 6.1 sets out a decision-making chart for the libraries and archives provisions.

6.2 Eligibility

In order to take advantage of the exemptions in Section 108, libraries and archives must meet certain ground rules laid out in Section 108(a). The first is that the library or archives must be either: (1) open to the public; or (2) accessible to nonaffiliated researchers working in a specialized field, even if it is not open to the general public. This means, for example, that a library in a for-profit business would be eligible to participate in the interlibrary loan system authorized in Section 108—provided that it was open to its competitors and met the other ground rules discussed below as well.

In addition to being open to the public, there may be the additional requirement that the organization actually have a physical presence. This is not expressly required in the words of Section 108, but could be said to arise

◆ **FLOWCHART 6.1**

Digitization Under the Libraries and Archives Provisions

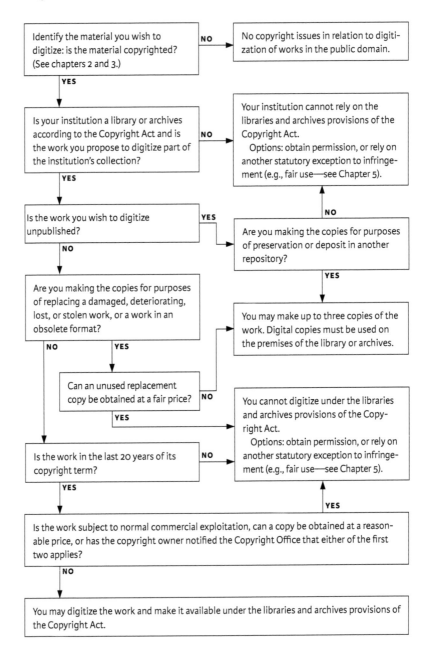

from traditional understandings of the terms "library" and "archives." For instance, the Senate report on the Digital Millennium Copyright Act noted that "Although online interactive digital networks have since given birth to online digital 'libraries' and 'archives' that exist only in the virtual (rather than physical) sense on Web sites, bulletin boards and homepages across the Internet, it is not the Committee's intent that Section 108 as revised apply to such collections of information."[2] That said, a purely virtual library that functioned as a normal library, had a professional staff, and followed the ethical norms and best practices of librarianship, arguably could be eligible for 108 protections.

QUESTION

Are museums covered by the libraries and archives exemptions?

There is no mention of museums in the wording or legislative history of Section 108, and so one would have to conclude that museums are not currently eligible to take advantage of these exemptions. Libraries and archives located in museums would, however, be able to use them—assuming that they are open to the public or to specialized researchers.

This position can be contrasted with that in Canada and Australia, in which the equivalent libraries and archives provisions can be relied upon by museums and galleries.[3] One of the recommendations of the 108 Study Group is that at least some museums be added to the law.

There are additional ground rules that must be satisfied before reproductions and distributions can be made under the libraries and archives exemptions. Unless a provision states otherwise:

▶ Only a single copy may be made
▶ The copy must be made "without any purpose of direct or indirect commercial advantage"
▶ Any copy must include either the copyright notice found on the original item or, if there is no copyright notice on the item, then a general legend stating that the work might be protected by copyright [17 U.S.C. § 108(a)]

■ **TIP**

If your institution intends to rely on an exemption in Section 108, it must not charge more than the actual cost of making a reproduction of a copyrighted work. Making money on reproductions invalidates the libraries and archives exemption, and places your institution at risk for the penalties associated with copyright infringement.

■ **TIP**

If a copyright notice (i.e., "Copyright 1965 Jane Doe") appears in a work you are copying, make sure you include it on any copies you make. If there is no copyright notice, use a general statement such as "This work may be protected by copyright (Title 17, U.S. Code)."

If the work is in the public domain, there is no need to include the notice.

■ **QUESTION**

How useful is the inclusion of for-profit businesses in the Section 108 exemption?

A court decision from 1994 suggests that the answer might be "not very." *American Geophysical Union v. Texaco* addressed copying practices at a Texaco research facility where researchers would either make copies of articles from technical and scientific journals themselves or receive them from Texaco's corporate library. The Court of Appeals for the Second Circuit did not address the issue of whether the actions of the library were exempt under Section 108. Instead it explored the issue of whether the researchers' use of the copies was a fair use. Because the researchers were requesting the copies as part of their employment, the Court concluded that the copies were made for indirect commercial advantage and thus the use was not fair. As a result, many libraries in for-profit businesses now rely upon annual licenses from the Copyright Clearance Center for permission for much of the copying done by their firms rather than attempting to rely on an argument under fair use or Section 108.

Nevertheless, for business archives that are open to the general public or to specialized researchers, the preservation and copying provisions of Section 108 are still very important.

In addition to conforming to the general eligibility requirements found in Section 108(a), any copying done under 108 must be isolated and unrelated [17 U.S.C. § 108(g)]. The library or archives is not allowed to make multiple copies of the same material when it is aware or has substantial reason to believe that it is engaging in the related or concerted reproduction or distribution of those copies. The library or archives could not fulfill a patron request for one chapter of a book on Monday, the next chapter on Tuesday, and so on—that copying would not be isolated and unrelated.

6.3 Preservation copying of unpublished works

The provisions regarding unpublished works in Section 108(b) are among the broadest exemptions found in the section. A library or archives can make up to three copies of any unpublished work found in its collections for either of two purposes:

▶ Preservation and security
▶ Deposit in another eligible library or archives for research use

There is no limitation on what format the reproduction may take. It could be a photocopy, microfilm, or digital reproduction. The three-copy restriction, found also in the section on replacement copies of published works, was adopted in recognition of microfilming practice. Best practice in microfilming stipulates that there should be three copies of a work made: the camera negative, the print master, and a service copy.

There are a number of important caveats about this provision. First, the copy must have been made *solely* for the purpose of preservation or supply to another repository. Second, any copy made in digital format must not be "otherwise distributed in that format" or "made available to the public in that format outside the premises of the library or archives" [17 U.S.C. § 108(b)(2)]. This is discussed in further detail in section 6.5, below. Finally, recall the general prohibition against direct or indirect commercial advantage (i.e., the repository cannot try to make money on the sale of the 108(b) copies) and the requirement that each copy include a copyright notice.[4]

6.4 Replacement copying of published works

Under Section 108(c), a library or archives can make up to three copies of a published work. The copies, however, can only be made to *replace* a work from the library's collection. A work can only be replaced when the original copy is one of the following:

▶ Damaged
▶ Deteriorating
▶ Lost
▶ Stolen
▶ In an obsolete format

An obsolete format is defined as one for which "the machine or device necessary to render perceptible a work stored in that format is no longer manufactured or is no longer reasonably available in the commercial marketplace" [17 U.S.C. § 108(c)]. An 8″ floppy disk, for example, would likely be considered to be an obsolete format. At least as late as 2003, however, the Copyright Office felt that whether a 5¼″ floppy disk was obsolete was an issue that a library would have to prove in court.[5]

If the work in question meets one of the criteria above, the library must also determine that "an unused replacement cannot be obtained at a fair price." The House Report of 1976, explaining the content of the new Copyright Act of that year, had this to say on the search for an unused copy:

> The scope and nature of a reasonable investigation to determine that an unused replacement cannot be obtained will vary according to the circumstances of a particular situation. It will always require recourse to commonly known trade sources in the United States, and in the normal situation also to the publisher or other copyright owner (if such owner can be located at the address listed in the copyright registration), or an authorized reproducing service.[6]

Assuming that a work is damaged, deteriorating, lost, stolen, or in an obsolete format *and* an unused copy cannot be obtained, then the library or archives can make up to three copies of the original. Any such copies must be made *solely* for the purpose of the replacement. Further, the copies can be made in digital format, provided that they meet the requirements discussed in section 6.5.

6.5 Digital preservation and replacement copies

The preservation copies of unpublished works made under Section 108(b) and the replacement copies of published works made under Section 108(c) can be digital. There are two restrictions on the uses that can be made of the digital copies, however. They are:

▶ There can be no subsequent distribution of the digital format
▶ The digital copy cannot be used "outside the premises of the library or archives"

This is significant for the manner in which an institution can supply other institutions with copies of unpublished works for research use. For example, a library that digitizes an unpublished movie for deposit in another library may not send a digital copy on a DVD to that library. It must instead generate an analog copy (for example, a VHS tape) and send that. In another example, if a library made a replacement copy of a textual work for another library, it would have to print out and send a hard copy rather than e-mail an electronic version—even if it scanned its original to produce the replacement copy.

Similarly, if a library made a replacement copy of a published audio CD, it would not be able to lend that CD to patrons (even though it could have lent the original). Instead, it would have to make a cassette copy for loan, since there can be no further distribution of the digital copy.

There is no definition of what constitutes "premises," but most analysts assume that this restricts use to a specific library building. Remember, too, the three-copy limit. If the library has one copy on a server and one copy on a backup tape, then only one patron at a time would be able to generate a third copy by copying the server copy to a local machine.

■ **QUESTION**

Can I legally make a backup copy of a movie published on VHS tape or on a DVD?

Not using Section 108. The replacement copy provision in Section 108(c) only applies if a work is already damaged, deteriorating, lost, stolen, or on an obsolete format. All media are always to some extent deteriorating, but the Copyright Office has argued that the law presumes that the damage must be greater than what is inherent in the format—otherwise, the exception would swallow the rule and *all* works would be considered to meet the standard.[7]

Some would argue that a different statutory exemption, most likely fair use, could be used to excuse anticipatory copying. Others would argue that since Section 117 contains explicit language permitting users to make a backup copy of software, this implies that this right is not authorized in the other statutory exemptions. If reliance were placed on fair use, of course the circumstances of the particular case would be significant.

6.6 Reproductions in response to patron requests

Sections 108(d) and (e) of the Copyright Act are provisions that allow a library or archives, without infringing copyright, to respond to requests from users to be provided with reproductions of either all or part of copyrighted works that are held in the institution's collection.

Flowchart 6.2 sets out the structure of Sections 108(d) and (e).

There are numerous requirements and exclusions that must be addressed before a copy can be made for a patron using Sections 108(d) and (e).

ELIGIBLE WORKS

Any copyrighted work can be reproduced using the preservation exemption for unpublished works found in Section 108(b) and the replacement provisions for published works found in Section 108(c). In contrast, only certain types of works can be reproduced for patrons using the provisions found in Sections 108(d) and (e). Musical works, pictorial, graphic, or sculptural works, and motion pictures and other audiovisual works are excluded from eligibility [17 U.S.C. § 108(i)]. (See the discussion of these terms in Chapter 2.)

◆ **FLOWCHART 6.2**

Request from user to be supplied with the whole or part of a copyrighted work in the collection of the institution

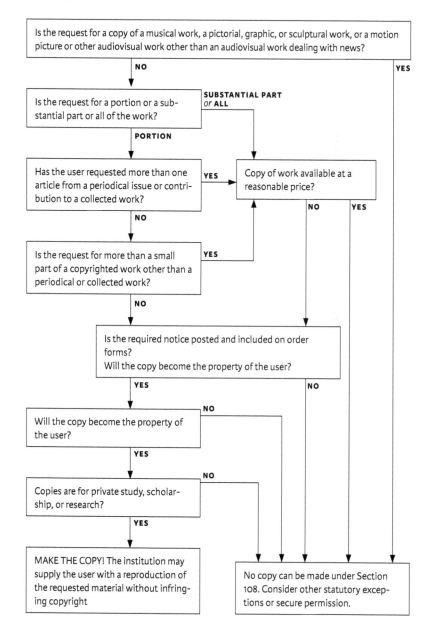

This means that copies of photographs for users cannot be made using Sections 108(d) and (e) since they are included within "pictorial, graphic, and sculptural" works. (An exception is made for illustrations and photographs that are part of textual works. If you are copying an article or chapter for a patron, you can also make copies of included illustrations.) Copies of musical sound recordings cannot be made for patrons unless the underlying scores (the musical work) are in the public domain. Copies of spoken sound recordings such as oral histories could be made under Section 108(d) and (e) since no musical work would be involved: see Case study 1 on oral histories. And in a limited exception to the ban on copying audiovisual works, audiovisual news programs such as television news broadcasts are eligible under Sections 108(d) and (e).

TIP

The prohibition in 108(i), which excludes some types of works from the operation of Sections 108(d) and (e) (making copies for users), refers to musical works, not sound recordings. Thus, you cannot make a copy of a recording of a copyrighted score or song under these provisions since that would infringe the copyright of the underlying musical work. You *can* make copies of recordings where the underlying musical work is in the public domain—assuming the other requirements of Section 108 regarding availability, etcetera, are met.

TIP

Just because some works such as photographs cannot be copied for patrons using Section 108 does not mean that they cannot be copied. Consider using other statutory exemptions, in particular fair use, to meet patron requests.

GROUND RULES

Regardless of whether a copy is made using Section 108(d) or (e), certain ground rules apply. They include:

▶ The copyrighted work must be in the collection of the library or archives.
▶ The copy must become the property of the user. The library or archives cannot use this provision to make copies to add to its own collection.

- The library or archives must have had no notice that the copy will be used for any purpose other than "private study, scholarship, or research."
- Warning notices must be displayed on the order form and at the place where the order is accepted.
- If articles or other portions of a work are being reproduced under Section 108(d), the copying done by the libraries and archives must not be systematic. The library, for example, cannot use Section 108 to establish a document delivery business that advertises that it will provide copies of articles from a set of publications.

■ QUESTION

What constitutes "notice" of a use other than for private study, scholarship, or research?

There is no clear explanation in the law of what constitutes "notice"—in particular what forms of "constructive notice" (i.e., facts that would put a reasonable institution on notice) are sufficient. The repository, therefore, will have to use its good judgment. Consider, for example, these two scenarios in which a library or archives is faced with the question of whether it should make a copy:

- **A film producer asks for a copy of an unpublished script. Later she films a performance of the dramatic work contained in the script without the permission of the copyright owner.** Just because someone is a film producer does not necessarily mean that she cannot also be engaged in private study or research. Without some evidence that the producer wished to use the requested copy for something other than private study or research, the copying would seem to be permitted under Section 108.

- **A scholar asks for a high-resolution scan of a document for publication in his latest book.** This would seem to constitute notice that the copy was going to be used for something other than private study, scholarship, or research. The institution has three options:

- ▼ Make the copy, but explain that it is only for private study, scholarship, or research, and that any other use requires the permission of the copyright owner.
- ▼ Use an exemption to copyright other than Section 108 to make the copy for the patron.
- ▼ Refuse to make the copy until the scholar provides a letter granting permission.

Which option the repository should follow is dependent on the level of risk they are willing to assume. Note that charging a publication permission fee would greatly increase one's risk—it is hard to argue that one had no notice that the copy was going to be used for a purpose other than private study, scholarship, or research if one is charging for publication.

Two different warning notices are specified in the law. First, the library or archives must display prominently at the place where orders are accepted a "display warning of copyright." Second, the institution must include an "order warning of copyright" on its reproduction order forms. The text to be used in the two notices is specified in 37 C.F.R. § 201.14:

Notice warning concerning copyright restrictions

The copyright law of the United States (title 17, United States Code) governs the making of photocopies or other reproductions of copyrighted material.

Under certain conditions specified in the law, libraries and archives are authorized to furnish a photocopy or other reproduction. One of these specific conditions is that the photocopy or reproduction is not to be "used for any purpose other than private study, scholarship, or research." If a user makes a request for, or later uses, a photocopy or reproduction for purposes in excess of "fair use," that user may be liable for copyright infringement.

This institution reserves the right to refuse to accept a copying order if, in its judgment, fulfillment of the order would involve violation of copyright law.

The Display Warning of Copyright must be printed on heavy paper or other durable material in type at least 18 points in size, and must be displayed prominently, in such manner and location as to be clearly visible, legible, and comprehensible to a casual observer within the immediate vicinity of the place where orders are accepted. An Order Warning of Copyright must be printed within a box located prominently on the order form itself, either on the front side of the form or immediately adjacent to the space calling for the name or signature of the person using the form. The notice must be printed in type size no smaller than that used predominantly throughout the form, and in no case can the type size be smaller than 8 point. The notice shall be printed in such manner as to be clearly legible, comprehensible, and readily apparent to a casual reader of the form.[8]

AMOUNT

Section 108(d) authorizes the making of a reproduction of a small portion of a copyrighted work: an article from a journal, a chapter from a collection of essays, or a similar small portion of any other work.

Section 108(e) authorizes the making of a reproduction of a substantial portion or all of a work. In order to make such a copy, the library or archives must first determine, based on a reasonable investigation, that a copy of the work cannot be obtained at a fair price. Note that there is no requirement that the copy be unused, as is found in 108(c); if there is a used copy available on the market at a fair price, the library or archives cannot make the copy.

> **TIP**
>
> We normally think of a single letter or memo in a collection as being a small part of that collection. In copyright terms, however, each document is likely to be an entire copyrighted work. Making a copy of a letter for a patron, therefore, is making a copy of an entire work and would fall under the provisions of Section 108(e). The law requires that the library or archives first conduct a reasonable investigation to determine that a copy cannot be found at a fair price before making a copy of that letter.
>
> In practice, most archives have assumed that the unpublished letters found in their collections are unique and that therefore the reasonable investigation can end before it even starts. There are a variety of materials found in manuscript and archival collections, however.

Many of the items included in collections may not be unique. Libraries and archives should not automatically assume, therefore, that they can reproduce anything in a manuscript collection without first conducting a reasonable search for copies.

■ QUESTION

Is the reproduction of unpublished works for patrons authorized by Section 108?

Most archivists would assume that the answer to this question is yes. In 1983, however, the Register of Copyright issued a report on Section 108 that suggested that the law did not authorize the reproduction of unpublished works for patrons, in spite of the clear stipulation in the law that copying could be done by "libraries *and archives*" (which presumably consist primarily of unpublished items).[9]

The archival community strenuously opposed this reading of the law,[10] and it has seldom resurfaced since. Still, it is a valuable reminder that even acts that seem clearly to be permitted may pose some risk.

FORMAT

Sections 108(d) and (e) are technology neutral. Assuming that all of the requirements of the sections are met, the reproductions made by the repository for the patron can be in any format, including digital.

■ QUESTION

Can patrons give copies made for them to other institutions?

The law stipulates that when a library or archives makes a copy of a copyrighted work for a patron, it may not keep a copy for itself; the copy has to become the property of the user. The goal is to ensure that libraries do not avoid purchasing additional copies of journals and books by retaining copies of items reproduced for patrons.

A copy made for a patron under Section 108 is a legal copy of the copyrighted work, however. This means that all of the rights found in Section 109 that are available to the owner of a legal copy of a work

are available to the user who requested the copy from the library. This
includes the right to give a copy of the work to another library or
archives. Legally made copies, even in digital form, can be given to
another institution by the patron of the first institution.

INTERLIBRARY LOANS

Section 108(d) presupposes that a patron makes a request for a copy directly
to the library or archives holding the original. Many users, however, request
copies through the interlibrary loan (ILL) system in which one library requests
on behalf of one of its users a copy of a portion of a work held by a different
library. Such behavior could be construed as systematic copying, which is
forbidden under this section. Therefore, Section 108(g)(2) was added to the
law to make it clear that ILL activities are permitted so long as the use of ILL
does not substitute for the subscription to or purchase of a work.

The National Commission on New Technological Uses of Copyrighted
Works (CONTU), which was created by Congress to explore issues related
to copyright and new technologies, created guidelines that govern ILL activity.[11] At the heart of the guidelines is the "rule of 5": in any calendar year, a
library may request up to 5 articles from the previous 5 years of any journal.
If a sixth article is requested, the library either needs to pay permission or
secure a subscription.

In addition to providing copies of portions of a work to users, ILL systems
also enable the physical loan of a book from one library to another. The loan
of a lawfully acquired copy of a book is authorized under Section 109.

AUDIOVISUAL NEWS PROGRAMS

Section 108(f)(3) permits libraries and archives to record audiovisual news
programs. The legislative history indicates that the exemption was intended
to apply to the daily newscasts of the national television networks. It may
apply to local television newscasts as well. It does not apply to documentaries, magazine-format broadcasts, or other public affairs broadcasts dealing
with subjects of general interest to the viewing public.[12]

Libraries and archives are allowed to lend copies of the recorded broadcasts to users. There is no mention of format, and so the copies could be
digital or on tape. Unlike copies of textual materials, which must become

the property of the user, copies of news recordings can only be lent to users. Performance of the broadcasts, either over the air or by streaming, is prohibited. So, too, is the sale of copies of the broadcasts.

If copies of audiovisual news programs have been acquired legally by means other than recording by the library or archives itself, then those copies can be treated the same as any textual item, and copies can be made for patrons just as if it was an article or entire book (with the same restrictions on copying described above). Section 108(i) stipulates that audiovisual news programs are eligible for all 108 exemptions.

UNSUPERVISED REPRODUCTION EQUIPMENT

In Chapter 4's discussion of indirect copyright infringement, the question was raised whether the actions of users on institution-provided photocopiers and other reproduction equipment could place a library or archives at risk. For instance, in a major Australian case in the 1970s, a library was held to have authorized copyright infringement by providing self-service photocopiers for use by patrons.[13] In the United States, Section 108(f)(1) makes the issue moot by absolving the institution of any liability arising from the unsupervised use of equipment "located on its premises," provided that "such equipment" displays a warning of copyright. In theory, this exemption would appear to extend to the user's own equipment, too, since the law states that the equipment must be "located on the premises," and not that the library must own it. Of course, it could be argued that one would have to place the warning label on the user's equipment to comply fully with the requirements of the section.

DIGITIZATION OF PUBLISHED WORKS IN THEIR LAST 20 YEARS OF COPYRIGHT

There is in Section 108 one provision that allows libraries and archives to digitize and make freely available on the Internet copyrighted works. Unlike the rest of the exemptions in 108, it is also available to nonprofit educational institutions that function like libraries or archives.

Section 108(h) allows libraries and archives to reproduce (including in digital form), distribute, and perform copyrighted works. The works can be in any format: textual, pictorial, sound, or audiovisual. There are, however, many important limitations on this right:

▶ The work must be published.
▶ It must be in its last 20 years of copyright term. If, for example, the work has a 95-year term, then during years 75 to 95 of that term, a library or archives could digitize the work and make it available. See Table 6.2.

In addition, the library or archives must conduct a reasonable investigation in order to determine if any of the following apply. If they do, Section 108(h) will not apply:

▶ The work is subject to normal commercial exploitation (i.e., that it is "in print" or being licensed)
▶ A copy can be obtained at a fair price
▶ The copyright owner has informed the Copyright Office that either of the first two conditions is true

Section 108(h) enables the kind of digitization that is of interest to most libraries and archives. The limitation concerning the availability of copies is substantial, however. Unlike Section 108(c), which mandates a reasonable search for *unused* copies, Section 108(h) stipulates that the search must be for *a* copy, implying that the copy can be new or used. And thanks to metasearch services such as AddAll.com, Bookfinder.com, and Vialibri.net, it is possible to find a copy of many books available for purchase. Furthermore, the question of what constitutes a reasonable investigation and what is a fair price are matters that could be the subject of litigation. Nevertheless, 108(h) represents the clearest and most generous digitization option for copyrighted works available to libraries and archives.

■ **TABLE 6.2**

When Works can be Digitized by Libraries and Archives using Section 108(h)[14]

Current Date	2009	2010	2011	2012	2013	2014	2015	2016	2017
Date of Publication of Eligible Works: 1923–32, plus these years	1933	1934	1935	1936	1937	1938	1939	1940	1941

6.7 Libraries and archives privileges found outside Section 108

Most of the exemptions for libraries and archives are found in Section 108, but specific exemptions for libraries and archives are found in other places in the Copyright Act. Most, however, are of limited utility in digitization projects.

The most important exemption has already been mentioned: Section 109, or the "first sale" doctrine, which allows libraries to display and loan physical items found in their collections. Section 109(b)(1)(a) contains an exemption specific to libraries and nonprofit educational institutions that allows them to rent or lend copies of "phonorecords" (meaning any physical object on which sounds are recorded)—actions that are otherwise forbidden by law. (This is why one can rent a DVD from a video store but cannot rent a musical CD from a music store.) Similarly, 109(b)(2)(a) allows nonprofit libraries to lend computer programs if a warning label is attached to the packaging containing the program.

Section 602(a)(3) grants an exemption to the general prohibition forbidding the unauthorized importation into the United States of copyrighted works acquired abroad. For example, if a work has authorized American and English distributors, it would be illegal to acquire copies from the English supplier for distribution in the United States. Nonprofit organizations operated for scholarly, educational, or religious purposes, however, are allowed to import one copy of an audiovisual work such as a movie "solely for its archival purposes." They can also import no more than five copies or phonorecords of any work other than a movie for its library lending or archival purposes.

▪ **KEY POINT**

It will come as a surprise to many librarians that the very common practice of importing from abroad for the lending collection copies of movies unavailable for purchase in the United States is of questionable legality. It is illustrative of a point made more fully in Chapter 10: namely, that cultural institutions have often knowingly or unknowingly skirted the letter of the law in order to serve their patrons and society. They have done so at little risk to themselves. No library has yet been prosecuted for lending to a patron a copy of a movie purchased abroad.

The digitization of library collections should be approached in the same way. Everyone needs to know the letter of the law (something these guidelines are intended to convey), but each library also needs to determine the risks and benefits involved in any planned digitization project. A project may be technically illegal but present no more risk to the institution than importing a movie from overseas for the circulating collection.

Section 1201(d) permits nonprofit libraries, archives, and educational institutions to circumvent access-control measures on a work for the sole purpose of determining whether it wants to acquire a copy of that work. In reality, of course, any library interested in evaluating a work with access controls would arrange a trial with the publisher rather than attempting to "hack" through the protection measures on its own. Section 1203(c)(5)(b) requires that courts waive the penalties for anticircumvention when it finds that a nonprofit library, archives, educational institution, or public broadcasting entity unknowingly violated the anticircumvention provisions of Section 1201 or the requirements to maintain copyright management information found in Section 1202. Section 1204(b) removes all criminal liability for these actions.

6.8 Checklist for libraries and archives provisions

☐ Is my institution a "library" or "archives"?

☐ Library	No definition of "library." Some provisions do not apply to libraries in for-profit entities.	108(a)
☐ Archives	No definition of "archives." Some provisions do not apply to libraries in for-profit entities.	108(a)
☐ "Virtual" libraries and archives	More than just a Web site, bulletin board, or online collection of information.	S. REP. No. 105–190[15]

☐ Does my institution meet the "ground rules" for eligibility?

	☐ Accessible to the public; ☐ Only single copies made; ☐ Copies contain © notice; and ☐ No direct or indirect commercial advantage.	108(a)

☐ Is digitization permitted by the libraries and archives provisions?

☐ Preservation	Unpublished works.	108(b)
☐ Deposit in another institution	Unpublished works for research use. Copy provided cannot be digital.	108(b)
☐ Replacement	Any published work that is damaged, deteriorating, lost, stolen, or in an obsolete format when the original was in the collection and no unused copy can be purchased.	108 (c)
☐ Web site use	Published works in their last 20 years of copyright that are not commercially available. Musical works; pictorial, graphic, or sculptural works; and motion pictures and other audiovisual works (other than an audiovisual news programs) are excluded.	108(h), 108(i)
☐ User requests and interlibrary loans	Articles from periodicals; essays from books; entire works.	108(d), 108(e)

☐ Can the public access electronic or digitized content?

☐ Digital copies made during the last 20 years of © term	Can be made accessible on the Web.	108(h)
☐ Digital copies made for preservation or replacement purposes	Access in digital form limited to the premises of the library or archives	108(b), 108(c)
☐ User requests, interlibrary loans	Can be supplied to a user in hard copy or electronic form.	108(d), 108(e)
☐ Articles and published works acquired in electronic form	Usually governed by license terms accompanying the material.	
☐ Audiovisual news programs recorded by the repository	A digital copy on physical media can be loaned to users.	108(f) (3)

7 Copyright Permissions and Licenses

7.1 Introduction

This chapter discusses the role of permission as a means of ensuring that a cultural institution's activities are copyright compliant. As we have seen, a cultural institution risks infringing copyright if it digitizes, or makes available online, material for which it is not the owner of copyright (see Chapter 4). In Chapters 5 and 6, we noted that there are certain statutory exemptions to copyright infringement, in particular fair use (Section 107) and the libraries and archives provisions (Section 108). However, many activities performed by cultural institutions are not covered by any of these exemptions. Instead, cultural institutions will need to obtain permission for the intended use from the owner of copyright.

This chapter will address questions such as:

▶ What is permission? Does permission differ from a license?
▶ What formalities are necessary for permission to be legally effective? For instance, does it need to be in writing?
▶ What sort of terms is it useful to have in permissions?
▶ What terms would be appropriate in an agreement on outsourced digitization?
▶ What are the various forms of online licenses?
▶ What are "Creative Commons" licenses, and how might they be relevant to cultural institutions?

The focus in this chapter is on how one structures an agreement with a copyright owner and what terms might be included in that agreement. The issue of how to locate a copyright owner in order to negotiate an agreement is discussed in Chapter 8.

In addition to securing permissions and licenses to use material in their own digitization projects, cultural heritage institutions may wish to license others to use collection material or other institution outputs. Detailed analysis of the issues associated with such third-party licensing is beyond the scope of these guidelines, although some of the general principles discussed here will be applicable. In addition, there are several excellent guides to managing the intellectual property of cultural heritage institutions.[1]

7.2 What is permission? What is a license?

GENERALLY

As we have seen, the Copyright Act grants the copyright owner the exclusive right to perform certain acts. If someone other than the copyright owner wishes to exercise one of those rights, they have two options: first, they can invoke one of the statutory exemptions; and second, they can seek the permission of the copyright owner. Permission allows someone who is not the copyright owner to do what would otherwise be an infringement of copyright.

Permission is normally given by granting the third party a license to use the work. A license is merely "a permission, usu[ally] revocable, to commit some act that would otherwise be unlawful."[2] The person who grants the license is often called the "licensor," and the person who is granted the license the "licensee." The license may be a formal document (what we normally think of as a license), but it can also be very informal. For example, when you give someone permission to forward to another party an e-mail message you wrote, you are in effect granting them a license to reproduce and distribute the work.

Licenses can apply to the entire bundle of exclusive rights included in copyright, or just to some. For example, it is possible for a copyright owner to license to a third party the right to reproduce a work, but retain the right to make derivative works.

Licenses come in a variety of forms and flavors:

▶ Exclusive versus nonexclusive
▶ Limited versus absolute
▶ Voluntary versus statutory/compulsory
▶ Negotiated individually versus collectively
▶ Paid versus free
▶ Written versus verbal
▶ Express versus implied
▶ Detailed versus cursory

The different approaches may be combined together in one license. For example, you can have a voluntary, free, cursory, written license. Each of the options is discussed briefly below.

EXCLUSIVE AND NONEXCLUSIVE LICENSES

Exclusive licenses are a bit of a misnomer. In the Copyright Act, the granting of an exclusive license is the equivalent of transferring copyright ownership of that right.[3] Exclusive licenses that grant to the licensee all of the rights of the copyright owner would in effect transfer ownership of the copyright to the licensee. Exclusive licenses exclude any other person—including the author or original copyright owner—from doing the acts granted in the license. And there are only limited opportunities under the Act to revoke an exclusive license

In most instances, cultural institutions will negotiate nonexclusive licenses. In contrast to exclusive licenses, under nonexclusive licenses copyright owners continue to own all copyright rights in their work. They can continue to do any of the acts they have permitted their licensees to do, and they can license others to do those same acts. That is, a copyright owner can negotiate multiple nonexclusive licenses permitting multiple parties to perform the same acts in relation to the same copyright work.

■ QUESTION

When is an author-friendly publishing contract not what it seems?

We recently reviewed a publishing contract from a major scholarly press. The contract specified that the author would retain copyright in the work, which seemed author-friendly. The contract also stipulated, however, that the author exclusively licensed to the publisher for the entire term of copyright two of the most important rights of copyright: the rights to reproduce and distribute the work. Because this was an exclusive license, the publisher became the owner of those rights, and the author could only get them back with difficulty (unless the publisher voluntarily reassigned them).[4]

The contract also stipulated that as long as the publisher kept the work in print, it had the exclusive right to exercise two more of the copyright owner's rights, namely the right to produce derivative works and the right to perform the work publicly. The only right the author retained was the right to display the work publicly—a right granted to her anyway by Section 109.

The result: the author retained copyright, but for all practical purposes in name only. The most important exclusive rights of the copyright owner belonged to the publisher.

LIMITED VERSUS ABSOLUTE

Both exclusive and nonexclusive licenses may be limited in certain ways. For example, the license may be of limited duration (e.g., for two years), only apply in a specific territory (e.g., conduct in the United States) or only permit certain uses of a work (e.g., one-time reproduction in a specific book of a fixed print run). Alternatively, the license can be more expansive. It is not uncommon, for example, to find permission granted in current contracts "in perpetuity, in all languages, in any and all media, whether now known or unknown, and throughout the Universe."[5]

DID YOU KNOW?

For a number of years, an award-winning documentary series on the history of the civil rights movement, *Eyes on the Prize*, was unavailable for purchase. When filmmaker Henry Hampton first created the series, he drew on film and photographs from a plethora of archives as well as many musical recordings. The owners of the still photos, video footage, and music used in the documentary granted permission to use the material for various lengths of time. Once their initial permissions had expired, the film had to be removed from circulation.

Fortunately, with $850,000 in grants in hand, the production studio was able to go through the onerous process of securing new permissions for all of the material used in the original film and it was rebroadcast on PBS.[6]

When granting or securing licenses to use content, cultural heritage institutions may want to consider the costs associated with time-limited grants.

VOLUNTARY AND STATUTORY LICENSES

A license may be voluntary, meaning that the copyright owner has freely granted the license to the licensee, or it may be required by copyright legislation. These compulsory licenses are commonly referred to as a "statutory licenses." In the case of a voluntary license, the parties are able to exercise a degree of control over the terms of the license (for example, what acts the licensee may perform, the duration of the license, the territory to which the license applies, etc.). In contrast, the terms and conditions of a statutory license are defined by law.

The Copyright Act provides for a number of statutory licensing arrangements. These include compulsory licenses or government-determined licensing fees for:

▶ Making and distributing new sound recordings based on existing recordings of nondramatic musical works [17 U.S.C. § 115]
▶ Performance of nondramatic sound recordings in a jukebox [17 U.S.C. § 116]
▶ Broadcast of sound recordings over the Internet [17 U.S.C. § 114]
▶ Retransmission by cable operators of television and radio broadcasts [17 U.S.C. § 111]
▶ Use of certain works by public broadcasting [17 U.S.C. § 118]
▶ Retransmission of television broadcasts by satellite carriers [17 U.S.C. § 119 and § 122]

The guidelines will not discuss statutory licenses in any further detail as the existing statutory licenses are quite technical and of limited, if any, relevance to digitization projects.

INDIVIDUALLY AND COLLECTIVELY NEGOTIATED LICENSES

Licenses can be arranged on an individual basis with copyright owners or their agents. Agents can include literary executors and organizations that specialize in negotiating on behalf of creators. Many of them are discussed in Chapter 8. Certain areas (most notably music) have also endorsed collective licensing. A collective licensing organization establishes fixed fees for the use of copyrighted material and collects and distributes those fees on behalf of the copyright owners. Collective licensing organizations are discussed further in Chapter 8.

PAID AND FREE LICENSES

The copyright owner may require a payment for permission to use one of the exclusive rights, but such a payment is not required for the permission to be legally effective. If a payment is requested, it can be through an up-front fee, through the form of ongoing fees or royalties, or both. Ongoing fees can be calculated in a number of ways. For example, a royalty might be payable on each sale of a product incorporating the licensed copyright work. Alternatively, a license fee could be calculated on the number of times a digital file is accessed, downloaded, or used.

■ KEY POINT

It is not necessary for a license fee to be paid in order for a valid license to be created. A simple grant of permission (called a "bare license" in legal terms) is enough to provide some protection. Many times, however, permission is granted through the use of a contract. To be effective and enforceable, contracts require three things: an offer, acceptance of the offer, and some "consideration" exchanged between the parties. Consideration is often monetary: for example, a permission to reproduce a work in return for payment. Contracts have certain advantages over bare licenses. Their terms, for example, are often clearer and they cannot be arbitrarily revoked (as, in general, can a bare license that does not require any payment of consideration).

WRITTEN AND VERBAL

Permissions do not have to be in writing in order to be valid, and therefore may be made verbally. Although a cultural institution may rely on an oral agreement, this may end up causing difficulties, and written permission should be sought wherever possible. This is because a written license is a far better record of the existence of a license and its terms than the recollection of a staff member.

TIP

Permission does not have to be in writing in order to be valid, but it is far better to have written evidence. Cultural institutions may choose to develop standard form license terms to streamline the permission process and to ensure consistency across departments and collection items.

EXPRESS AND IMPLIED

Licenses are commonly "express," in the sense that the terms are reviewed and agreed to by the parties (either orally or in writing). However, license terms may also be "implied" by "the kind of license being granted, by the conduct of the licensor, or by the licensor's apparent refusal to exercise its exclusive rights to the licensed property."[7] For example, when a person writes a letter to the editor of an opinion page in a newspaper, there is an implied license granted to publish the letter. When viewing a Web page, a reproduction of the HTML file is stored (at least temporarily) on your computer; we can assume that the author of the Web page has granted an implied license for you to make this reproduction.

It is conceivable, though not particularly likely, that a cultural institution could argue that it has an implied license to digitize certain collection items and then make them available on the Web. For example, an oral history project that was structured from the start to provide the widest possible access to generated material might be able to argue that it had an implied license from the interviewees that would allow transcripts to be made available on a Web site. In general, however, it is far preferable for an institution to rely on the terms of an express license rather than invoke an implied license.

LEVEL OF DETAIL

The amount of detail in an expressed license can vary greatly. Some may take the form of a letter. Others may take the formal structure of a contract, but even here the differences can be great. Some licenses are just one or two pages long; others are highly detailed and lengthy documents. A license with very little detail can still be legally effective—as a matter of law, the main issue is whether the licensor has granted the requisite permission (either as a bare license, or part of a contract).

As is discussed below, at a minimum, a license used by a cultural institution should include:

- ▶ Identification of the parties to the agreement
- ▶ A description of the work to which the license applies (including the creator and title, and any preferred form of attribution of the creator)
- ▶ The date the license was made
- ▶ The rights granted by the licensor
- ▶ The territory and duration of the license

7.3 Negotiating licenses

STRUCTURE

As noted earlier, permissions and licenses do not need to be detailed in order to be legally binding. In some instances, cultural institutions use short, user-friendly agreements. These may be less than a page long.

Brief licenses often stipulate a standard set of terms, perhaps with options to cover various situations, in the body of the agreement and then record information particular to the transaction—such as the name of the licensor, the title of the work, and so forth—in a schedule attached to the end of the license.

As in discussed in detail in Part 7.4, licenses can also be highly intricate agreements. The main benefit of using a longer license is clarity and certainty. However, such a lengthy document may be intimidating and seem overly legalistic to some potential licensors. In contrast, short-form licenses may be easier to deal with on a day-to-day basis. But if not properly drafted, they may be less definitive and possibly less helpful if a dispute arises about the license.

Cultural institutions may find it beneficial to have a number of different standard form agreements for use in different circumstances. Which agreement is used in any given case will depend on the nature of the work, the profession and interests of the creator, and the proposed uses of the work. For example, a longer agreement may be appropriate when dealing with a professional photographer selling works to a gallery, but not for a family donating snapshots to a social history museum. Similarly, where an institution is dealing with a key work or iconic item, it may be beneficial to use a long-form agreement in order to gain maximum certainty regarding allowed uses.

RIGHTS

The clause setting out the permitted uses of the licensed work is at the core of the license and should be given careful consideration. The permitted acts may be described narrowly or broadly. Where descriptions are narrower, licenses may need to be renegotiated should a new use or technology arise (see below).

The permitted acts should take into account the exclusive rights of the copyright owner, the proposed uses of the cultural institution, and the profession and interests of the copyright owner. The license may permit the licensed work to be reproduced, copied, published, or communicated for a variety of purposes, such as exhibition, promotion and advertising, inclusion on a Web site, use in educational materials and programs, inclusion in the institution's publications or merchandise, and so forth. In some instances, institutions may request unremunerated licenses for noncommercial activities, and agree to negotiate separately with the copyright owner for commercial uses.

As seen in Chapters 5 and 6, some uses of works are permitted under statutory exemptions in the Copyright Act. However, it may be useful to supplement these with rights under a license—such as a provision allowing digital content to be migrated to a new format when existing software is superseded or becomes obsolete or a right to reproduce the licensed work for the purpose of preservation.

It is important to consider the consequences that flow from the rights granted. For example, if the cultural institution has the right to alter, adapt, or modify the licensed work, will it own all of the intellectual property in the alteration, adaptation, or modification? If so, the license should include provisions concerning further developments and improvements of the licensed material. Similarly, does the cultural institution have the ability to *sublicense* use of the work (i.e., enter into a license with a third party in relation to the work)? And will the cultural institution need to take measures to prevent members of the public from reproducing the work (such as banning or limiting photography)?

MANAGEMENT

As should be obvious by now, cultural institutions can engage in a broad range of licensing arrangements. Each arrangement carries with it its own administrative burden. For example, some institutions seek nonexclusive, royalty-free, perpetual licenses at the point of acquisition for particular uses. These licenses commonly permit noncommercial activities and bypass some of the administrative difficulties involved in retrospectively obtaining copyright licenses for collection items. At times, however, the institutions may have to enter into other types of licenses. These may be of fixed duration or only relate to use in a particular project (e.g., a license that permits a copy of a movie to be used in an exhibition). Should the licensee desire to extend the duration of the use beyond the term of the license, or should the licensee wish to use the copyright material for a different purpose, the license may need to be renegotiated.

TIP

It is important to have a good management system in place in relation to copyright licenses, particularly those of fixed duration. For example, if a cultural institution is granted a two-year license to publish a certain image on a Web site, it is important that the institution knows when the license expires so that the license can be renegotiated or the image removed. If this process does not occur, the image on the Web site may infringe copyright once the license lapses.

7.4 Sample licenses

PERMISSION LETTERS

Perhaps the simplest way to secure permission is via a simple letter to a copyright owner seeking authorization to use a work. Kenneth Crews while at the Copyright Management Center at Indiana University–Purdue University at Indianapolis (IUPUI), developed a number of sample permission letters that can be adapted to any individual project; they have moved with him to Columbia University.[8] These provide a useful starting point for cultural heritage institutions—bearing in mind that it is also important to obtain legal advice in relation to the content of any legal documentation (such advice being beyond the scope of guidelines such as these). Here is the body from his model for a general permission letter:

IUPUI COPYRIGHT MANAGEMENT CENTER GENERAL PERMISSIONS LETTER MODEL[9]

I am in the process of creating [*Describe project*]. I would like your permission to include the following material with this [*Project*]:

[Citation with source information]

The [Project] will be used [Describe how the project and material will be used]. It will be accessible by [Describe users].

If you do not control the copyright on all of the above mentioned material, I would appreciate any contact information you can give me regarding the proper rights holder(s), including current address(es). Otherwise, your permission confirms that you hold the right to grant the permission requested here.

Permission includes nonexclusive world rights in all languages to use the material and will not limit any future publications—including future editions and revisions—by you or others authorized by you.

I would greatly appreciate your consent to my request. If you require any additional information, please do not hesitate to contact me. I can be reached at:

[Your contact information]

A duplicate copy of this request has been provided for your records. If you agree with the terms as described above, please sign the release form below and send one copy with the self-addressed return envelope I have provided.

Sincerely,
[Signature]
[Typed name]

Permission granted for the use of the material as described above:
Agreed to: _____ Name & Title: _____
Company/Affiliation: _____ Date: _____

This simple letter addresses most of the key elements of any permission agreement. It identifies the parties, establishes that they are authorized to enter into this agreement, describes the work for which permission is being granted, gives the date permission was granted, and describes the geographic scope of the permission. It lacks an explicit description of the duration of the agreement, but this could be added by an institution adapting this letter. Such an institution would also want to spell out in some detail how the digitized material will be used in order to make it clear what permissions the licensor is conferring. For instance, if material will be made available on the Internet, this should be expressly mentioned.

This sort of agreement is often nonthreatening to the licensor and can usually be negotiated fairly quickly. A downside to such agreements is that they are often very narrow in the rights they convey. Although they may allow one to meet an immediate project goal, they are poor at anticipating future uses of digitized content. For example, a standard permission letter might allow a cultural institution to digitize content to display on a Web site. At a later point, however, the cultural institution may want to do more with that content. For example, it may want to automatically convert text into sound, or establish a print-on-demand function, or combine the text with other resources into a new product. Any of these activities may require another permission letter.

TIP

Model permission letters are helpful, but every digital project manager will need to devise a customized letter based on the nature of the material, the goals of the project, and the potential concerns of the licensors. In drafting a letter, try to secure permission for your immediate needs as well as any future uses you may wish to make of the work. Repeatedly returning to seek additional permissions is time-consuming, expensive, and at some point becomes counterproductive.

BRIEF LICENSES

Many institutions rely on a formal brief license, often accompanied with a cover letter explaining the purpose of the project, in order to secure permission. The DSpace Non-Exclusive Distribution License used by MIT is a good example of a brief license:

THE DSPACE NON-EXCLUSIVE
DISTRIBUTION LICENSE[10]

In order for DSpace to reproduce, translate, and distribute your submission worldwide your agreement to the following terms is necessary. Please take a moment to read the terms of this license, fill in the information requested (and sign and submit this license to DSpace at _____).

By signing and submitting this license, you (the author(s) or copyright owner) grants to Massachusetts Institute of Technology (MIT) the non-exclusive right to reproduce, translate (as defined below), and/or distribute your submission (including the abstract) worldwide in print and electronic format and in any medium, including but not limited to audio or video.

You agree that MIT may, without changing the content, translate the submission to any medium or format for the purpose of preservation.

You also agree that MIT may keep more than one copy of this submission for purposes of security, back-up and preservation.

You represent that the submission is your original work, and that you have the right to grant the rights contained in this license. You also represent that your submission does not, to the best of your knowledge, infringe upon anyone's copyright.

If the submission contains material for which you do not hold copyright, you represent that you have obtained the unrestricted permission of the copyright owner to grant MIT the rights required by this license, and that such third-party owned material is clearly identified and acknowledged within the text or content of the submission.

IF THE SUBMISSION IS BASED UPON WORK THAT HAS BEEN SPONSORED OR SUPPORTED BY AN AGENCY OR ORGANIZATION OTHER THAN MIT, YOU REPRESENT THAT YOU HAVE FULFILLED ANY RIGHT OF REVIEW OR OTHER OBLIGATIONS REQUIRED BY SUCH CONTRACT OR AGREEMENT.

MIT will clearly identify your name(s) as the author(s) or owner(s) of the submission, and will not make any alteration, other than as allowed by this license, to your submission.

Note that this brief license contains many of the elements found in most licenses. It identifies the parties to the agreement and specifies the rights granted to MIT. It does not formally identify the work to which the license applies nor date the agreement, but identification and dating occurs as part of the electronic submission process. The agreement also adds provisions to indemnify MIT against any contributory copyright infringement. This brief license does not include information on its duration; this would be a matter for the court in the event that there was a legal action brought on the terms of the license.

DETAILED LICENSES

Detailed licenses are formal contracts, usually developed on a case-by-case basis with the support of legal counsel. They are particularly appropriate if the material at issue is of great economic or cultural importance. They are also frequently used in conjunction with digitization outsourcing. A good example is the digitization agreement between Google and the University of Virginia that governs Google's digital conversion and use of a portion of the Virginia library collections.[11]

In addition to the information found in a permission letter or brief license, a detailed license might have clauses that allow for future or unanticipated uses. It might spell out who authorized users of the material are, and what they can do with the material. There may be information on any fees and royalties to be paid for the use of the content, and specification of the reporting and auditing requirements. The duration of the license is likely to be spelled out, along with information on what happens if there is any breach or default of the agreement. There are likely to be provisions for the termination of the contract prior to expiration of term. There may be expanded provisions about warranties and indemnification. What happens, for example, if the licensor claims to have the authority to grant the permissions found in the license but in reality does not that authority? Finally, such licenses often specify the choice of law and jurisdiction in case any action is brought forward.

TIP

If you are contracting for outsourced digitization services, be sure to include clauses on the physical ownership of the digital files produced during digitization as well as any copyright that may have been produced. The contractor should be expected to return or destroy all copies it has made during the digitization project when they are no longer needed for production purposes. Although outsourced scanning itself is unlikely to create a new copyrighted work (for the reasons discussed in Chapter 3), other services provided by a contractor could conceivably generate a copyright that could belong to the contractor. The agreement should make clear that the contractor transfers all rights it may have in the digitized content to the institution.

7.5 License terms

This section consists of a table of examples of clauses and elements that might be included in a license. It focuses on a license between a cultural institution and the owner of copyright in a collection item. A detailed license may include many or all of these clauses, whereas a brief license or permission letter may only contain some of them. We have marked some clauses as essential; these should be included in all licenses.

TABLE 7.1

Common terms appearing in copyright licenses

☐ **General information** (essential in any license)

☐ The parties to the license.	☐ Full name of individuals, companies, or institutions that are parties to the license. ☐ Address of each party.
☐ The work to which the license applies.	☐ The work should be clearly described. ☐ Some institutions use a boilerplate license in which the licensed work is described as the "Work" throughout the license, and a definition of the "Work" is included in a schedule or definitions section. ☐ A photograph of the work could be attached to the license for identification purposes.
☐ The date the license was made.	☐ This should be inserted when the parties sign the license.

☐ **Recitals**

☐ The background to the license.	☐ Recitals tend to be used in longer agreements.
	☐ Recitals are not legally binding terms within the license—they merely describe the parties and summarize the reason for entering into the license.
	☐ Recitals give a license a legalistic tone, and may be inappropriate and/or unnecessary for many licenses used by cultural institutions.

☐ **The rights granted** (essential in any license)

☐ The rights granted to the licensee.	☐ If the license is exclusive, the license actually transfers ownership of that right to the licensee.
	☐ It may be preferable for terminology to be technology-neutral, to help reduce the need for renegotiation.
☐ The use that others may make of the licensed work	☐ If the licensee is required to limit access to a specific group, the identification of what constitutes authorized users.
	☐ Identification of what users of the work are authorized to do with it. For example, is the work made available under a Creative Commons license?

☐ **Extent and duration of the grant of rights**

☐ The territory of the license	☐ The license may specify that it only applies to a defined geographic area.
	☐ If a cultural institution proposes to make digital content available over the Internet, it should seek worldwide rights.
☐ The duration of the license.	☐ The duration may be perpetual, for the life of the copyright, or for a fixed term.
	☐ If the license is of fixed duration, does the proposed use of the work extend beyond the term of the contract? If so, the license may need to be renewed or renegotiated upon expiration.
	☐ Can the license be renewed? If so, what is the procedure for renewal?

☐ **Delivery**

| ☐ Delivery of material to the licensee. | ☐ If cultural institutions are licensing the use of material they do not own, there must be a transfer of the material to the institution. If the institution is contracting with someone to perform digitization services, there must be transfer to the service. |
| | ☐ There may be a clause specifying the media, format, and delivery of the item. |

☐ **Warranties and indemnities** (desirable, but can make the document appear legalistic)

☐ Warranties given by the licensor.	☐ A warrant that the person granting the license is legally capable of doing so. (If that person is not the owner of copyright, or does not have authorization by the copyright owner to enter into the license, any license is likely to be invalid and leave the cultural institution exposed to a claim of copyright infringement.)
	☐ A warrant that the rights granted in the license do not infringe the rights of any third parties.
	☐ These warranties are particularly important where the licensed work contains underlying rights, such as most films and sound recordings.
☐ Indemnity given by the licensor.	☐ A provision in which the licensor indemnifies the licensee against any liability, costs, damages, etcetera, if any of the licensor's warranties turn out to be false.

☐ **Fees and royalties** (essential when applicable)

☐ Up-front fee.	☐ Is the licensee required to pay an up-front fee?
	☐ If so, the manner of payment and amount of the fee should be stated.
☐ Ongoing fees or royalties.	☐ Are ongoing fees payable?
	☐ If so, the manner of payment and calculation of the fee should be stated (e.g., pay-per-use, blanket fee for specified period, etc).

☐ **Assignment and sublicensing**

| ☐ Assignment. | ☐ If assignment is permitted, are there any limitations on the exercise of the right (for example, the written consent of the other party)? |
| ☐ Sub-licensing. | ☐ If sublicensing is permitted, are there any conditions for exercise of that right, or any processes that must be complied with? |

☐ **Termination**

☐ Is termination allowed?	☐ A termination provision enables a license to be terminated prior to the expiration of its term. ☐ Depending on the wording of the clause, the licensor, the licensee, or both may be able to terminate the license. ☐ Is termination without cause permitted (that is, without justification), or only termination upon the happening of certain events (e.g., specified breaches, bankruptcy or insolvency, or a warranty turning out to be false)? ☐ Under general legal principles, it may be possible to terminate a license even if there is no express termination clause.
☐ Termination process.	☐ Where termination is allowed without cause, the typical process is that a notice must be served on the other party stating the intention to terminate. The license will usually set out the minimum period that must transpire between receipt of the notice and the date termination comes into effect.
	☐ Where termination is for a specified breach, the typical process is that a notice setting out the breach is served on the other party, and that party is given a time to remedy the breach (this time is usually stipulated in the license). If the breach remains uncured, the license can be terminated. ☐ Do the parties need to embark on a dispute resolution procedure before the license can be terminated?
☐ Consequences of termination.	☐ Do any rights survive the termination of the license? ☐ Can the licensor retain copies of the work after termination of the license?

☐ **Miscellaneous**

☐ Governing law.	☐ This clause (sometimes referred to as a choice of law clause) specifies the jurisdiction that governs interpretation of the license. For example, the clause may state that the license is governed by the law of a particular state, such as New York.
☐ Severability.	☐ A "severance" clause states that if part of the license is found to be legally invalid, this clause can be "severed" from the license, and the remaining clauses in the license continue to operate.

☐ Entire agreement.	☐ Specifies that the written license constitutes the entire agreement between the parties and supersedes any prior arrangements, agreements, or understandings between them with respect to the subject matter of the license.
☐ Notices.	☐ Sets out the contact details of the licensor and licensee for delivery of any notices that are required or permitted under the license.
	☐ May also specify how a notice may be sent (e.g., hand delivery or certified mail) and when a notice is deemed to have been received (e.g., upon successful completion of a facsimile transmission).

7.6 Clickthrough and browse-wrap licenses

The bulk of this chapter has discussed the use of licenses to secure the permission of a copyright owner in order to digitize and make available on the Internet copyrighted content. Sometimes the copyright owner will only allow digitization to occur if there are restrictions placed on the subsequent use of the files. For example, a copyright owner might allow her works to be digitized for noncommercial, educational uses, but wish to prohibit any commercial uses. Similarly, the cultural heritage institution that does the digitizing may wish to impose its own requirements on downstream use of the digital files. It may, for example, want to receive proper credit for any subsequent use of the material.

What is required is a license between the cultural institution and the user: a document that stipulates the terms by which the user may exploit a digital work. It is not possible, however, to arrange for individual licenses with each potential user of a Web site. Instead, a provider must rely on some combination of a clickthrough license and/or a statement of terms and conditions that governs the use of a site.

The term "clickthrough license" derives from the "shrink-wrap license" commonly used with software products. With a shrink-wrap license, since the license terms are sealed inside shrink-wrapping, they cannot be viewed until after the product has been purchased and the shrink-wrap broken. Sometimes there is a notice on the outside the shrink-wrap that warns that breaking the wrapping shall be deemed acceptance of the license by the consumer. Terms are nonnegotiable: you must accept the license or decline to use the product. One variation often used with software is an end user license agreement, or EULA. One must agree to the terms of the EULA in order to install the software.

A clickthrough license (sometimes also called a clickwrap license) is a nonnegotiable online license. Users must signal their acceptance of the license terms by clicking their mouse on an "I AGREE" button or similar icon or link before they are allowed to enter the Web site. An example of a clickthrough license in action is found at the Johns Hopkins University's site devoted to digital surrogates of three manuscripts of the *Roman de la Rose*. The page devoted to "Conditions for Use of this Site" begins this way:

> Before beginning your research, we ask you to read and agree
> to abide by the following conditions. You may enter the site by
> clicking on the agreement statement at the end of this page.[12]

A fairly long list of requirements governing the use of the images follows, at which point the following directions appear:

> To view the images now, please click on the agreement below:
> I accept the conditions listed above.[13]

Browse-wrap licenses are the newest iteration of the nonnegotiated license. A browse-wrap license stipulates that merely by continuing to view a Web site, you agree to abide by any terms and conditions governing the use of that site. Normally such terms are included in a page entitled "Terms and Conditions," "Acceptable Use," or simply "Copyright." The page of terms is frequently linked from the bottom of each page on a Web site. Sometimes it is found on an "About" page describing the purpose of the Web site, and sometimes it is hidden away and can only be found with a site map.

Critics of clickthrough, shrink-wrap, and browse-wrap licenses argue that these licenses are unenforceable because they are not the product of negotiation between parties but represent a one-sided "take it or leave it" approach to licensing. However, several court cases have upheld the legality of shrink-wrap, clickthrough, and browse-wrap licenses. In addition, Maryland (where Johns Hopkins University is located) is one of two states (the other being Virginia) that have passed legislation that make these licenses expressly enforceable.

TIP

The legal enforceability of a clickthrough or browse-wrap may not be of great importance to cultural heritage institutions in their capacity as licensors of content. Nevertheless, a good statement on "Terms and Conditions" is imperative for any Web site. If you expect users to respect your wishes regarding the use of digitized material, it is incumbent on you to make those wishes explicit, clear, and easily accessible.

7.7 Alternative licenses

Over the past few years, a number of alternative models have arisen in relation to copyright management. These include free software licenses, open-source licenses, copyleft licenses, and Creative Commons licenses. These licenses have been developed because of perceived problems and limitations with copyright law and traditional licensing models. Some institutions have paid considerable attention to the possibility of using principles from Creative Commons in their licenses.

A Creative Commons license is a license that has been created by Creative Commons, a nonprofit U.S. corporation.[14] Creative Commons is founded on the idea that some copyright owners may not want to exercise all of the intellectual property rights available to them under the law because they want others to know about or build upon their work, because they wish to contribute to an "intellectual commons," or because they believe that Creative Commons licenses can help attract commercial interest in their work. Creative Commons seeks to promote the creative reuse of intellectual works with a minimum of transactional effort, thereby facilitating the distribution of content online and making access to that material easier and cheaper. A Creative Commons license sits somewhere between "all rights reserved" and the public domain, where no rights are reserved; as their graphic notes, in Creative Commons licensed materials, "some rights are reserved."

Creative Commons licenses do not involve giving up copyright protection; they are, in fact, based on the availability of copyright and the ability of copyright owners to license selectively some or all of their rights. For example, some creators might choose to permit wide noncommercial uses of their work under a Creative Commons license while retaining full rights in relation to any possible future commercial uses of the work.

The Creative Commons Web site contains a number of different licenses that copyright owners can use without charge to enable others to make certain uses of the copyright material. There are even licenses that can dedicate the work to the public domain or stipulate that copyright in the work will only endure for the period of copyright found in the first Copyright Act of 1790 (14 years, renewable for another period of 14 years). They can be used for any sort of copyright material, but these licenses can very easily be embedded in digitally published material. Licenses with broadly equivalent scope exist for many different countries. As noted in the preface and preliminary pages, a Creative Commons license has been used for these guidelines.

The advantages of Creative Commons licenses to cultural heritage institutions are numerous. For example, if the copyright owners were willing to license their works with a Creative Commons license, it would obviate the need to draft and negotiate individual licenses with them, at least for the uses specified in the license; this may well include many digitization activities. It would also make clearer the conditions under which users of the digitized work could access and exploit the work.

Yet the Creative Commons licenses are not the panacea for all licensing issues found in cultural heritage institutions. First, owners may not wish to apply Creative Commons licenses to their works, even where they would be willing to allow similar uses by a cultural institution under an individually negotiated license. Second, the Creative Commons model does not assist with *retrospective* licensing issues: i.e., material already in the collection for which copyright is problematic. Third, because a Creative Commons license is based on copyright rights, it is not an option when a work is in the public domain. A cultural institution that wished to include in a digitization project public-domain material could not use a Creative Commons license to regulate access since there is no copyright to license; a different agreement would be needed.[15]

In spite of these limitations, Creative Commons licenses remain an important tool for cultural institutions. They are an option for owners and institutions to consider in their negotiations, as well as a possibility for institutions when managing their own copyright.

7.8 Conclusion

Licenses are becoming of ever greater importance to cultural heritage institutions as they both try to secure the rights to use the copyrighted works of others as well as market and promote their own collections and services. Familiarity with the rudiments of licensing is becoming a fundamental skill for many information professionals.

It is important to create or agree to licenses that are legally acceptable. It is also fundamentally important to be sure that the terms of the license are understood by, and acceptable to, the licensors. It is equally (if not more) important to make sure that the terms and conditions in the agreement are compatible with the fundamental mission and principles of the organization. The release of Google's contracts with its digitization partners, the recent controversy over the Smithsonian's agreement with Showtime, and the struggle over the license terms (and possible public domain status) of some digitized Smithsonian images have turned the attention of many to the proper nature of the terms that should govern such agreements.[16] Especially controversial is the degree of control repositories should seek to assert over the use of public domain materials in their holdings.[17] Some have argued that freely releasing public domain material to the world is in the best interest of the institution;[18] others have argued that it is appropriate to try to recover some of the costs of preserving and digitizing the material.[19] There are as yet no commonly agreed upon standards of best professional practice, though some recent reports contain useful recommendations to be followed when working on digitization contracts.[20] Each institution, therefore, will need to decide on its own how best to ensure that the licenses it agrees to or grants best serve its mission.

8 *Locating Copyright Owners*

8.1 Introduction

In Chapter 7, we discussed mechanisms for securing the permission of copyright owners to digitize works when the statutory exemptions described in Chapters 5 and 6 are not available. It is of course impossible to negotiate permission if one cannot first identify the copyright owner or the owner's representative. This chapter discusses some of the paths you may wish to follow when trying to locate a copyright owner in order to seek permission to use a copyrighted work.

The exact strategy you should follow will depend in part on the nature of the work. The procedures for locating the copyright owner of a published text will vary from those required for sound recordings or works of art. They will also vary according to the circumstances of creation. In general, more effort should be spent in trying to locate the owner of copyright in a professional photograph, for example, than in an amateur snapshot in a photo album since the former author made or makes his or her living from the exploitation of copyrighted works.

It is important to develop a strategy for locating copyright owners prior to starting a digitization project. The costs of locating copyright owners can vary tremendously. In an important study exploring the copyright permission process, Denise Troll Covey reported that depending on the strategy followed at Carnegie Mellon University, the costs of securing permission to digitize printed books ranged from $0.69 to $200.00 per title.[1] Other users who have wanted to use copyrighted works have reported being forced to hire professional genealogists and private investigators in their quest to locate copyright owners.[2] It is easy for a search for copyright owners to spin out of control; forming a clear strategy in advance can help avoid this problem.

This chapter will address questions such as:

▶ How can I determine whom I need to contact to secure permission?
▶ Whom do I need to contact when there are multiple owners of copyrights in a work?

▶ What procedures should I follow to locate copyright owners?

▶ What tools exist to assist me in my search?

▶ What role can reproduction rights organizations and copyright collectives play in my efforts?

▶ What can I do if the work is an "orphan work"—one whose copyright owner cannot be identified or cannot be found?

The issues discussed in this chapter are closely related to concerns discussed in Chapter 10 on risk management. In some cases it is easy to locate a copyright owner. In many cases, however, it is unclear who owns the rights in a work. You may locate individuals who claim, either innocently or fraudulently, to be copyright owners when in reality they have no claims to copyright. The decision as to whether to accept their claims is part of the risk-management calculus discussed in Chapter 10.

8.2 Identifying copyright owners

GENERALLY

All efforts to locate copyright owners must begin with the identification of the original copyright owners. The discussion in Chapter 3 on copyright ownership is of fundamental importance to this determination. The default rule is that copyright initially belongs to the author, but there are complexities to this rule (for instance, for works made for hire, where the employer, rather than the creator, is considered the author), and in any event, copyright can be transferred or inherited by others. You will need to determine who initially owned copyright and what has happened to ownership since that time. Unfortunately there is no requirement that transfers of copyright need to be recorded, and so your detective skills will be put to the test. Different types of material will likely require different strategies.

If the work is published, it likely will have a copyright notice (since this was a requirement to secure copyright permission, at least in the United States, until 1989). The copyright notice is an important starting point; it is evidence of who owned the copyright at the time of publication.

The absence of a copyright notice on the copy of a work that you are considering digitizing does not necessarily mean that it was initially distributed without one. It may have been distributed with a copyright notice that your copy lacks or, especially with photographs, your copy might be a reproduction that did not include the original copyright notice. It is therefore useful to conduct a search on the Internet for the author, title, or portions of the text in order to discover whether it was ever distributed as a copyrighted work. Google's Book Search (http://books.google.com) is especially valuable since it indexes the full text of both in-copyright and out-of-copyright works. Visual materials, sound recordings, and audiovisuals are harder to search on the Internet, but portions of lyrics, captions, or general descriptions might help identify copyright owners.

Of course, identifying the copyright owner at the time of publication does not indicate who owns the particular exclusive right that one may need for a digitization project. For example, an author might have retained copyright but given her publisher an exclusive license to reproduce and distribute a work. Since a digitization project involves reproduction and distribution, in this example a cultural heritage institution should actually negotiate with the publisher and not with the author. Alternatively, a book might be published with the publisher identified as the copyright owner, but when the book went out of print, the copyright reverted to the author. (This was a fairly common provision in scholarly publishing contracts.) Permission to digitize the work would therefore need to be secured from the author.

TIP

Given the inability to determine who owns the exclusive rights that digitization may possibly infringe, it may sometimes be wise to identify and locate all possible copyright owners, including the author and her heirs as well as the publisher and its successors.

As the duration of copyrights has increased, the likelihood that the original copyright owner will still own copyright late in the copyright term has decreased. Authors die, copyrights are inherited, firms go out of business or are sold, and the ownership of copyright passes from hand to hand. There is no requirement that the details of copyright contracts or transfers of ownership be centrally recorded. The ownership of copyright from the date of original publication, therefore, can be a mystery and it can require great detective skills to identify and locate the current ownership.

Two resources available through the Copyright Office can provide important clues in the copyright hunt. The first is information on copyright renewals. Copyright could only be renewed by the author of a work or by his or her heirs. Many copyright renewals, therefore, are in the name of the immediate copyright heirs of deceased authors. These renewed copyrights could also be assigned to a publisher (and in some cases the original publishing contract might have required that renewed copyrights be transferred to the publisher upon renewal). Nevertheless, the renewal record can identify the copyright owner at the moment of renewal and should take initial precedence over what may appear in the published work itself.[3]

Renewal information is not the only valuable source of information found in the Copyright Office. Although it is not mandatory, it is possible to record voluntarily with the Copyright Office transfers of ownership, mortgages, nonexclusive licenses, and other assignments.[4] The Copyright Office's online database includes an index to assignments and other documents recorded since 1978; earlier index entries can be examined in the Copyright Office.[5] As with the renewal records, the recorded transfers and other documents can identify who owned the copyright at the time of the recordation of the document, and so can serve as a starting point for locating the current copyright owner.

FALSE COPYRIGHT NOTICES

A copyright notice can be an important clue in identifying a copyright owner, but such notices should not be taken at face value. Including a fraudulent copyright notice on an item is a federal criminal offense under 17 U.S.C. § 506(c), but the penalties are low in comparison to copyright infringement (up to $2,500) and the crime has seldom been prosecuted. As a result, many authors and publishers include copyright notices on material that is either in the public domain or whose copyright they do not own.

The mere presence of a copyright notice should not be taken as absolute proof that a valid copyright exists and is owned by the person claiming it. It can be important evidence for a risk assessment, however. A claim to copyright in a work, however, even when it is not true, still suggests that the presumptive owner may take umbrage at the use of that work by others.

■
■

DID YOU KNOW?

On the 4th of July each year, the *Boston Globe* newspaper prints as an editorial the full text of the Declaration of Independence. At the bottom of the page in the online version available through boston.com, one finds a copyright notice: "© Copyright 2008 Globe Newspaper Company." Just because they have included the notice does not mean that one would have to seek the permission of the Globe Newspaper Company in order to reprint the Declaration of Independence!

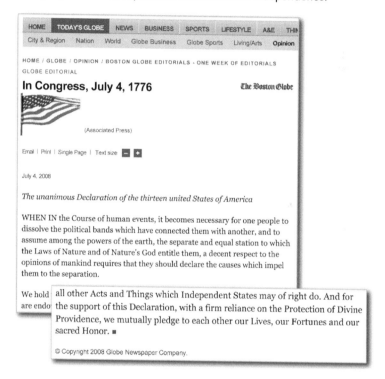

MULTIPLE RIGHTS OWNERS

Sometimes there are a number of people who own one or all of the exclusive rights of the copyright owner. This could be because the work was created as a joint work of authorship, with two or more authors sharing the copyright. Or it could be because inheritance of other transfers of ownership assigned the exclusive rights to multiple rights holders. Fortunately, as was discussed in Chapter 3, it is only necessary to secure permission from one of the multiple rights holders. Any part owner of a copyright can exercise any of the exclusive rights in which he or she shares—including authorizing others to use the work. It is not necessary to track down all of the copyright owners—finding one will be enough, if all you are seeking is a nonexclusive license.

TIP

When negotiating copyright transfer agreements with a donor, consider whether that donor owns all or part of the copyright. If the donor, for example, had inherited only a partial share in a copyright, that is all he or she can transfer to the institution. The institution would then assume the responsibility to account to the other copyright owners for their share of any profits generated from exploiting the copyright.

MULTIPLE RIGHTS IN ONE WORK

Remember, too, that there can be multiple copyrights included in one work. As part of the process of identifying the copyright owners, it is also necessary to identify all of the copyrights that may be found in the work under consideration. A photograph of a sculpture, for example, may require two different permissions: from the owner of the copyright in the photograph and from the owner of the copyright in the sculpture. A musical sound recording is likely to encompass a number of different copyrights: in the underlying score, in the performance, and perhaps in the recording. A movie might have different copyrights in the movie itself, the script used in the movie, and in novel on which the script was based. There can be additional copyrights in the music used, items depicted in the movie, etc. Permission from all of these copyright owners would need to be secured unless the movie studio had secured a blanket license to authorize reproduction and distribution of the works as part of its initial licensing. If this is the case, the cultural institution should secure from the publisher or distributor a warranty that they have secured the necessary permissions from the owners of any underlying copyrighted works to authorize the permission they are granting. This warranty should be backed up with an indemnity protecting the cultural institution from liability if the warranty turns out to be false.

Digital Image Rights Computator

A useful tool for thinking about the multiple rights found in copy photographs is the Digital Image Rights Computator from the Visual Resources Association found at http://www.vraweb.org/resources/ipr/dirc/. The Computator guides you through a series of questions relating to:

▶ The copyright status of the underlying work represented in the image
▶ The copyright status of the photographic reproduction
▶ The source from which the image has been obtained
▶ Any contract terms that might govern the uses of the image
▶ The intended use(s) of the image

It then provides guidance on whether and from whom you need to seek permission.

8.3 Strategies for locating copyright owners

GENERALLY

Once the last known copyright owners have been identified, the process of locating those copyright owners can begin. In many cases, communication with the presumed copyright owner will reveal that the copyrights have been transferred or assigned to a third party and that individual or corporation will need to be contacted to secure permission.

Locating individual *authors* is perhaps the most challenging assignment. *Publishers* are perhaps easier to locate, though they have their own challenges. *Collective Rights Organizations* can simplify the search for the copyright owners of some works, especially in music and fine arts. The issues associated with locating each type of copyright owner are discussed below.

LOCATING AUTHORS

A variety of approaches can be followed for locating authors and their copyright heirs and executors. The best approach to follow is dependent on a number of factors:

▶ The profession of the author (a professional writer or artist versus an amateur)
▶ The type of work (whether it is published or unpublished)
▶ The nationality of the author

■ **TIP**

The WATCH File

For professional authors and artists, an excellent starting point is the WATCH File. WATCH, for "Writers, Artists, and their Copyright Holders," is a database jointly maintained by the Harry Ransom Center of the University of Texas at Austin and the University of Reading Library. The database tracks information about the copyright owner of works from prominent individuals, with an emphasis on American, British, French, and other European authors and artists. One can find in the database the contact information for either the current holder of the copyright or the authorized representative charged with administering those copyrights. The WATCH file is found at http://www.watch-file.com or http://tyler.hrc.utexas.edu/.

What if the prominent author you are searching for is not in the WATCH file? The WATCH file team has provided some excellent suggestions on how to proceed,[6] which we have modified and present in Table 8.1. Although they were developed with unpublished works in mind, many of the suggestions are applicable to locating the authors of published works as well.

▮▮ **TABLE 8.1**

Locating Prominent U.S. Copyright Owners

☐ Do accession files contain information on copyright ownership?	☐ Check the accession files for information on the donor of unpublished works. Were they heirs to a copyright owner? Was copyright ownership discussed?
	☐ Check with other institutions that hold works by the author. They may have obtained material from a copyright owner or executor, or may have cleared a copyright in the past.

☐ Examine scholarship	☐ Look at works by scholars on the author. The notes may contain acknowledgements or other information as to copyright ownership. ☐ Check with societies devoted to the author's work. The International James Joyce Foundation, for example, maintains an FAQ devoted to copyright issues surrounding James Joyce's work.[7] ☐ Check online for copies of works by the author to see if any carry a credit line indicating copyright status. Be careful, however. Even the most reputable institutions can make mistakes when it comes to assessing copyright.[8]
☐ Ask the publisher	☐ We recommend asking the publisher to determine whether it has any rights in the work. ☐ The publisher may also be paying royalties to the author or her heirs, and could help locate them.
☐ Ask the literary agent	☐ If it can be determined (perhaps from acknowledgements in published works), identify and ask the author's literary agent.
☐ Check with membership organizations for writers	☐ The Authors Registry will search its author records for one or two names for free.[9] ☐ Even if an author is not found in the Authors Registry, it may still be helpful to check with some of the organizations it represents: ☐ The Authors Guild, although primarily a writer's advocacy group, includes literary agents and estates among its members.[10] ☐ The American Society of Journalists and Authors represents professional freelance writers.[11] ☐ The Dramatists Guild represents over 6,000 playwrights, composers, and lyricists.[12]
☐ Check with relevant reproduction rights organizations (RROs)	☐ The RROs discussed in this chapter may have information on an author.
☐ Write to the author's last known address	☐ If the author is recently deceased, a survivor may still be living at the address.
☐ Use reference sources to locate information on where an author lived or her family (who may have information on her copyrights)	☐ Literary tools such as author directories and *Contemporary Authors* are especially valuable for writers. ☐ Other general biographical tools such as *Marquis Who's Who* and the *Biography and Genealogy Master Index* are good sources of general information. ☐ Google Book Search (and Google in general) may have leads you can follow.

☐ Use genealogical and probate investigations	☐ Genealogical resources (including local obituaries) may be good resources for tracking partners and/or heirs.
	☐ If you can identify when and where a person died, check the probate records for the author. They may indicate who inherited copyrights.
☐ Publish queries in appropriate journals	☐ Some publications such as the *New York Review of Books*, the *New York Times Book Review*, and the *Times Literary Supplement* will publish author queries.

Once again, it is important to stress that not all steps are appropriate for all works. In most cases, for example, there would be little need to publish a query seeking the author of an undated, unidentified photograph found in a family scrapbook. If the photograph, however, was going to be at the heart of a multimillion-dollar advertising campaign, a more thorough search might be warranted. Balancing the expense of copyright investigations with potential risk of infringement will be discussed in more detail in Chapter 10.

WATCH THIS SPACE

WorldCat Copyright Evidence Registry

The WorldCat Copyright Evidence Registry, currently in its pilot phase, is a new project that holds the potential of becoming a major source of information on copyright. The registry hopes to gather information from libraries about the copyright status of individual works. This can include information on copyright owners and whether works by certain authors have entered the public domain. See http://www.oclc.org/us/en/productworks/cer.htm.

LOCATING PUBLISHERS

Publishers are an important resource for securing permission. In many cases, it will be the publisher, and not the author, that owns the copyright in the work, either because copyright was transferred to the publisher or because the work was created as "work made for hire" and hence the publisher is considered to be the author. Even if it does not own the full copyright, the publisher may own the exclusive rights required for digitization. Lastly, the publisher may be able to provide current contact information for a copyright owner—especially if the publisher has to send royalty checks to that individual.

There are two major advantages to starting a search for copyright owners with the publisher. First, it may be easier to find an old publishing house or its successors than it is to find an individual author or her heirs. The directories of publishers are extensive, and the publishing literature often records what happens to major publishers. Publishers may also have a greater willingness than authors to be found—publishers, after all, are interested in marketing their products. Second, publishers know about copyrights. Many of them have departments that specialize in permissions; you can usually find the address for that department on the publisher's Web site.

The task of locating a publisher may be slightly less daunting than finding an author, but it is not always easy. The recent report on the efforts of Carnegie Mellon University to locate publishers to seek permission to digitize books from the collections makes this clear. The report describes three different projects to secure permission to digitize works. Each project consisted of different types of material and followed different methodologies. Two of the projects were attempts to digitize groups of individual titles. In the first project, they were unable to contact 21 percent of the publishers. In the second project, 31 percent of the publishers could not be located.[13]

Even if the publisher could be located, the publishers' knowledge about the copyright status of the works they owned varied widely. In some cases this might be because the titles were acquired when another publisher was absorbed into the current firm. In other cases, it may have been due to poor record keeping. As Denise Troll Covey, the report's author, noted:

> The Posner study also made us aware that many publishers do not keep good records. Some do not really know what they have published. On several occasions, we had to photocopy the title page of a book and fax it to the publisher because it claimed it had not published the book. Frequently, publishers reported that they did not know whether they had the right to grant nonexclusive permission to digitize and provide open access to their books.[14]

Particularly problematic are the frequent changes in ownership of publishing houses. Firms are acquired, merge, or go out of business with increasing rapidity. With the passage of time, it becomes harder and harder to locate successor firms. The first project undertaken at Carnegie Mellon was particularly impacted by changes in publishers:

> With rare exceptions, the older the work, the more difficult it was to locate the publisher. We could not find the publishers of most of the books published between 1920 and 1930 and of almost half of the books published between 1940 and 1950. Publishers of more than a third of the books published from 1950 to 1960 and 1960 to 1970 could not be found. By contrast, few of the publishers of books published 1980 or later could not be found.[15]

TIP

Firms Out of Business Database

A new tool may make searching for defunct publishing firms easier. In 2007, the University of Reading and the Harry Ransom Center at the University of Texas, the groups that created the WATCH file, unveiled the FOB (Firms Out of Business) file. FOB records information about printing and publishing firms, magazines, literary agencies, and similar organizations that have gone out of existence. Whenever possible, it identifies the successor organizations that might own any surviving rights. Although FOB is newer and less complete than WATCH, one can hope that with community input and support it may grow into just as important a resource. FOB is found at http://www.fob-file.com/.

In spite of the difficulties in identifying and contacting publishers, Carnegie Mellon's experience in its three projects as well as similar efforts at Cornell University in support of CHLA, the Core Historical Literature of Agriculture project, suggest the effort may be worth it. Depending on the project, for example, Carnegie Mellon was able to secure permission to digitize works in 38 percent, 54 percent, and 70 percent of the completed transactions. They were able to achieve greater degrees of success with different types of publishers, with more permissions granted by scholarly associations and university presses than by commercial publishers. The popularity of the idea of the "long tail"—that previously ignored titles may become economically viable thanks to the Internet and print on demand—may change the willingness of commercial publishers to grant permission, however.[16]

QUESTION

Can a copyright be abandoned?

When a firm goes out of business, many people assume that its copyrights are abandoned and the works it created enter the public domain. This is incorrect. First, most bankruptcy proceedings liquidate the assets of an organization (including any intellectual property) by selling them to another party or transferring them to a debtor. Copyrights are an asset, and hence are normally transferred. Second, as was discussed in Chapter 3, copyright transfer can only take place via written agreement or operation of law. Physical property can be abandoned;[17] copyright cannot. If there is no written dedication of copyright to the public, the copyright still subsists. It may be difficult to locate the current copyright owner, but the work is not in the public domain.

REPRODUCTION RIGHTS ORGANIZATIONS

A reproduction rights organization (RRO) is a society that acts as an agent for a large number of copyright owners. Collecting societies administer copyright owned by their members and collect and distribute income generated from those copyrights. They commonly also collect and distribute royalties from statutory licensing schemes.

Some copyright owners do not wish to be bothered with permission requests and authorize a collecting society to manage the entire business. Therefore, it is possible, and sometimes mandatory, to negotiate permissions and licenses with collecting societies rather than with the individual owners of copyright. For cultural institutions, one of the key benefits of collecting societies is that they offer a streamlined procedure for rights administration, thus reducing the administrative difficulties in locating and contacting individual owners. All of the previous discussion on locating authors and publishers can be ignored if their copyrights are managed by a reproduction rights organization.

Copyright collectives can simplify the permissions process, but they are not a total panacea. For one, not all organizations are authorized to license all possible uses. Rights to license electronic and Internet distribution in particular often remain with the publisher or author. The transaction costs associated with securing permission can often be high, and the organization will usually charge fees even if the use is educational or noncommercial. In some cases the copyright owner may permit noncommercial, educational uses at a cost lower than would be charged by the reproduction rights organization.

> **TIP**
> Even though a reproduction rights organization may manage copyrights for an author or publisher, cultural institutions can still attempt to contact the copyright owner directly for permission to use a work.

There are many reproduction rights organizations in the United States and abroad. Several Web sites, including those managed by Georgia Harper and the Copyright Management Center at I.U.P.U.I., provide information on and links to many of them.[18] The following highlights some of the RROs of greatest utility to cultural heritage institutions:

TEXTUAL WORKS

Copyright Clearance Center (CCC): http://www.copyright.com/
CCC manages the copyright for thousands of text-based works including books, magazines and journals, newspapers, etcetera. Traditionally CCC has been a clearinghouse for securing permission for commercial course packs, interlibrary loan uses that exceed the CONTU guidelines, classroom use that exceeds fair use, commercial document delivery, and the general commercial use of copyrighted material (through its annual business license). More recently it has moved into the business of granting permission to republish textual material, first in print and now online. Even if your desired use is not licensed by the CCC, it can still be a good place to determine who at least is claiming copyright and the authority to license a work.

> **QUESTION**
> ## Is the CCC Academic License a solution to securing permission?
> In June, 2007, the CCC announced that it would begin to offer an annual copyright license for academic institutions. The license, it is promised, will provide "faculty and staff with convenient,

preapproved permissions to use content in course management systems, paper and electronic course packs, electronic library reserves, research collaboration and more."[19] Questions have been raised, however, about the cost, breadth, and impact that the license may have on fair-use analysis.[20]

For most digitization projects in cultural heritage institutions, the academic blanket license would not be a viable option. Most of the permissions that a digitization project would require are excluded from the license, including:

▶ Creation of a database or a repository of works that is available for multiple people's use outside the context of a class
▶ "Cover-to-cover copying of whole works"
▶ "Any use of the work that results in manipulation or change of the original, or that does not result in a reproduction that is substantially identical visually to the original" (thus limiting the institution's ability to link digitized works into new and exciting products)
▶ Interlibrary loan
▶ Advertising or marketing[21]

ARTISTIC WORKS

There are two primary organizations that serve as the rights agents for artists. They are:

Artists Rights Society (ARS): http://www.arsny.com/
Founded in 1987, ARS represents the intellectual property rights interests of many American visual artists (painters, sculptors, photographers, architects, and others). Through its membership in CISAC (Confédération Internationale des Sociétés d'Auteurs et Compositeurs), the Paris-based umbrella organization that oversees the activities of international copyright collecting societies in all media, it also represents up to 30,000 foreign artists in the United States.

Visual Artists and Galleries Association (VAGA): http://vaga.org
Founded in 1976, VAGA is the first U.S. organization to represent visual

artists' copyrights on a collective basis. It represents approximately 500 American artists and estates and also thousands of foreign artists and estates through reciprocal agreements with sister organizations worldwide.

MUSICAL WORKS

Securing permission for the online reproduction and distribution of musical works involves the participation of multiple collective rights organizations:[22]

The performance right in the musical composition is often licensed by one of three collective rights organizations. The choice of which organization to join is at the option of the composer or publisher of the work. All three organizations are developing rates and licenses for Webcasting or Internet use. ASCAP and BMI also have song title databases in which you can search by title, composer, or publisher.

▶ **ASCAP:** http://www.ascap.com/
▶ **BMI:** http://www.bmi.com
▶ **SESAC:** http://www.sesac.com/

The reproduction and distribution right in the composition is often licensed by the Harry Fox Agency: http://www.harryfox.com/. They maintain an online database called Songfile that can be used to secure permission to make 2,500 or fewer recorded copies (CDs, cassettes, LPs, or digital downloads) of a musical work. It is also possible to search the Songfile database for information on titles, songwriters, and publishers of songs.

The *reproduction, distribution, and performance rights in a sound recording* are often managed by the Recording Industry Association of America through its SoundExchange program: http://www.soundexchange.com/. It collects and distributes digital performance royalties for sound recording copyright owners (usually a record label) when their sound recordings are performed on digital cable, satellite television, Internet radio, and satellite radio. For other Internet uses, you will normally have to contact the individual copyright owners of the sound recordings.

■
■

EXAMPLE

Digitizing Early Recordings[23]

Let's say that you are interested digitizing Fred Waring's recording for Decca of Jerome Kern's 1943 song "And Russia Is her Name," with lyrics by E. Y. "Yip" Harburg. You determine that the Kern's and Harburg's composition was registered and renewed; it is still protected by copyright. In the ASCAP database on the Internet, you see that the Publisher and Administrators of the song are the Glocca Morra Music Corporation and Universal Polygram International. You determine which ASCAP license would best meet your needs.

And Russia is Her Name

Music by Jerome Kern, Lyrics by E. Y. Warburg

© 1943 by Chappell & Co., renewed 1970.

Source of the image: http://www.tias.com/7042/PictPage/1922871671.html, which (incorrectly) maintains that Ladybugs Antiques & Collecticbles has a copyright in the scan.

License: Included under an assertion of fair use.

Remember that this license only covers the public performance of Kern's and Harburg's work. You therefore go to the Songfile database managed by the Harry Fox Agency and discover that they manage the mechanical reproduction rights for the music publisher. You select the appropriate license from them.

Lastly, you need to think about the rights in the recording of Fred Waring's performance of the song. You aren't interested in limiting yourself to the uses allowed under a statutory license and administered by SoundExchange, and so you need to contact the permission department at Decca, the original record label, which owns the rights in the recording itself. From Decca (or any successor company that may have acquired the rights), you need to obtain permission to reproduce, distribute, and perform Decca's sound recording. They should also be able to tell you if the Fred Waring estate itself has any copyright interest in the sound recording in case you need to secure permission from them as well.

INTERNATIONAL REPRODUCTION RIGHTS ORGANIZATIONS

The equivalent of many of these U.S.-based collective rights societies can be found in other countries. They can be an important resource in locating copyright owners for foreign works. Many of them are members of the International Federation of Reproduction Rights Organizations (IFRRO), found at http://www.ifrro.org/. Others belong to CISAC (Confédération Internationale des Sociétés d'Auteurs et Compositeurs), the Paris-based umbrella organization that oversees the activities of more than 200 international author copyright collecting societies. Directories of members of both organizations are available on their Web sites.

Among the most important international text licensing agencies are Access Copyright: the Canadian Copyright Licensing Agency (http://www.accesscopyright.ca/); CLA: the Copyright Licensing Agency Ltd., representing publishers in the United Kingdom (http://www.cla.co.uk/); and ALCS: Authors' Licensing & Collecting Society, UK, created to provide collective administration for writers (http://www.alcs.co.uk/).

NEW INITIATIVES

The explosion of the Internet as a publication and distribution medium has led to the development of many new initiatives to license collectively online content. Whether these initiatives attract enough content to become viable licensing options remains to be seen. Two deserve mention:

iCopyright: http://info.icopyright.com/
iCopyright was created in 1998 to be an automated copyright licensing system for digital content. It licenses permission to users to e-mail, print, and save content—but not to republish or redistribute the content. Associated Press articles are one of the items that can be licensed through iCopyright.

PLUS Coalition: http://www.useplus.com/
The PLUS (Picture Licensing Universal Coalition) is not a collective rights organization itself, but is developing tools to assist in the licensing of visual images. The system is based around the idea of embedding standardized rights metadata into digital images that identify the rights owner, describe the license terms, and make it easy to track future licensed and unlicensed

uses of the images. As part of the project, PLUS has been developing an online registry of artists and licensors that is expected to be released in 2009.

OTHER LICENSING AGENCIES

In addition to the reproduction rights organizations, many other professional organizations and commercial businesses license the reproduction and distribution of copyrighted works. In some cases, they are able to license works for online distribution; in other cases, they may only be able to provide limited licenses (for example, for the performance of a work in a church or the showing of a movie in a school). Licensing organizations include publishers of dramatic works, photo stock houses, and cartoon and comics syndicates. The online resources referenced in note 18 contain many links to major sources of content.

8.4 Orphan works

In spite of one's best efforts, it may be difficult or impossible to locate the owner of copyright in a work. This may be because the work is anonymous, the company that owned copyright is defunct, it is impossible to trace copyright through multiple bequests and transmissions, or because the copyright owner's identity is known but the owner or the owner's representative cannot be located. These items are commonly referred to as "orphan works."

When current creators and users cannot locate a copyright owner, they cannot negotiate over the use of the older work. Potential users, therefore, can be extremely reluctant to incorporate orphan works in new creative efforts or in projects (such as library digitization efforts) that would make the older works available to the public. Users, publishers, libraries, archives, museums, and other institutions worry that reproducing and/or distributing copyrighted works without the permission of the current copyright owner may leave them open to the draconian monetary, statutory, and criminal penalties found in current copyright law. The result is that orphan works often are not used—even when there is no one who would object to the use.

Recognizing that there might be a problem associated with orphan works, the Copyright Office undertook a study of the orphan works issue. Public comments were solicited, and many of them documented how concerns over the orphan status of copyrighted works led cultural institutions to exclude them from digitization projects.[24]

After considering a wide range of possible solutions to the problem, the Copyright Office chose to recommend a fairly simple solution:

▶ Users would be expected to conduct a reasonably diligent investigation to locate the copyright owner before they could exploit an orphan work.
▶ If such an investigation is done, and a copyright owner later surfaces, the user would only have to pay reasonable compensation for the use of the work—not the high penalties that can be associated with copyright infringement.
▶ Libraries, museums, and other noncommercial users could avoid even those fees if they stopped using the item immediately.

Some had hoped for more specific guidance on what constitutes a "reasonably diligent" search for the owner of an orphan work, but the report echoed the argument made in this chapter: namely that it will vary according to the nature of the material, the age of the item, and the expected use. Different communities will have to establish what they consider to be best practice.

The Orphan Works Act of 2006, H.R. 5439, included the heart of the recommendations. It met strident opposition from photographers, who were worried that because their work can easily lose all identifying markings, it would be easy for users to label them "orphans" and widely distribute them on the Internet. As a consequence, the bill failed to pass before Congress adjourned. New, compromise bills that supposedly addressed the concerns of all parties were reintroduced into the House and Senate in 2008, but they, too, encountered opposition from critics who fear the impact of the legislation on their businesses, and only the House Bill passed. The solutions that have been proposed would make it too costly for any large-scale digitization program to avail themselves of the protections in the law. It is likely, therefore, that the digitization of orphan works will continue to entail some risks.

9 *Other Types of Intellectual Property, Contracts, and Jurisdictional Issues*

9.1 Introduction

Up to now the guidelines have primarily addressed issues associated with copyright. Copyright is the most common form of intellectual property found in the holdings of cultural heritage institutions, and therefore copyright issues will be of particular concern in their digitization projects. Yet copyright infringement is not the only way that a digitization project could put a cultural institution at risk.

This chapter will consider some of the non-copyright related legal issues of importance to digitization projects. An obvious place to start such analysis is with forms of intellectual property other than copyright. They include:

▶ Trademark
▶ Patents
▶ Trade secrets
▶ Industrial design rights

Of these four types of intellectual property, only trademark is likely to be at issue in most digitization projects, and hence is the only type discussed in this chapter: see section 9.2. These guidelines do not address trade secrets, on the basis that most collection items being digitized would not contain such information, but there are three points about sensitive and restricted information that are worth emphasizing more generally.

First, there are a number of areas of tort law that pertain to the distribution of information that identifies an individual, reproduces their personal information or likeness, or impacts on their reputation. The following three will be discussed in these guidelines in sections 9.3 and 9.4:

▶ The right of publicity
▶ The right of privacy
▶ Defamation (which includes libel and slander)

Second, some collection items have restrictions on access and use by virtue of the terms in donation and loan documentation (and, as well shall see, institution-imposed terms of access). The capacity to impose such restrictions typically arises from ownership or control of the physical item, not ownership of copyright (indeed, the work could be in the public domain). Thus, regardless of whether there are any copyright issues surrounding the digitization of restricted items, there may be legal consequences for acting contrary to donation or loan conditions. These issues are discussed further in the text on contracts in section 9.5.

Thirdly, care should be taken where proposed content contains potentially sensitive information—for instance, where cultural heritage material or items from indigenous collections are being digitized. There is a long history of research conducted with such populations without true informed consent or benefit sharing, meaning that items now held by cultural institutions may have been created or removed without the agreement of indigenous owners. Although not necessarily implicating legal issues, there are strong ethical and cultural aspects associated with the management of these items, as reflected by domestic and international developments in indigenous rights in cultural heritage and intellectual property. This is discussed further in section 9.7.

A final point: so far, the guidelines have focused on American law and have assumed that digitization, access, and use takes place in America. The Internet, however, is international in scope. It is appropriate to inquire, therefore, what obligation, if any, does a cultural institution have with regard to the laws of other countries. This is considered in section 9.6.

This chapter will address questions including:

▶ When can an institution digitize trademarked works?
▶ Can I digitize and distribute a photograph of a famous individual?
▶ What responsibility do I have to protect the privacy and reputation of individuals named in records I may wish to digitize?

▶ How can we use contracts with users to maintain control over our digitized materials?

▶ Do I need to worry about copyright and other laws in every other country in the world?

9.2 Trademarks

Imagine the following scenario: Your institution has a world-class collection of Coca-Cola bottles. You decide that you want to digitize and make available on the Internet photographs of the bottles. Your staff photographers take the photographs, so you know you don't have to worry about copyright: it is work for hire, and your institution owns the copyrights. (Fortunately none were taken by contract photographers!) But you know that the Coca-Cola Company owns trademarks in its name, logo, and bottle shape. Do you have to worry about their rights in your digitization project?

To answer that question, we need to look more closely at the nature and purpose of the intellectual property known as trademarks.[1] Trademarks are used in commerce to do two things. First, they identify and distinguish the goods of one manufacturer or seller from goods manufactured or sold by others. In addition, trademarks indicate the source of the goods. In short, trademarks are brand names or similar indications of origin. Thanks to trademarks, you know that the cola you are drinking was made by an authorized Coca-Cola bottler and not by Pepsi.

Trademarks are often distinctive symbols, pictures, or words, but they can also be distinctive and unique packaging, color combinations, product styles, and even building designs. The TransAmerica Pyramid in San Francisco, for example, is a trademark as well as being a building; so is the Rock and Roll Hall of Fame and Museum in Cleveland. Even sounds can be trademarked: for example, the roar of the MGM lion or the three chime tones used by NBC.

Closely related to trademarks are service marks. Trademarks distinguish different *goods* from each other, and service marks identify and distinguish the *services* of one provider from the services offered by others. As with trademarks, they also identify the source of the services. In this chapter, we will use the term trademark to refer to service marks as well.

There is no requirement that trademarks be registered with the federal

U.S. Patents and Trademark Office (USPTO). Even without registration, a trademark owner can acquire state statutory or common law rights in a mark simply by using the mark in commerce.[2] Trademark owners can also use the trademark symbol "TM" or the service mark symbol "SM" any time they wish to alert the public that they feel they have a trademark, regardless of whether they have filed an application with the USPTO (though such use is not required in order to have an enforceable trademark). Trademarks owners who register their marks with the USPTO may use the federal registration symbol "®." Unlike copyrights, trademarks never expire as long as they are continuously used in commerce.

DID YOU KNOW?

The "devil" on Underwood canned ham is reputedly the oldest existing food trademark still in use in the United States. It has been recognized as a trademark since 1870 (Trademark no. 82).

The owner of a trademark has the exclusive right to use the trademark on the product it is intended to identify and often on related products. The owner may bring an infringement suit against anyone who uses a trademark in a manner likely to cause confusion in the marketplace. In addition, the trademark owner may bring action against users that *dilute* the mark, either by blurring its distinctiveness or by tarnishing the reputation of the product.

In order to retain its mark, it is normally required that trademark owners bring infringement actions against widespread use of their trademarks by third parties. Failure to stop misuse of a trademark may lead to the annulment of the original trademark grant. (This differs from copyright, where there is no requirement that copyright owners pursue copyright infringers in order to maintain their copyrights.)

Could digitization and distribution of works containing trademarks place a cultural institution at risk of being charged with direct or contributory trademark infringement? For example, could digitizing and distributing a photograph of the Rock and Roll Hall of Fame result in court action, even if the institution possessing the photograph owned the copyright in the work? In theory, the answer is yes. It is quite common for movie studios, for example, to worry that the inclusion of trademarked objects in their films might suggest endorsement of the film by the trademark owner. As a result, they (or more likely their insurance companies) will frequently require that trademarked objects be removed from a scene. In one example, a studio removed the TransAmerica Pyramid from the skyline of San Francisco.[3]

Fortunately, as with copyright, there are exceptions to the exclusive rights of the trademark owner that make a lawsuit against a cultural heritage institution highly unlikely.

Most important is the fair use exception to trademark. It is not an infringement of trademark to use a mark simply to describe a good or service [15 U.S.C. § 1115(4)]. Nor is it an infringement to use a mark outside commerce (so long as the use does not suggest sponsorship or endorsement). Trademark is primarily a consumer-protection statute: it is intended to ensure that potential customers are not confused by a competing product. So long as the use is noncommercial and does not imply sponsorship or endorsement by the trademark owner, the use would likely be fair.

As for dilution, there are similar exemptions. 15 U.S.C. § 1125(c)(4) stipulates that no dilution action can be brought for the following uses:

▶ Fair use of a famous mark by another person in comparative commercial advertising or promotion to identify the competing goods or services of the owner of the famous mark.
▶ Noncommercial use of a mark.
▶ All forms of news reporting and news commentary

Again, noncommercial use is a statutory shelter against a charge of dilution.

In sum, a noncommercial digitization project should be immune from most dangers of trademark infringement. So long as the hypothetical digital collection of photographs of Coca-Cola bottles mentioned at the start of this section is a noncommercial product and there is no suggestion that the Coca-Cola Company has sponsored or endorsed the project, trademarks are unlikely to have been infringed. Commercial use of trademarks is a more complicated issue. Any cultural heritage institution that wishes to sell access to digitized collections containing trademarked items should consult with a trademark attorney in advance. Similarly, legal advice should be sought if the institution's use of commercial marks might reflect badly on a product or the company behind it.[4]

9.3 Right of publicity

Imagine the following scenario: Instead of wanting to digitize photographs of cola bottles, your institution wanted to digitize photographs of early baseball players. All of the photographs were published before 1923 and so there is no fear of copyright infringement. But do the subjects of the photographs have any non-copyright interest in their use? Do you need their permission before you can reproduce and distribute the works through digitization?

To answer this question, it is necessary to examine the right of publicity.[5] Publicity rights are a relatively new concept in intellectual property law, emerging in the United States as a separate subject from the right of privacy (discussed in the next section) in the 1950s. The right of publicity prevents the unauthorized commercial use of an individual's name, likeness, or other recognizable aspects of one's public image. It gives an individual the exclusive right to control the commercial use of his or her identity, and permits individuals to bring action to recover damages from unauthorized use of one's public persona.

The right of publicity is largely protected by state common and/or statutory law. Currently 29 states recognize some form of personality rights. Eighteen have explicit statutes recognizing a right of publicity: California, Florida, Illinois, Indiana, Kentucky, Massachusetts, Nebraska, Nevada, New York, Ohio, Oklahoma, Rhode Island, Tennessee, Texas, Utah, Virginia, Washington, and Wisconsin.[6] Other states rely on common law or sometimes privacy law to protect publicity rights. In some states the right of publicity is protected through the law of unfair competition.

To the surprise of many people, Indiana, and not California or New York, the traditional homes of public figures, has the strongest right of publicity. It protects the right of publicity for 100 years after a person's death, and protects not only an individual's name, image, and likeness but also signature, photographs, gestures, distinctive appearances, and mannerisms. The reason for Indiana's interest in publicity law is simple: it is home to CMG Worldwide, one of the first and largest publicity rights management firms. Its client list includes Babe Ruth, Marilyn Monroe, Mark Twain, and Amelia Earhart.[7] The statute in Tennessee (home to the estate of Elvis Presley) is also notable: it protects publicity rights "as long as the right holder continually exploits the commercial value of the identity."[8]

The economic value of publicity rights has been increasing dramatically. In 2006 Muhammad Ali sold 80 percent of his publicity rights to the entertainment rights firm CKX for $50 million.[9] Earlier the same company spent $100 million to acquire an 85 percent share in the publicity rights of Elvis Presley, the perennial top-earning deceased celebrity.[10]

■ **DID YOU KNOW?**

Publicity rights do not just apply to world-famous celebrities. For example, Nan Wood Graham has registered her publicity rights with California's Secretary of State's office. Graham is "famous" for being the sister of artist Grant Wood—and the model for the wife (or daughter) in Wood's most famous painting, *American Gothic*. Anyone who wishes to use *American Gothic* must consider whether their use would impinge on her estate's ability to market her image.

Grant Wood, American Gothic, 1930,

License: © claimed by the Art Institute of Chicago in the art and reproduction, but publication without notice or renewal placed the work in the public domain.
Source: http://www.artic.edu/aic/collections/artwork/6565

The right of publicity could be a nightmare for cultural institutions: a right that varies from state to state, with no central registry of rights and incredibly long periods of compliance. Fortunately there is an important limitation on the right of publicity: it is primarily an *economic* right, restricted to the *commercial* use of an individual's persona.[11] It is intended to prevent third parties from exploiting for financial gain an individual's image or personality. Publicity rights, therefore, should not apply to noncommercial, educational use of a person's image. This is an area that is developing and changing rapidly, however, and should be monitored.

Commercial use of the likeness of others is a different matter, and would require the institution to consult with an attorney specializing in the right of publicity.

TRICKY AREA

Commercial Use of Public Domain Materials

The most requested reproduction at the National Archives and Records Administration (NARA) has long been a photograph of a meeting between Richard Nixon and Elvis Presley on 21 December 1970. The topic is so popular, in fact, that NARA has created an online exhibition dedicated to the meeting entitled "When Nixon met Elvis."[12]

The photographs of the meeting were taken by Ollie Atkins, Nixon's chief photographer and a member of the White House Photographic Office. As with other works by government employees, the photographs are in the public domain. Because NARA's use in the exhibit is for noncommercial purposes, there should not be a problem with publicity rights.

The Richard Nixon Library and Birthplace Foundation also offers versions of the White House photos

Photograph of Richard M. Nixon and Elvis Presley at the White House, 12/21/1970 (cropped).

Photographer: Ollie Atkins

License: Public domain

Source: National Archives and Records Administration, http://arcweb. archives.gov/arc/action/ExternalId Search?id=1634221

through its Museum Store. They have fifteen items for sale that carry the photograph, including coffee mugs, mouse pads, playing cards, magnets, and of course T-shirts.[13]

Nixon and Elvis Pen

Uncredited photograph

Source: The Richard Nixon Library & Birthplace Foundation Museum Store, http://www.nixonlibraryfoundation.org/index.php?src=directory &view=products&category=The%20Day%20Nixon%20Met%20Elvis

License: Used under an assertion of fair use.

These commercial products may impinge on publicity rights and might require the authorization of the respective estates. As the NARA site notes, although the photographs are in the public domain,

> . . . the estates of Richard Nixon and Elvis Presley may claim rights in their likenesses and images, and further use of these photographs may be subject to those claims. Anyone who

intends to download these images and use them commercially should first contact the appropriate representatives of former President Nixon or Mr. Presley or consult with his own legal counsel.[14]

9.4 Right of privacy and defamation

Imagine the following scenario: You have in your collections the papers of a local member of Congress. You would like to digitize the papers and make them available on the Internet. Among the papers are communications from staff at various government agencies (including the Social Security Administration and the Department of Veterans Affairs) in response to requests for assistance that the member of Congress sent on behalf of individual constituents who were having financial, medical, and other problems. The memos from the government officials are in the public domain because of Section 105 of the Copyright Act (which does not allow copyright in works of the Federal government). But should you digitize the memos?

The preceding scenario introduces us to the concept of the right of privacy. Many archivists are familiar with explicit statutory privacy regulations including FERPA, the Family Educational Rights and Privacy Act, which protects student information; HIPAA, the Health Insurance Portability and Accountability Act of 1996, which protects certain medical records; and the Gramm-Leach-Bliley Act, which protects some financial information. There is also a general right of privacy found in tort law. Unlike the right of publicity, which is generally thought to be a property right, the right of privacy is a personal right. Damages in a publicity case are based on the economic harm suffered; damages in a privacy case are assigned based on emotional distress. Privacy actions attempt to assess the harm to one's dignity.

The standard authority on privacy torts recognizes four types of invasions of privacy:[15]

▷ "Intrusion upon seclusion"
▷ Public disclosure of private facts
▷ False light
▷ Appropriation of name or likeness

Let's consider each in turn:

INTRUSION UPON SECLUSION

In order to have an action based on "intrusion upon seclusion," three factors need to be present. First, there must be an intrusion, physical or otherwise. There is no requirement that the results of the intrusion must be publicized (that is covered by the second type of privacy tort listed above: public disclosure of private facts); merely intruding is enough. Second, that intrusion must be into an area where a person is entitled to privacy. Third, the intrusion must be highly offensive to a reasonable person. Looking into an upstairs window with binoculars would be intrusive; so would opening someone's mail.

PUBLIC DISCLOSURE OF PRIVATE FACTS

An action for invasion of privacy can be brought when someone makes known to the public matters that would be highly offensive to a reasonable person and which are not of legitimate concern to the public. The method used for publicizing the fact is immaterial: it could be in writing, orally, or via a Web site. The important thing is that a fact concerning a person's private life is communicated other than in private conversation or in such a way as that is likely that it will become public.

FALSE LIGHT AND DEFAMATION

An action for placing someone in a *false light* is similar to the public disclosure of private facts, but in this case the private "facts" that are revealed to the public are false. Alternatively, the facts could be true, but presented in such a way as to misrepresent the person's character, history, or beliefs. The false light must be highly offensive to a reasonable person, and normally the person who revealed them must act with reckless disregard or actual malice for an infringement to have occurred.

Closely related to false light is *defamation*. With defamation, a false claim that is likely to hurt the reputation of an individual or corporate entity is communicated orally (constituting the tort of *slander*) or in print or other fixed medium (known as *libel*). Truth is a defense to a charge of defamation: if the publicly revealed information is true, no defamation occurred. In addition, where the defamation concerns a "public figure" or "public official," it must be proven that the publisher acted with actual malice, that is, acted with knowledge that the fact was untrue or with serious doubts about its truth. However, even if an offensive fact is true, it might still be presented in such as way as to constitute an invasion of privacy—either through the public disclosure of private facts or by using them in a way so as to present a third party in a false light.

TRICKY AREA

Republishing Defamatory Works

The risk of invading privacy is greatest when digitizing unpublished or private communications. A digitization project conceivably could, however, republish defamatory accusations.

This may have happened in California. Rabbi Lipner sued the Regional Oral History Office in the Bancroft Library at the University of California. He claimed that program had defamed him by recording, printing, and distributing an interview with Richard Goldman in which Goldman made a number of allegedly false and defamatory statements about Lipner. A court found the statue of limitations (one year in California) had expired and dismissed the case.

But when does publication occur? This was an issue in another case involving Rabbi Lipner and the oral histories. The appeals court in that case concluded that the limited distribution of an oral history prior to the commencement of the suit did not constitute publication for the purposes of California law. Late in 2007, the California Supreme Court reversed this opinion. The court ruled that the Bancroft did indeed "publish" the oral histories many years ago when it distributed a few copies to other repositories.[16] In addition, the court rejected the plaintiff's argument that the clock to file an action should only commence when an alleged defamation is discovered, and not when it was published. (*Hebrew Academy v. Goldman*)

APPROPRIATION OF NAME OR LIKENESS

The appropriation of someone's name or likeness sounds very much like the right of publicity. The right of publicity, however, is an economic right. Privacy law protects against unauthorized use of someone's name or likeness even when there is no commercial use.

DEFENSES

There are generally three defenses to charges of invasion of privacy: death, newsworthiness, and permission. Traditionally (and in contrast with some versions of the right of publicity), all rights of privacy expire when you expire. If the subjects in the documents are deceased, they can be digitized. If the private facts that are revealed are of legitimate public interest or concern, then an invasion of privacy action should fail. Repositories can always seek the permission, preferably in writing, of the individual whose privacy might be hurt by a digitization project.

Curators in cultural heritage institutions have long been sensitive to privacy issues when administering their collections. Digitization doesn't change the problem, only exacerbates it. It is one thing to "disclose" private facts to an occasional researcher in a reading room. It is quite another to make those items universally available on the Internet. The staff in cultural heritage institutions must stay alert to possible privacy issues when selecting material for digitization to ensure that they are not unintentionally making available online material that ordinary people would find to be offensive.

TRICKY AREA

Correcting the Historical Record

One of the great appeals of digitization is that it can make material that previously was difficult to discover and retrieve easily accessible to a broader audience. In doing so, however, it may make factual errors more broadly known.

The *New York Times* has faced this issue because of the easy searchability of its digital edition. Here are examples of the complaints that they have received about the online version of the paper:

▶ A person arrested years ago on charges of fondling a child said the accusation was false and the charges were dropped. The Times reported the arrest but not the disposition of the case.
▶ A woman said her wedding announcement 20 years ago gave the incorrect university from which she graduated. She is afraid prospective employers who Google her will suspect résumé inflation.

- A woman quoted years ago in an article about weight loss said, tearfully, that she never was a size 16, as the article stated.
- The husband of a school administrator in the Midwest complained that a news brief reporting her suspension was published after officials had already publicly said she did nothing wrong.[17]

No cultural institution wants to alter the historical record, but it would be wise to establish a policy outlining what the institution will do in response to a request prior to its receipt. One digital repository reports that although it will not remove an offending article from page images, it will remove the text of the article from the metadata provided to search engines, making the item much harder to find. Other solutions include:

- Inserting in the item errata or cross-references to explanatory essays
- Encouraging the aggrieved party to create their own explanatory Web site that could be indexed by search engines and retrieved at the same time

9.5 Contracts

These guidelines have been primarily about the impact of copyright on digitization projects. However, laws relevant to the physical embodiment of the collection item can also be important, most notably personal property law and contract. For example, it is common for material held by an institution to have been acquired according to a deed of gift, loan agreement, or other transfer document. Such documentation may include restrictions on how the repository may use the material. There are a number of implications of this:

- Failure to comply with such conditions may have significant legal consequences for the institution, for instance as a result of breach of contract. In some cases, it could even result in property in an item returning to the donor. This is not to mention the relationship management issues that may arise if an institution agrees to donor conditions, only to ignore or override them at a later stage.

▶ By and large, restrictions specified in contract take precedence over any rights specified in copyright. This is particularly true for the Section 108 libraries and archives exemptions; Section 108(f)(4) states explicitly that nothing in the section overrides any "contractual obligations assumed at any time by the library or archives when it obtained a copy . . . of a work in its collections."

The upshot is that institutions should be careful when accepting gifts subject to conditions, and when reviewing loan contracts, to ensure that any such obligations and restrictions are reasonable and consistent with institutional missions. Where a condition or contractual provision is no longer workable, it may be necessary to obtain legal advice on the best way to proceed.[18]

Of course, many cultural institutions themselves use contract law when licensing copyright or to mimic the exclusive rights found in copyright when they are not the copyright owner or if the work is in the public domain. For example, a repository may create "terms of use" on a Web site, or have recipients of copies of collection items sign a user agreement (in effect a contract) that stipulates that they may not further reproduce that work, or give the copy to others, or publicly display the work, without first getting permission of the cultural institution. Reproduction, distribution, and public display are normally the exclusive rights reserved to the copyright owner, but here the cultural institution is using contract law to mimic those rights in order to create what has been called a kind of "quasi-copyright."[19]

We should emphasize, again, that the cultural institution's ability to restrict subsequent use of reproductions provided from its collections is based not on copyright but on the institution's physical ownership of the material. The cultural institution tells users that they may have access to the physical item, and may receive copies of that item, but only if the users agree to abide to the terms specified by the institution. In a physical repository, this contract is usually established by providing to the user a copy of the institution's rules and regulations regarding use of the material. For digital collections, such agreements are often established by means of the click-through and browse-wrap licenses discussed in Chapter 7. As noted in that chapter, measures that regulate or restrict public access to collection items can be highly controversial, in particular where the underlying material is in the public domain.

Despite this controversy, quasi-copyright contractual agreements are likely legal.[20] The key issue is the scope of the limitations on use in the contractual agreement. Thus, a contract agreement that attempted to mirror perfectly all copyright rights would not be acceptable. Section 301 makes it clear that the Copyright Act preempts all state laws, including contract laws, that are "the equivalent to any of the exclusive rights within the general scope of copyright." Most commentators, however, feel that the typical agreement with a user is not the equivalent of the exclusive rights in copyright. An exclusive right, for example, is the right to stop *anyone* from reproducing a copyrighted work. The typical user agreement stipulates that *the user*, and not the general public, is prohibited from reproducing a work.

What does this mean in practice? Assuming that a cultural institution specified in its agreements that there could be no subsequent reuse of reproductions provided by the institution to users, the institution could bring legal action against any user who reproduced and distributed copies provided to that user. The institution could not, however, bring legal action against any third party who may have gotten a copy of the reproduction and further reproduced it: there is no binding legal agreement between the institution and the third party.

Concerns about the limited legal options available to them regarding control of public domain material have led some cultural institutions to restrict the amount of material that they place online. In some respects, this fear is misdirected. With online resources, it is possible to use server logs and other tools to determine if a possibly infringing user secured the material from the institution's Web site. If they did, a legal action is theoretically possible. It is impossible, however, to identify the source of digital copies made from analog originals provided to users by the cultural institution. A photographic reproduction provided to the user by the institution can be easily digitized and distributed on the Web by a third party. It would be almost impossible to determine that the third party got the copy of the digitized image from the known user. Analog reproductions, and not digital copies, perhaps present the greatest threat to an institution's control over its collection.

That said, cultural institutions can use contracts and technological measures to attempt to control subsequent use of public-domain collection material, but in the end it is likely to be a losing struggle. Once a reproduction is made available, whether to an individual user or to the public more generally, the possibility of "leakage" (i.e., distribution or reuse contrary to terms of use) is open. At a practical level, perhaps the most useful thing institutions can do is release content in a form or resolution that would be unsuitable for commercial reuses—though this may greatly limit the utility of the resource for educational and scholarly uses.

> **TIP**
> When formulating use agreements, be sure to make it clear whether you are asserting rights based on copyright ownership or physical owner-ship of the material. The scope of the agreement will differ depending on the basis for the agreement. For example, a cultural institution asserting copyright ownership can license use of material under a Creative Commons license (discussed in Chapter 7), whereas such licenses would not be applicable if the agreement is based on physical ownership.

9.6 International issues

These guidelines discuss copyright and digitization in terms of U.S. law. The Internet, however, is international. As noted in Chapter 4, both copyright law and the protection of moral rights can be qiute different outside of the U.S. Are cultural heritage institutions expected to follow the copyright laws of other countries?

The question is becoming less and less theoretical. At least one digitiza-tion project in the United States has received requests that it remove from its Web site works that are in the public domain in the United States but are protected overseas. Recently, a Canadian Web site that made copies of public-domain digitized sheet music available on the Internet was threat-ened with a lawsuit by an Austrian sheet music publisher; the works were still protected by copyright in Austria. Unable in that instance to restrict access to the material just to Canadians, the student managing the site removed it from the Internet.[21]

The issues of concern in these cases relate to "governing law" (i.e., under which country's law should a claim be assessed) and jurisdiction of courts (i.e., does a particular court have the capacity to hear a claim). For instance, if digital content is created in the United States and is stored on a U.S. server but can be accessed overseas, can a foreign court hear an action in relation to that content? And if so, should it apply its own law, or that of the U.S.?

Few questions are currently more unsettled in "cyberlaw" than the area of Internet jurisdiction. From the perspective of a cultural institution, having to adhere to international as well as American copyright laws could be thought to be a disaster. The institution might be forced to identify the most restrictive copyright and privacy laws in place anywhere in the world and then limit its digitization efforts to materials outside that restrictive boundary.

There are two factors that limit the "chilling effect" that might be feared to arise from potential infringement of foreign laws. First, for many types of lawsuits to proceed in a foreign country, often the courts in that country would have to agree that the cultural institution has a real and substantial connection to that country (a common standard for jurisdiction). A digitization project involving material from the country and targeted at users there could establish such a connection.

Second, even if a foreign court concluded that it had jurisdiction and then ruled that the cultural institution infringed copyright or some other law, the foreign plaintiff would still have to apply to an American court to have that foreign judgment enforced—an action that is costly and not without difficulties. In any event, it is unlikely that a U.S. court would enforce such a judgment if the foreign law was markedly different from U.S. civil law. These issues about U.S. enforcement will not arise, of course, if the cultural institution has a substantial presence in the other country, as many do. The Guggenheim Museum, for example, has a branch in Bilbao, Spain; many universities maintain campuses overseas. If an infringement suit occurred in a country where a cultural institution had substantial assets, those assets could be seized as part of a judgment; there would be no need to approach a U.S. court to enforce the ruling.

There are two things that cultural institutions can do to minimize the risk they face:

▶ First, on any Web site of digitized materials, when describing the rights status of the material (as recommended in Chapter 10), specify that all actions are taken in accordance with American laws. Foreign users should be encouraged to understand the copyright laws in their own countries before they download the material.

▶ Second, before proceeding with a digitization project involving materials from another country where your institution has a presence, confirm that your project is compatible with the laws of that country. Consult with your institution's legal advisers to ensure that they concur with your assessment.

It is also possible that cultural heritage institutions will adopt "zoning" or geolocation techniques that restrict access to their digital collections for users in some jurisdictions. The use of geolocation is developing rapidly across many aspects of Internet communication, and is becoming ubiquitous in advertising and common in many major audiovisual sites (such as the BBC's iPlayer service in the UK).

9.7 Traditional knowledge

As noted in the introduction, care should be taken when digitization efforts include certain items from cultural heritage and indigenous collections. There is a long history of research on indigenous populations being conducted without true informed consent or benefit sharing. Indigenous peoples commonly lack access to information about the types and location of information that may have been collected about them and is now held by cultural institutions. Further, the history of acquisition of cultural heritage items is replete with examples of such items being removed without the agreement of the country of origin and/or indigenous owners. These items may contain secret or spiritual information or information that is otherwise regulated under indigenous knowledge systems. Digitization of any of this material may deeply offend the communities that are the source of the material.

At the same time, digitization can offer a means to bring to the attention of indigenous peoples elements of their past. Such digitization projects may be able to proceed effectively through consultation, cultural consents, repatriation of copy documentation in addition to original artifacts, collaborative projects, and so on.[22]

Note that these practices are not required by law. The Native American Graves Protection and Repatriation Act (NAGPRA), the governing federal legislation, requires the return of Native American cultural items and human remains to their respective peoples, but does not impact representations of artifacts. There are movements both domestically and at the international level to afford new rights in cultural heritage to indigenous peoples. At the 2007 International Council of Museums (ICOM) meeting, a general resolution was passed to "to support the efforts of WIPO and other relevant organizations to develop and implement a new WIPO Convention and other Conventions aiming to ensure the protection of the collective moral rights of the originators, inheritors, transmitters, and performers of the world's traditional cultural expressions, and traditional knowledge."[23] It remains to be seen whether any of these efforts will result in legally binding obligations; cultural institutions should stay abreast of developments.

Yet regardless of the legal requirements, there is much that institutions can do to adopt more culturally sensitive practices. Institutions that desire to digitize the traditional knowledge of indigenous peoples should be aware of the issues raised in the relevant literature, such as the proposed "Protocols for Native American Archival Materials."[24] Through consultation and dialogue, it should be possible to bring the benefits of digitization without offending or causing harm.

10 *Risk Management*
How to Digitize Safely

10.1 Introduction

As should be apparent by now, many digitization projects are likely to entail some risk to the cultural heritage institutions undertaking them. The reasons for this risk are many, and include:

- ▶ The copyright status of the work may be unclear
- ▶ It may not be possible to identify all of the subsisting copyrights incorporated into one work
- ▶ It may not be possible to locate copyright owners and secure permission
- ▶ Works that are in the public domain in the United States may be protected by copyright in other countries
- ▶ Individuals and groups may believe they have more rights in material than the law allows, and take umbrage when an institution digitizes the material

In the face of such uncertainty, some cultural institutions might become "spooked" and conclude that they should avoid digitization projects. This would be an unfortunate overreaction.

A better alternative is to identify the possible risks associated with a digitization project prior to its commencement and identify strategies to mitigate some of those risks. Research might also lead one to conclude that although the contemplated action might technically infringe copyright, the likelihood that anyone would complain is small. After assessing and mitigating risks, each cultural institution can determine whether it is comfortable with the level of risk associated with each project before proceeding.

How an institution assesses risk will vary with the institution and the particular project under consideration. Relevant factors might include the nature of material being digitized, the accessibility of digital content, the likely remedies in the event of legal proceedings, the availability of sovereign immunity arguments (for state institutions, see Chapter 5), the arguable existence of an implied license, the likelihood of a complaint being made, the potential impact of the project on the institution's reputation or relationship with current and future donors, the institution's level of comfort with risk, the availability of legal advice, and the perceived social utility of proceeding with the project. Furthermore, there may be steps that the institution can take to minimize its risk profile.

This chapter discusses the risk analysis calculus with which institutions must engage. It addresses questions such as:

- ▶ What factors increase the risk my institution faces?
- ▶ How likely is it that I might be sued?
- ▶ What are the potential damages?
- ▶ What strategies can my institution follow to minimize risk?
- ▶ What role do disclaimers and other notices play?

The risk-analysis calculus must be institution- and project-specific. For example, a state institution, because of the availability of a sovereign immunity argument (see Chapter 5), might conclude that it is at a lower risk than a private institution and be more willing to undertake a project. An institution with in-house legal counsel and copyright insurance might be more willing to accept risk than would a small organization that would have to rely on outside pro bono assistance in the event of a lawsuit. No general rules, therefore, on what is an acceptable level of risk can be formulated; each institution must decide on its own.

10.2 Recap of potential risks

Table 10.1 below summarizes some of the ways that a digitization project can place an institution at risk:

▮▮ **TABLE 10.1**

Factors that indicate your institution is at risk of infringing copyright

☐ Copyright subsists in the collection item.	☐ The item is protected, having regard to its originality, place of authorship or publication, and so forth. ☐ Copyright has not yet expired.	See Chapters 2 and 3

☐ The cultural institution does not own copyright.	☐ General rule is that the "author" is the copyright owner. Note special rules, e.g., for works made for hire. ☐ There has been no assignment of copyright to the cultural institution.	See Chapter 3
☐ The cultural institution engages in one of the exclusive rights of the copyright owner.	☐ The exclusive rights vary with the material under consideration. ☐ Exclusive rights include digitization and online distribution.	See Chapter 4
☐ The act does not fall within an exemption under the Copyright Act	Examples of exemptions include: ☐ Fair use ☐ Libraries and archives provisions	See Chapters 5 and 6
☐ Permission has not been secured from the copyright owner	☐ Express permission has not been obtained from the copyright owner ☐ No implied permission can be discerned	See Chapter 7
☐ Options:	☐ Do not proceed with the use (or select other material which raises no copyright issues); or ☐ Proceed with use under a risk management strategy.	

10.3 Elements working to minimize risk: the litigation calculus

The risk of litigation against cultural institutions varies, but historically has been very low. There have been very few court decisions that address the reproduction and distribution activities of cultural institutions.[1]

DID YOU KNOW?

Court cases involving copyright infringement by cultural heritage institutions are rare. When they occur, there is often an unusual twist to them: either the institution itself is unusual or the contested activity is not part of normal services. Some of the most prominent recent cases include:

▶ *Hotaling v. LDS*: The court concluded that the Church of Jesus Christ of Latter-Day Saints illegally distributed a copyrighted work (a microfiche) by including in its catalog a record for an unauthorized copy. Most copyright-infringement cases involve reproduction; this is one of the few to address the distribution right.

▶ *Sundeman v. Seajay Society*: The Seajay Society, a private foundation associated with the University of South Carolina, copied all of its copy of Marjorie Rawling's unpublished first novel for a researcher (who was also an officer of the Society). The court found the foundation's copying of the entire manuscript for the researcher to be a fair use based on the researcher's use of the material, in effect equating the researcher and the foundation of which she was an officer.

▶ *Internet Archive v. Suzanne Shell*: Shell, the proprietor of a Web site at www.profane-justice.org, sued the Internet Archive, which is sometimes considered to be a library, for copyright infringement and breach of contract for violating the site's terms of use when the Archive's robotic spiders copied Shell's site for display in the Archive's WayBack Machine. The case was settled out of court. Few cultural institutions currently harvest third-party Web sites without permission, but they may face similar challenges if the practice becomes more common.

▶ *Hoepker v. Kruger*: Barbara Kruger, an artist specializing in collages and other composite works, used a photograph by German photographer Thomas Hoepker in one of her works. Kruger gave permission to the Museum of Contemporary Art LA and the Whitney Museum to use the image on newsletters and brochures publicizing an exhibit as well as on postcards, note cubes, magnets, and T-shirts. Hoepker and his model sued Kruger and the museums

Barbara Kruger.

Untitled (It's a small world but not if you have to clean it), 1990. The Museum of Contemporary Art, Los Angeles.

License: No copyright information provided, but presumably copyright is owned by Kruger. Kruger added the text to the photograph taken by Thomas Hoepker. Used here under an assertion of fair use.

Source: http://www.moca-la.org/museum/pc_artwork_detail.php?acsnum=90.4

> for copyright infringement and invasion of privacy. The court dismissed the copyright charge, concluding that Hoepker's work was in the public domain in the United States. The privacy action was also dismissed because the products depicting the work were sold to disseminate Kruger's artistic expression.[2]

There are a number of reasons for this dearth of case law, but one of the most important is what we might call the "litigation calculus" that the copyright owner engages in. That is, in deciding whether or not to bring a court action, a copyright owner will usually weigh the costs of litigation (e.g., the time and expense of bringing court proceedings) against the potential benefits (e.g., the size and nature of potential remedies). This analysis will vary according to the type of material under consideration, the profession of the copyright owner, the nature of the allegedly infringing use, and so forth. For example, where copyright is very financially valuable to the copyright owner (examples might include architectural plans and contemporary art and design), owners might be concerned when an institution reproduces their works without permission or without paying remuneration, particularly in commercial products. In contrast, authors of private diaries or letters and the takers of family photographs may have less concern about enforcing copyright—although privacy concerns may arise for some of them, others may be excited that their works are being preserved and accessed.

As indicated above, the costs of copyright litigation can be high. All copyright actions must be brought in federal (as opposed to state or small claims) courts, and they are usually litigated by highly specialized (and hence well-compensated) intellectual property lawyers who typically charge hundreds of dollars an hour. There are many steps to complete before trial takes place (such as drafting pleadings, making discovery of documents, filing and responding to motions, etc), and even after a decision has been handed down, appeal may be possible. Costs in the vicinity of tens of thousands of dollars are not uncommon.[3] The decision to begin an infringement action, therefore, should not be made lightly. (Of course, although the high cost of copyright litigation may work to limit the number of actual lawsuits filed, it also is one reason why cultural institutions should act responsibly in avoiding such lawsuits.)

■

DID YOU KNOW?

Because some copyright decisions include the award of attorneys' fees to the prevailing side, we can see the actual costs for one side of these high-profile instances of copyright litigation:

▶ $813,724.25 (*Matthew Bender v. West*)
▶ $1,825,886.09 (*Mattel, Inc. v. Walking Mountain Productions*)
▶ $1,347,519.15 (*Fantasy Inc. v. Fogerty*)
▶ $2.9 million (*Religious Technology Center v. Scott*)

Most judgments for attorneys' fees are for much less than the above amounts. These figures, however, give an indication of how expensive some litigation can become!

Balanced against the potentially high cost of bringing proceedings are the low returns that are likely to come from a successful action against many cultural heritage institutions. As was discussed in Chapters 4 and 5, three provisions of the Copyright Act limit the remedies available to a copyright owner:

▶ Section 504(c)(3) stipulates that nonprofit educational institutions, libraries, and archives are not subject to statutory damages for copyright infringement when they have reasonable grounds for believing that their use is a fair use.
▶ Section 412 states that there can be no award of statutory damages or attorneys fees for infringement of unpublished works prior to registration.
▶ The 11th Amendment to the Constitution makes it possible for libraries, archives, and museums that are part of state governments to raise a sovereign immunity argument in relation to copyright claims for monetary damages (see Chapter 5).

From a monetary viewpoint, these provisions make it financially risky to bring legal action against a library or archives. (Museums may make for slightly better targets unless they are also nonprofit educational institutions.) It may be possible to stop infringing conduct through a court-ordered injunction, but the amount of money that a successful plaintiff can recover by way of damages may be limited. In many cases, it will only be the actual monetary loss that the copyright owner has suffered—usually the license fee that would have been required had permission been secured in advance. Given that in many cases the material that a cultural institution is likely to want to digitize is going to have low commercial value, any damages that a repository would be forced to pay would not warrant the expense of a suit.

A final note should be added. As a general rule, most legal disputes, regardless of the subject, settle well before trial or final judgment; indeed, many are resolved before the institution of proceedings. The reported decisions of the courts only reflect a very small percentage of the total number of disputes. On the positive side, this demonstrates that there are many opportunities to reach a resolution with the copyright owner prior to litigation or judgment. This may be through payment of a retrospective licensing fee, removing content from a Web site, supplying the copyright owner with copies of the publication in which their material is reproduced, and/or adding an attribution indicating the owner of copyright: see section 10.4. However, this also means that the cost of *dispute resolution* (leaving aside any litigation) should be factored into an institution's risk analysis. Indeed, it is also wise to have considered how the institution might respond to claims from copyright owners early in a project, and certainly before it publicly releases content. This is discussed further in section 10.6.

10.4 Cease-and-desist notices

Very rarely will the first notification of an aggrieved copyright owner arrive in the form of a filed lawsuit. It is much more common for a cultural institution first to receive a letter complaining of a perceived violation, and steps the institution can take to rectify the alleged harm (such as payment of money, destruction of infringing copies, and/or removal of material from the Internet).

Such a "letter of demand" or "cease and desist" notice may take the form of a letter or an e-mail directed to someone in authority at the cultural institution. It might also take the form of a DMCA "takedown" notice (sometimes called a DMCA 512 notice, after the section of the Copyright Act where its provisions are spelled out). Section 512 allows copyright owners to ask an

Internet Service Provider (ISP) to remove from its servers material that is allegedly infringing. If the ISP responds expeditiously, it is immune from any claim of contributory infringement.

This raises an initial question—is a cultural institution an ISP for the purposes of this provision? As discussed in the Tip below, the answer would generally be no. That said, many copyright owners are familiar with the DMCA takedown notice provisions and use them for all infringement complaints. It is therefore useful to be aware of their existence and designated content.

The component parts of a DMCA takedown notice as found in 17 U.S.C. 512(c)(3) are:

▶ The name, address, and electronic signature of the complaining party
▶ The infringing materials and their Internet location
▶ Sufficient information to identify the copyrighted works
▶ A statement by the owner that it has a good faith belief that use of the material has not been authorized by the copyright owner
▶ A statement that the information in the notice is accurate and, under penalty of perjury, that the complaining party is authorized to act on the behalf of the copyright owner

TIP

A cultural institution that mounts digitized material on its own servers would not generally be eligible for Section 512 safe-harbor protections. This is because Section 512 is directed to entities that maintain servers on which third parties can place content. It gives the hosting entity some protection from liability for *contributory* infringement. This is very different from most digitization projects, where the institution selects and publishes the material online.

There is no harm, however, in registering a DMCA designated agent with the Copyright Office. You are protected in the event that any third-party material should ever be added to your servers. Furthermore, including the name of a "DMCA designated agent" somewhere on your Web site makes it clear who on your staff should receive copyright complaints.

Instructions on how to register a designated agent are found at http://www.copyright.gov/onlinesp/.

If a cultural institution receives a complaint about an alleged infringement of copyright or a DMCA takedown notice, there are a number of options for settling the dispute. These include offering to:

▶ Take down infringing content from the Internet
▶ Pay a retrospective license fee
▶ Pay monetary compensation
▶ Provide free copies of books or other items in which the copyright owner's material appears
▶ Insert an attribution line indicating the copyright owner's rights

It may be possible to negotiate an acceptable outcome for the institution and copyright holder without involving lawyers. However, it may be useful to brief a lawyer on difficult cases or if you are have questions about how to draft settlement terms. For instance, it may be important that the agreed terms expressly state they comprise the full and final settlement of the dispute, to ensure that the copyright owner does not later commence proceedings in relation to the same complaint. It is also common for parties to sign terms of settlement on the basis that they do not admit liability. A lawyer can advise on the terms most appropriate for your institution.

Litigation is most likely to follow a cease-and-desist letter when the legal issues are uncertain, the stakes in bringing the litigation are high, or the plaintiff has noneconomic concerns and wants to use its copyright to address them. A classic example of the latter is when someone uses control of a copyright to enforce his or her sense of privacy. A copyright owner may also commence litigation when the alleged infringer delays in responding to a complaint. It is therefore advisable to deal with disputes in a timely manner (even if you believe that you are not at fault or that the dispute can be resolved easily).

DID YOU KNOW?

Just because someone complains about an alleged infringement or forwards a DMCA takedown notice to the institution does not mean that the cultural institution is automatically at fault. Sometimes the aggrieved party complains about uses that are arguably excused.

The Web site "Chilling Effects" (at http://www.chillingeffects.org) has been collecting cease-and-desist letters and DMCA takedown notices that have been sent to Web sites. In 2005, the Free Expression Policy Project at the Brennan Center for Justice at NYU School of Law conducted a study of 320 letters on the site. They concluded that "more than 20% either stated weak copyright or trademark claims, or involved speech with a strong or at least reasonable free expression or fair use defense. Another 27% attacked material with possible free expression or fair use defenses."[4]

10.5 Workflow for minimizing risk

Flowchart 10.1 depicts a workflow designed to minimize the possibility of violating copyright.

The amount of risk involved at each stage increases (perhaps with the exception of digitization under a license, which tends to promote certainty, but has other logistical issues), as the following brief discussion of each of the eight steps indicates.

YOU OWN ALL THE COPYRIGHTS

If you are the copyright owner of a work, you are free to digitize it. The key issue is making sure that you actually are the copyright owner; that any copyright transfers are valid; and that you have not inadvertently transferred copyright to someone else. For instance, if the work is from employees of your organization, make sure that separate employment agreements do not change the normal work-made-for-hire arrangements. In many environments, authors believe that work belongs to them when it actually belongs to their employers. Remember, too, that there can be layers of copyright in a work, and it is necessary to have the permission of the owners of the copyrights in all of the layers before proceeding. Lastly, make sure that there are no privacy, publicity, or other non-copyright rights that may pose a challenge.

THE COPYRIGHTS ARE IN THE PUBLIC DOMAIN

A work may be in the public domain either because it was never protected by copyright in the first place or because all of the copyrights have expired.

◆ **FLOWCHART 10.1**

Safe Digitization Workflow

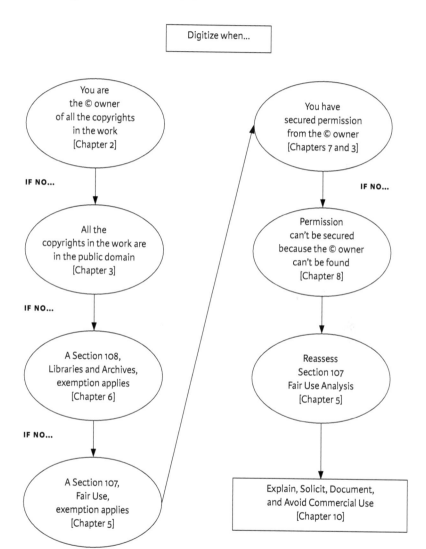

The biggest risk when digitizing public domain works is that you have miscalculated the copyright status of the work. When thinking about copyright term, keep the distinctions between published and unpublished in mind. Many works that we might think are published (such as a radio broadcast or a play) can actually be unpublished for purposes of copyright. Remember, too, that works first published abroad may have had their copyright restored (even if the American edition of the work you are examining appears to be in the public domain). Again, be sure to consider all of the copyrights when dealing with a work with multiple layers.

ONE OF THE SECTION 108 EXEMPTIONS APPLY

Most digitization projects seek to provide public access via the Internet to digitized materials. Using Section 108, you may be able to do this for published material in its last 20 years of copyright term. For other digitization projects, you are restricted to on-premises use (if relying solely on Section 108).

YOU CONCLUDE THAT DIGITIZATION IS A FAIR USE

As discussed in Chapter 6, it is difficult to employ fair use as a justification for the digitization and general public distribution of entire copyrighted works. Nevertheless, by carefully tailoring a project in accordance with the fair-use factors found in Section 107, it may be possible to decrease the risk of infringement in other types of projects. For instance, limiting access to a small defined community for a specific research purpose might help, as might limiting the amount of material that can be retrieved (Google's "snippets" argument) or only making content available in a low-resolution format. Developing new products such as visual indexes and catalogs that are more than substitutes for the original works could also potentially qualify as a fair use. If you decide to adopt a fair-use rationale for digitization, be sure to work closely with your legal advisers in advance.

YOU SECURE THE PERMISSION OF THE COPYRIGHT OWNER

The safest, but also potentially the most expensive, way to minimize risk is to digitize with the permission of the copyright owner. The primary risk associated with this approach is that someone may claim to own a copyright when in reality it belongs to someone else. Requiring warranties and indemnification with any grant of permission can decrease risk, but indemnities are not infallible, and they may decrease the likelihood of securing permission if documentation looks too legalistic.

Perhaps the bigger issue associated with securing permission from the copyright owner is logistical: the impact on your budget. Identifying and locating copyright owners can be expensive. It may make little sense to spend $100 to locate an owner of a work if you would only spend $0.05 in a license fee or if the penalties for an infringing use are similarly low. There are a number of internal mechanisms that institutions can implement to help reduce transactions costs of licensing (such as information management tools and obtaining licenses for some activities at acquisition). Collective management by copyright owners can also help streamline the process.

THE WORK YOU WANT TO DIGITIZE IS AN ORPHAN WORK

Orphan works are materials for which the copyright owner is difficult or impossible to identify or locate. Two key questions arise for management of orphan works: (1) what level of search must be undertaken before a work is designated as orphaned; and (2) what are the consequences of such a designation (for instance, what sort of digitization efforts might be undertaken for orphaned material)?

In relation to the first question, some investigation of the copyright status of a work is always in order. Almost all discussions of orphan works start with the assumption that the user conducts at a minimum a "reasonable" search for a copyright owner. It would be wise to document in writing the rationale for the approach you have taken, and to keep a paper trail of individual searches.

In relation to the second question, this will come down to the usual risk-management factors: the nature of the orphaned material, the purpose of the use, the level of public accessibility, and so on. It may also depend on how viable a fair-use argument is, as discussed next.

REASSESS FAIR USE AND THE OVERALL RISK

If, after conducting a reasonable search for the copyright owner of a work, the owner still cannot be found, conduct a fresh fair-use analysis. If an owner cannot be found, it suggests that the market impact of your proposed use is low, perhaps lower than you initially assumed. This is highly relevant to analysis of the fourth fair-use factor, and may alter your conclusion about the likely determination of a fair-use defense.[5] A digitization project that may have initially seemed to be unfair may now be judged to be fair. As already discussed, there may also be ways of structuring your project to tailor it to the fair-use factors—it may be worthwhile to revisit these.

■ QUESTION

When is it permissible knowingly to infringe copyright?

These guidelines have assumed that cultural heritage institutions do not wish to knowingly violate copyright. There are situations, however, when it is conceivable that an institution may wish to infringe. As an example, imagine a collection that has a large number of artworks created by African craftspeople during the first half of the twentieth century. There is no documentation extant to indicate whether the works were "published" for copyright purposes. The institution wishes to digitize the works and then make the images accessible via a Web site that requires a subscription for access. It also intends to market the images individually. In recognition that the works are part of the cultural heritage of Africa, the institution intends to provide free access to the database to African institutions.

Because the works are anonymous and may be unpublished, it is likely that they are still protected by copyright in the United States. A fair-use analysis of the institution's plans would suggest that the proposed use is infringing. The purpose is commercial rather than educational; the works are creative and unpublished; the entire work is being duplicated; and the market impact would be great since a copyright owner would be affected in his or her ability to market or license the work once it was broadly available. All four factors would appear to weigh against a finding of fair use.

The likelihood is extremely small, however, that the heirs of the Africans who created the works will realize that they own the copyright in the works under U.S. law, learn that the works have been digitized and are available electronically, and proceed to bring a copyright-infringement suit in a U.S. court. In addition, African institutions would have free access, and through them African users would also be more likely to gain access. Thus, there would be an arguable public benefit to the wider communities from which the works came. In this situation, given the extremely low risk present and the wider perceived benefits, the institution may decide to proceed.

10.6 Explain, solicit, document, and contribute

Regardless of which of the approaches listed above an institution prefers for any given project, there are certain general recommendations that should be followed in all instances. The recommended actions may lower the risks associated with digitization. In addition, they suggest that you are a "good actor." There is no general exemption for "good intentions" or "innocent infringement" in copyright (remember the discussion in Chapter 2 of the strict liability provisions of copyright), but judges tend to look more favorably on litigants who have acted responsibly. The suggestions also represent general good practice in digitization.

The four key elements are:

▸ Explain what you are doing
▸ Solicit information from copyright owners
▸ Document your copyright investigations
▸ If you don't have clear copyright title, avoid commercial use

EXPLAIN WHAT YOU ARE DOING

Regardless of the justification that you use for your digitization project, be sure to explain what you have done on your Web site. If you believe that there are no known copyright restrictions on the work, say so. If you are using Section 108(h) to make materials available during their last 20 years of copyright, say so. At a minimum, you should make information on the general copyright status of the project available to potential users. It is a service to your patrons to provide them with information on your copyright investigations of individual items.[6]

TIP

Here is an excellent explanation of why works were digitized, from the Web site for the *Prosperity and Thrift* collection at the Library of Congress's American Memory project. Note that they have determined that some items are in the public domain; others are made available with the permission of the copyright owner; and still others, after an extensive search for the copyright owners, are made available under an assertion of fair use:

> The Library of Congress has exhaustively researched the contents of this collection to ascertain any possible legal rights embodied in the materials. Items included here with the permission of rights holders are listed below. Many of the items in this collection are in the public domain, that is, not subject to copyright protection such as the works of employees of the federal government of the United States.
>
> Despite extensive research, the Library has been unable to identify all possible rights holders in the materials in this collection. Thus, some of the materials provided here online are made available under an assertion of fair use [17 U.S.C. § 107]. Therefore, we stress that this collection and the materials contained therein are provided strictly for noncommercial educational and research purposes. Again, responsibility for making an independent legal assessment and independently securing any necessary permissions ultimately rests with persons desiring to use particular items in the context of the intended use.[7]

LEAVE THE DOOR OPEN TO ORPHANED COPYRIGHT OWNERS

You never want your first contact with an aggrieved copyright owner to be via a lawsuit, so make other avenues available. Announce on your Web site that you would like to hear from unidentified copyright owners. Information they can provide will increase your knowledge about objects in your collections. The dialogue may also begin a mutually beneficial discussion of permission, licensing, or takedown.

The Kheel Center for Labor-Management Documentation and Archives at Cornell University has a good example of this approach on its Web page for labor photographs, most of which are orphan works:

> The Kheel Center would like to learn more about these images and hear from any copyright owners who are not properly identified on this Web site so that we may make the necessary corrections. If you have any additional information about the images or would like to suggest a correction, please contact Barb Morley at kheel_center@cornell.edu. Please include the photo identification number (e.g., 5780pb32f14a).[8]

DOCUMENT YOUR INVESTIGATIONS

Many of the existing and proposed protections for libraries, archives, and nonprofit educational institutions require that either an institution has a "reasonable belief" that its use is fair or has first conducted a "reasonable investigation." It is fundamentally important to document any copyright investigations you conduct as part of the digitization process.

Documentation can vary according to the nature of the project. If, for example, you are making material available during its last 20 years of copyright under Section 108(h), a memo to the file explaining why and how you concluded the selected works were in their last 20 years of copyright would be sufficient.

For a fair-use analysis, you will want to document your assessment of the four factors found in the statute, along with any other applicable factors. The Copyright Management Center at IUPUI has developed a "Fair Use Checklist" which is very helpful in documenting fair use analyses. A copy is found in Table 10.2; an online version is available from Columbia University.[9] The University of Minnesota has constructed a similar online fair-use-analysis tool: see http://www.lib.umn.edu/copyright/checklist.phtml.

It is certainly permissible to adapt the sample checklists for specific projects. For example, it may not be necessary to complete a form for every letter in a manuscript collection, but rather complete one form for a group of items that have identical copyrights and will be used in the same way.

Remember, too, that not all elements have to weigh in favor of fair use—the important thing is that the preponderance of the elements favors fair use. Most of all, remember that the analysis does not have ultimately to be correct, but merely reasonable. The important thing is that you conduct a serious analysis of each fair-use factor that you document and retain.

AVOID COMMERCIAL USE

Perhaps the most fundamental step you can take to minimize risk is to avoid making commercial use of reproductions of copyrighted works. With works in the public domain or works whose copyright you clearly own, you can of course charge whatever you want for their use. And when you have secured permission from a copyright owner to digitize a work, you can also negotiate the right to commercialize the work.

Generally, no commercial use should be made of copyrighted works without the permission of the rights holder. Commercial use eliminates any 108 defense, and makes it much harder to claim that a use is a fair use. A hefty check from a motion picture company or commercial publisher may look appealing at the time it is received, but the amount of the check is likely to pale in comparison to the damages that could be assessed in a successful copyright-infringement suit. If you want to generate revenue through the digitization, reproduction, and distribution of copyrighted works found in your collections, then your obligation to search for the copyright owners will be much stronger.

QUESTION

Is it possible to avoid all risk?

Unfortunately, the answer is no. In spite of your best efforts to determine copyright status, identify copyright owners, and follow the most rigorous practices, someone may nevertheless commence an action against you.

A recent lawsuit against Cornell University demonstrates this. In 1983, two sentences appeared in the university's newspaper stating that a student had been arrested for burglary. In 2007, the Cornell University Library digitized that paper and made it available online.

TABLE 10.2

IUPUI Checklist for Fair Use

CHECKLIST FOR FAIR USE

Please complete and retain a copy of this form in connection with each possible "fair use" of a copyrighted work for your project

Name:_____   Date:_____   Project:_____

Institution:_____   Prepared by:_____

PURPOSE

Favoring Fair Use

- ❑ Teaching (including multiple copies for classroom use)
- ❑ Research
- ❑ Scholarship
- ❑ Nonprofit Educational Institution
- ❑ Criticism
- ❑ Comment
- ❑ News reporting
- ❑ Transformative or Productive use (changes the work for new utility)
- ❑ Restricted access (to students or other appropriate group)
- ❑ Parody

Opposing Fair Use

- ❑ Commercial activity
- ❑ Profiting from the use
- ❑ Entertainment
- ❑ Bad-faith behavior
- ❑ Denying credit to original author

NATURE

Favoring Fair Use

- ❑ Published work
- ❑ Factual or nonfiction based
- ❑ Important to favored educational objectives

Opposing Fair Use

- ❑ Unpublished work
- ❑ Highly creative work (art, music, novels, films, plays)
- ❑ Fiction

AMOUNT

Favoring Fair Use

- ❑ Small quantity
- ❑ Portion used is not central or significant to entire work
- ❑ Amount is appropriate for favored educational purpose

Opposing Fair Use

- ❑ Large portion or whole work used
- ❑ Portion used is central to work or "heart of the work"

EFFECT

Favoring Fair Use

- ❑ User owns lawfully acquired or purchased copy of original work
- ❑ One or few copies made
- ❑ No significant effect on the market or potential market for copyrighted work
- ❑ No similar product marketed by the copyright holder
- ❑ Lack of licensing mechanism

Opposing Fair Use

- ❑ Could replace sale of copyrighted work
- ❑ Significantly impairs market or potential market for copyrighted work or derivative
- ❑ Reasonably available licensing mechanism for use of the copyrighted work
- ❑ Affordable permission available for using work
- ❑ Numerous copies made
- ❑ You made it accessible on Web or in other public forum
- ❑ Repeated or long-term use

This document is provided as a courtesy of the Copyright Management Center, IUPUI, 530 W. New York St., Indianapolis, IN 46202. For further information and updates please visit http://www.copyright.iupui.edu/. This document last updated March 10, 2003.

There were no copyright issues; the paper had been produced by employees of the university.

The student, now a practicing California attorney, discovered the article through Google and filed two suits against the University, one for $1 million and the second for $10 million.[10] In the suits, the former student asserted libel and public disclosure of private facts through the alleged "republication" of the article. (These torts are discussed in more detail in Chapter 9.) The judge dismissed both suits on a number of grounds, not the least of which was that the plaintiff had pled guilty to a lesser charge of burglary in conjunction with the thefts.[11] The judge also ordered the plaintiff to pay Cornell's legal fees for both cases.[12]

The absence of any apparent substantial legal basis for proceeding in the two suits did not stop them from occurring. Any digitization project runs the same sorts of risks. One can hope that a judge will quickly dismiss frivolous charges, but there is no panacea that can protect against all actions.

Blotter Barton

Department of Public Safety officials have charged Kevin G. Vanginderen of 603 Winston Court Apartments with third degree burglary in connection with 10 incidents of petit larceny and five burglaires on campus over a period of a year. Safety reported recovering some $474 worth of stolen goods from him.

Also, according to the morning reports of the department for the period March 7 through 13.

"Blotter Barton," *Cornell Chronicle*, 3/17/1983, p. 6.

License: published without a © notice, so presumed to be in the public domain.

Source: http://ecommons. library.cornell.edu/bit-stream/1813/5350/14/014_24.pdf

10.7 Conclusion

The approach to risk assessment outlined in this chapter is intended to reduce the risk associated with digitization projects, but the danger of a lawsuit can never be eliminated. Cultural heritage institutions have long existed in an environment of risk—often, however they just may not have been aware of it. For years, for example, the best practice for preservation microfilming in libraries stipulated that the library make three copies of a work: the camera negative, the print master, and the service copy. It was not until 1998, however, that the permission to do this was made explicit in copyright law. Prior to this, each library that followed the standard accepted the risk that this might not be considered to be a fair use.

It is important that cultural institutions respect the rights of copyright owners. We should never forget, however, that first, copyright exists to benefit the public good, and second, cultural institutions have long occupied a special place in copyright law, due to their missions of preserving and facilitating access to intellectual and creative works. It would be unfortunate if, in their desire to avoid *all* risk, those same institutions failed in their fundamental missions.

11 *Case Study 1*
Interviews and Oral Histories

11.1 Introduction

Many cultural institutions have documents in which people are interviewed to establish a body of information about particular cultures, events, subjects, or geographical areas. These interviews are commonly recorded, often on audiotape and sometimes on video. The interviews are often, though not always, transcribed. In some instances, the interviewee speaks without interruption. In others, an interviewer may guide and encourage the development of the story being told. Often the interviews are conducted as part of a structured oral history project; in other cases, they may have been interviews conducted by a reporter or author as part of background research.

The following issues arise in relation to copyright:

▶ In what expression does copyright subsist? The transcription, the recording, the words on the recording, or all three?

▶ Who is the author of each copyright work? The interviewee (whose story is being recorded), the interviewer (who is providing the prompts for the story), the person recording the interview (often, but not always, the interviewer) or the transcriber (who is taking the spoken words of the interviewee and interviewer and reducing them to a written form)?

▶ Who is the owner of copyright in each work? Does the cultural institution ever own copyright?

Having discussed these legal issues, this case study concludes with a copyright checklist for digitizing oral history recordings.

11.2 Identification of potentially protected material

The first step in analyzing whether digitization of oral history interviews raises a copyright issue is to identify all possible copyrighted works (see Chapter 2). There are three potential copyright works in this scenario:

- The words of the interview (a *literary work*)
- The recording itself (a *sound recording* or *audiovisual work*)
- The transcript (a *literary work*)

Recall that the copyright in a sound or audiovisual recording is separate from any literary, dramatic, or musical work that was recorded. That is, it is possible that one person owns copyright in the *recording* (either the audio recording or the video recording), but another owns copyright in the *recorded material*. This is relevant to cultural institutions because digitization reproduces both works. It may therefore be necessary to obtain consents from multiple parties.

11.3 Does copyright subsist in any of these items?

Copyright will only subsist in an item if the following conditions are met:

- For all works—the work is fixed in some tangible form
- For all works—the work is original
- For sound recordings or audiovisual items—the process of "fixing" the recording requires some creative choices (i.e., it is more than purely "mechanical" recording)

In light of these conditions, does copyright subsist in each of the three works identified above?

THE INTERVIEW

For the purpose of this case study, it will be assumed that the words of the interview are original; an exception might arise where, for example, the interview includes readings from a text written by another person.

There is nothing in the definition of "literary work" to suggest that it does not apply to a speech or interview merely because the words are spoken extempore; oral expression can be original. Furthermore, when recorded on tape or subsequently transcribed, that expression becomes fixed. Since original expression is fixed, federal copyright protection is afforded to the interview itself.

THE RECORDING

A recording is obviously fixed, so it would meet one of the requirements to be afforded copyright protection. But what of originality?

The act of talking can be a form of performance. One need only think of the difference between a good and bad audiobook to know how much the performance of the speaker matters. It is likely, therefore, that the speakers in an interview would have a copyright in their performance as recorded. If sound or video engineers record the interview, and if they make judgments on how best to capture the interview or subsequently alter, edit, or remix the interview, then they might be an author of a copyright in the recording as well.

THE TRANSCRIPT

We have suggested above that the words spoken in an oral history interview when fixed by recording are copyrighted. But can a transcript of that interview have its own copyright, separate from the words themselves?

Transcripts clearly exist in material form, and so meet one of the two requirements for copyright protection. It is much harder to conceive of a transcript that contains the requisite originality. If a transcript is a mere factual expression of the words spoken on the tape, then there would be no separate copyright in it; the only copyright would exist in the words spoken in the interview. With most oral history transcriptions, it would seem unlikely that a separate copyright could exist in the transcript.

If, however, the transcriber expends significant skill and effort to create the transcript, a court might conclude that an original literary work had been created.[1] For example, deleting irrelevant text, editing the expression (e.g., removing "ums" and correcting grammar and syntax), and in particular changing the order in which text appears in order to produce the final work might create a work that is different from the original interview, and hence copyrightable in its own right. It might be bad oral history practice, but good for copyright ownership.

11.4 Who is the author of the work?

Copyright can conceivably subsist in the interview itself, the recording of that interview, and in an edited transcript of the interview. Who would be the owner of the copyright in each instance?

THE INTERVIEW

In most interviews, the most important contribution comes from the interviewee, and it is almost certain that he or she owns at least a part of the copyright in the interview. As John Neuenschwander notes, when the tape stops rolling, "the interviewee is usually deemed to be the sole author of the tape and the singular copyright holder."[2]

Interviews involve an interviewer as well. Whether the interviewer's own contributions are original enough to warrant copyright becomes a question of fact. When the interviewer merely gives a general framework for the interview and the interviewee essentially speaks uninterrupted, then the interviewer's contribution may not be original enough for him or her to be considered an author. But if the interviewer is an important figure in his or her right and the interview is as much about his or her contributions as it is about the interviewee, or if the questions the interviewer poses are creative and original, then it is possible that the interviewer would own a copyright in his or her own words.[3]

It is also theoretically possible that the work of the interviewer and the interviewee could be considered to be a "joint work," which is defined in copyright law as "a work prepared by two or more authors with the intention that their contributions be merged into inseparable or interdependent parts of a unitary whole" [17 U.S.C. § 101]. If a joint work, copyright would be shared equally between the interviewer and the interviewee, and either of them could exercise any of the exclusive rights of the copyright owner. The interviewer, if a joint copyright owner, could assign his or her copyright to the repository—or authorize a repository to digitize the work and make it available online.

Some recent oral history theory has stressed the collaborative nature of authorship in the oral history process—and in the process, laid the groundwork for at least a theoretical argument for joint authorship. Kathryn

Marie Dudley, for example, has argued that authorship is a tenuous concept in oral histories:

> . . . the production of oral testimony is always a collaborative, dialogic, jointly orchestrated affair. Out of this social interaction emerges a document of which it can rightly be said that the author function is up for grabs . . . What gives the author function its critical edge in oral history and ethnography is the fact that no one 'authors' the texts we produce, yet the truth conditions of our discourse require that *someone* step forward to claim that authorship, with all the legal, political and moral ramifications it entails.[4]

Eliot Mazé notes that "If the interview is most productively understood as a dialogic event, formed by the narrative strategies of both the interviewer and interviewee, then any archived representation of that event must somehow grant equal authorship to those on all sides of the microphone."[5]

Recent court cases on joint authorship have identified the intent of the parties as being the key element. In the oral history context, this would boil down to one key fact: did the interviewer and interviewee intend to create a joint work with each as a joint author? Intent is especially important when "one person . . . is indisputably the dominant author of the work and the only issue is whether that person is the sole author or she and another . . . are joint authors."[6] For example, an editor and a writer may intend their contributions to be merged into an inseparable whole, "yet very few editors and even fewer writers would expect the editor to be accorded the status of joint author, enjoying an undivided half interest in the copyright in the published work."[7] Intent can be established by examining the facts surrounding authorship and ownership, including who had final decision-making authority, the agreed-upon credits for the work, the description of authorship in written agreements with third parties, and other additional evidence.[8] In a rare case, it may be possible to argue that the intent of the parties in an oral history interview was to create a joint work.

Remember, too, that if the interviewer is an employee of an oral history organization and the interview is conducted as part of his or her employment, the "author" of the copyright would be the oral history program, not the interviewer.

THE RECORDING

The ownership of copyright in a recording of an interview is complex. It should at a minimum include the contributions of the "performers" (the interviewee and possibly the interviewer) who are captured on tape.

It may include as well the contribution of the recording engineers and/ or producers responsible for setting up the recording session, capturing and processing the sounds, and compiling and editing them to make the final sound recording. If a video recording, it could include the director and video engineers who oversee the shoot. If the sound or video engineers recording the interview engage in any creative work eligible for copyright protection, it is likely that it would merge with the interviewee and potentially inter- viewer in a joint work of copyright.

Although in theory a recording engineer (or his or her employer) could own the copyright in the recording, what they can do with that recording is very limited. Since there is an underlying copyright in interview, in order to reproduce or distribute the recording, the permission of the copyright owner of the interview (most likely the interviewee) would be needed. CBS Television, for example, could not use the video it had shot of Martin Luther King, Jr., delivering the "I have a dream" speech without first securing per- mission from the Martin Luther King, Jr., estate, which owns the copyright in the text captured on the film (*Estate of Martin L. King v. CBS*).

THE TRANSCRIPT

Again, there are two possible copyright authors for the transcript. The work could be considered to be a joint work between the interviewer, the interviewee, and the transcriber—assuming that all intended to create a joint work in which they shared equally. Alternatively, each individual could own the copyright in his or her contribution, but not have an interest in the others' work. That would mean, for example, that the interviewer could not authorize the reproduction of the transcript that could contain copyrightable contributions from the transcriber. On the other hand, the transcriber could not solely authorize the reproduction of the transcript, since it would contain the interviewer's original contributions as well as those of the transcriber.

Transcriptions are frequently conducted by outside contractors. It is unlikely that they would contribute enough original content to warrant a copyright of their own, but it would be wise to stipulate as part of the contract that they transfer to the organization commissioning the transcription any copyright they may have in the material

11.5   Has copyright in the work expired?

THE INTERVIEW

The duration of copyright in a literary work varies depending on when and where it was created and whether it has ever been published. If considered a joint work, the longest possible duration for each contributor determines the last possible date of copyright protection.

▶ If *unpublished*, copyright in the interview would expire 70 years after the death of the interviewee.

▶ If *unpublished*, copyright could also expire 70 years after the death of the interviewer, assuming his or her contributions were enough to warrant a copyright interest.

▶ If either the interviewee or interviewer were acting as an employee, their employer would own any copyright they created, and it would expire 120 years after creation.

What constitutes publication of an oral history interview is a very difficult question to answer. Certainly selling copies of transcripts would constitute publication. Distribution does not have to be extensive. In *Hebrew Academy v. Goldman*, the court found that the nationwide distribution of ten copies of an oral history (nine of which went to other libraries) constituted publication. Offering to sell or loan the tapes of the interviews may constitute publication of the underlying literary work as well (*La Cienega Music Co. v. ZZ Top*).[9]

If the interview was published, either as transcripts or via distribution of the recordings, then for much of the twentieth century the various copyright formalities would have had to have been followed. Copyright notice would have had to appear on the copies distributed, and the interviews would have had to have been registered and renewed. The duration of works can be determined by following the principles set forth in Chapter 3.

THE RECORDING

Where duration is concerned, it is necessary to distinguish between sound recordings and audiovisual recordings.

Sound recordings only received federal copyright protection starting in 1972. Few if any of the pre-1972 recordings will enter the public domain prior to 2067. Unpublished sound recordings made since 1972 are protected for 70 years after the death of the author or 120 years after creation if the work was done by an employee.

Sound recordings *published* between 1972 and 1989 had to follow the requirements for notice. If the proper copyright notice did not appear on the piece, the sound recording entered the public domain. (Note, however, that this did not automatically also place the underlying work in the public domain. It could have been registered separately.) If published with the copyright notice, none of these published sound records will enter the public domain until 2049 at the earliest.

Audiovisual recordings have received copyright protection since 1912. The rules governing copyright duration of a filmed interview are the same as those for the interview itself. If the work is unpublished, copyright would endure for either the life of the author plus 70 years or for 120 years (if a work of corporate authorship). If published, the recording would have had to follow the notice requirements required of all published items (unless the recording was published after 1 March 1989).

THE TRANSCRIPT

If there is a separate copyright in the transcript, it would follow the same rules governing copyright duration as those for the interview itself.

11.6 Does the institution wish to perform one of the "exclusive acts" of the copyright owner?

For the purpose of this case study, we will concentrate on the digitization of oral history sound recordings, as this appears to be a topical issue for cultural institutions.

The exclusive rights of the copyright owner include making a "reproduction" of a literary work and making a "copy" of a sound recording or audiovisual. This encompasses making a digital version of an item held in analog form. Digitization clearly makes a copy of the sound recording or film, meaning that a cultural institution risks infringing copyright unless it is the owner of copyright, has the permission of the copyright owner, or the digitization falls within an exemption in the Copyright Act. Digitization also reproduces the underlying literary work (that is, the interview), raising the possibility of infringing copyright in that work. If digitized copies are made available from a publicly accessible server, digitization may also impinge on the distribution and public performance rights of the copyright owner.

11.7 Does digitization fall within any exemptions to infringement in the Copyright Act?

There are a number of scenarios under which a cultural institution could use the exemptions available in the Copyright Act to digitize an oral history interview, either as a transcript or in recorded form (audio or film).

▶ If a library or archives owns an *unpublished* transcript or recorded interview, that interview may be digitized for purposes of preservation. Access to a digital copy can be provided on the premises of the library or archives [17 U.S.C. § 108(b)]

▶ A library or archives may also digitize an unpublished interview in order to make an analog copy for deposit in another library or archives [17 U.S.C. § 108(b)]

▶ In response to a request from a user, a library or archives can provide a digital copy of an entire oral history transcript if it has first determined, on the basis of a reasonable investigation, that a copy of the interview cannot be obtained at a fair price. The library or archives is not allowed to retain a copy of the digital file [17 U.S.C. § 108(e)]

▶ Similarly, a library or archives can provide to a user upon request a digital copy of an entire sound recording of an oral history interview. Again, it must determine that a copy of the recording is not available in the market. Note that this only applies to sound recordings; it does not apply to video interviews [17 U.S.C. § 108(b) and 108(i)]

▶ During the last 20 years of a work's copyright term, a library or archives may post on its Web site a digitized copy of a published oral history transcript, sound recording, or film, provided that certain requirements are met [17 U.S.C. § 108(h)]

This analysis suggests that an oral history can be digitized without the consent of the copyright owners for some purposes, but that other uses will require permission from the owners of copyright in the recording and the interview.

11.8 Are there other considerations than just copyright to consider?

As discussed in Chapter 9 of these guidelines, there are rights other than copyright that should be considered when undertaking a digitization program. Certainly the privacy issues associated with oral history interviews leap to mind.

An oral history program may have letters of release from the interviewees and interviewers that would legally authorize them to digitize and post to the Web oral history interviews. The "Principles and Standards of the Oral History Association," however, stipulate that programs should make good faith efforts "to ensure that the uses of recordings and transcripts comply with both the letter *and spirit* of the interviewee's agreement" (emphasis ours).[10]

Before commencing an oral history digitization project, cultural institutions should consider whether the interviewees anticipated this level of general access to their remarks. It is one thing to add an oral history to a scholarly institution where it is likely to be used in a restricted setting. It is quite another to find one's remarks readily accessible via Internet search engines. A repository may have the legal right to make something available, but it would still not be ethical.

In addition to privacy issues, cultural heritage institutions would also need to consider whether anything in a digitized interview could be considered to be defamatory. If the interview had been previously published, the statute of limitation on defamation suits might protect the institution (as was the case with *Hebrew Academy v. Goldman*, discussed in Chapter 9).[11] If digitization constitutes first publication of the oral history, however, the digitizing institution could be liable.

11.9 Practical suggestions arising from this chapter

☐ Obtain copyright permissions (or, where appropriate, assignments) from participants in oral history interviews at the time of the interview. This should include the interviewer, the interviewee(s), and any individuals who recorded the interview.

☐ Obtain copyright permissions (or, where appropriate, assignments) from people involved in transcribing interviews when the transcripts are made.

☐ Fragile unpublished recordings can be digitized immediately under the preservation copying provisions in the Copyright Act. However, there are limits on the uses of materials produced under exemptions in the Act.

☐ If you have a collection of oral history recordings for which the copyright information is missing or incomplete, you may need to consider a copyright risk management strategy for certain acts of digitization or making digitized content available to the public. For example, a person's participation in an interview project designed to copy and make accessible to the public the recorded work might constitute an "implied license" to perform certain copyright acts (see Chapter 7). In any event, the risk of a copyright infringement action may be low. That said, copyright owners may become concerned when personal or culturally sensitive material is made available to the public or where transcripts are used in commercially successful products.

12 *Case Study 2*
Dissertations, Theses, and Student Papers

12.1 Introduction[1]

Most academic institutions have collections of doctoral dissertations, master's theses, and/or honors papers from students. Thanks to over two decades of work by groups such as Virginia Tech University[2] and the Networked Digital Library of Theses and Dissertations,[3] many institutions now routinely ask students to deposit theses and dissertations with their schools in electronic form. The availability of dissertations in electronic form dramatically increases their accessibility and is consistent with the general academic assumption that doctoral scholarship should be published and shared. Dissertations also reflect the intellectual heritage of the institution. They document the type and quality of research that has been done at the university over time. It is little wonder, therefore, that many schools, in addition to encouraging current students to add their writings to an electronic repository, are also exploring digitizing the historical collections housed in the library or archives.

The following issues arise in relation to the digitization of dissertations, theses, and student papers:

▶ Who owns the copyright in the work: the student, the funding agency that supported them, or the school?

▶ What is the copyright status of the work? Are dissertations unpublished or published? If published, have they entered the public domain?

▶ Do laws designed to protect student privacy, most notably FERPA, affect whether a school can digitize?

▶ Do commercial efforts to digitize dissertations provide any guidance to the schools themselves?

Having discussed these legal issues, this case study concludes with a copyright checklist of items to consider when digitizing dissertations, theses, and student papers.

12.2 Definitions

For the purpose of this chapter, we will distinguish between dissertations, theses, and student papers (DTSPs) as follows:

- ▶ Dissertations will refer to written work documenting the research conducted as part of the requirements for the completion of a doctoral degree. Dissertations are normally prepared with the expectation that their results will be shared with the larger community of scholars.
- ▶ Theses will refer to written research prepared as part of the requirements for the award of a master's degree. Many master's theses are eventually published, but there is not the same general assumption that master's work needs to become part of the scholarly commons as there is with dissertations.
- ▶ Student papers refer to the written work created by undergraduate and K–12 students. Many cultural institutions have collections of honors papers, award-winning papers, or even undergraduate theses that they may wish to digitize and make available. Occasionally faculty members will seek the help of a library or archives to digitize current student papers in order to build an online library of student work for the benefit of subsequent classes.

12.3 Can copyright subsist in DTSPs?

Copyright will only subsist in an item if the following conditions are met:

- ▶ The work is fixed in some tangible form
- ▶ The work is original

Clearly both conditions would apply to DTSPs: they must be written (or at least be tangible), and the research and writing presented in them must be original. DTSPs are therefore subject to copyright protection.

12.4 Who owns the initial copyright in a DTSP?

As was discussed in Chapter 2, normally the author is the initial owner of copyright. In the case of DTSPs, therefore, the default assumption must be that the author of the dissertation, thesis, or student paper owns the copyright in the work.

Several factors, however, could alter that default assumption. Foremost among these is the "work made for hire" doctrine. Remember that for copyright purposes the author of works written by employees is the employer. It is possible that a PhD or master's candidate might be both a student and an employee of either the university or an outside firm. In that case, there is the remote possibility that his or her employer would be considered to be the author of the dissertation or thesis. MIT, for example, asserts ownership in student theses if the thesis research is supported in whole or in part by "wages, salary, stipend, or grant funds administered by the Institute."[4] Most graduate students at MIT receive research stipends, and so most of the MIT theses are owned by the University.

It is less likely that undergraduate students would ever be considered employees of their school merely because they have matriculated. If the research and writing for an undergraduate honors paper was conducted as part of paid university employment, however, the copyright in the paper might belong to the school and not the student.

It is slightly more likely that rather than claiming full copyright ownership of student work, a university or school might insist as a condition of enrollment or completion of a degree that the school be given a license to use and exploit any copyrighted work created by the student during his or her tenure. For example, it is quite common for graduate schools to require that doctoral students grant to the school the right to house in a library, reproduce, and distribute their dissertations.[5] Regulations on the submission of certain honors papers or the granting of awards may carry similar stipulations of license terms. It is best to check the regulations of the individual school.

At many schools, financial support for study may carry with it license requirements as well. Most undergraduate schools seem to exclude general financial aid from creating any sort of special arrangement with students. The University of California Copyright Policy, for example, stipulates that registered students own the copyright in their work when it is produced "without the use of University funds (other than Student Financial Aid)."[6]

With graduate students, it is much more likely that their education, and in particular their dissertation research, would be supported with funds from the university or external sources. The terms of those grants may affect the scope of rights that the students have in their theses or dissertations. For example, federal grant regulations require that research supported with federal funds grant to the government "a royalty-free, nonexclusive and irrevocable right to reproduce, publish, or otherwise use the work for federal purposes, and to authorize others to do so."[7] Grants from other sources can carry their own stipulations, and thus potentially alter the default position that students own the entirety of the copyright in their work.

One would hope that any variation from the normal assumption that authors own the copyright in their DTSPs would be reflected in the DTSP itself. We will therefore continue this chapter working on the assumption that the students are the initial authors and copyright owners of their work.

12.5 Is the work published or unpublished?

The publication status of a DTSP has great implications for the duration of copyright (discussed in the next section). As was discussed in Chapter 3, for most of the last century published works had to comply with the strenuous requirements for notice, registration, and renewal. Failure to follow these requirements put published items in the public domain. Formal publication of a dissertation may also alter who owns the copyright in the manuscript version. The publication status of DTSPs, therefore, is of prime importance.

FORMAL PUBLICATION

There are two mechanisms by which a DTSP could become published. The first is if the author of the DTSP arranged with a publisher to reproduce and issue the work either in its entirety or as journal articles. Publication as a book or journal articles publishes the underlying manuscript as well. A typescript dissertation or thesis sitting on an archives shelf may appear to be unpublished, for copyright and digitization purposes, but it should be treated the same as any other volume sitting in the library if it has been subsequently published.

> ### TIP
> Do not be misled by the physical format of the item in front of you. It may look as if you have a manuscript letter or unpublished dissertation, but if that work has ever been published with the authorization of the

copyright owner, a different set of rules regarding copyright duration, preservation copying, fair use, and possibly copyright ownership, apply.

Subsequent formal publication of a DTSP complicates the use that can be made of the typescript version usually found in libraries and archives. Book and journal publishers often require the transfer of copyright in the manuscript to the publisher or the grant of extensive licenses. This means that the publisher could also own the copyright in the underlying typescript DTSP housed in the archives. Unless the archives had secured an irrevocable license to reproduce and distribute the typescript version, digitizing a published dissertation and making it available on a Web site would be an infringement of the publisher's reproduction, distribution, and display rights.

What happens to ownership when, as is especially common in the humanities, graduate authors extensively rework and rewrite their dissertations before publication and transfer copyright ownership of this new version to the publisher? If the dissertation and the published version were entirely distinct and separate, with no common expression between them, the author could still own the copyright in the dissertation while the publisher owned the copyright in the book.

Usually, however, there is something of the original manuscript included in what is published. In that case, the publisher could be given copyright ownership in all of the new material as well as in that portion of the dissertation that carries over to the published edition. Duplicating or digitizing the typescript original could in theory infringe on the publisher's ownership of part of the dissertation—even though the author may still own the rights to that portion of the manuscript that was not included in the publisher's version. In this scenario, one needs to think of the original dissertation as consisting of two copyrighted works, one of which is owned by the author and the other which is owned by the publisher.

■ **TIP**

Subsequent publication as a book or article is most likely to be an issue with dissertations and some master's theses, but it can apply to student papers as well. Michael Beschloss's *Kennedy and Roosevelt: The Uneasy Alliance*, for example, started as a senior honors thesis at Williams College; Melanie Thernstrom's book *The Dead Girl* began as her senior honors thesis at Harvard.

INFORMAL PUBLICATION

In addition to formal publication, an argument could be made that most DTSPs are published almost immediately upon completion. How could a typescript dissertation or thesis in an archives or library be considered published? The answer is dependent on the peculiar concept of "publication" embraced by the 1909 Copyright Act.

As was discussed in Chapter 2, publication for copyright purposes consists of making copies of a work available to the general public through sale or loan. Publication could occur by formal publication—but it could also occur if copies were provided to an authorized distributor, and it could arguably occur just by listing an item in a library catalog.[8]

Dissertations in particular seem to live in a netherworld between informal publication and unpublished status. On one hand, dissertation requirements almost always stipulate that copies of dissertations should be provided to the library in order that they can be made available to interested researchers. In addition, publication of dissertations—as a means of becoming part of the community of scholars—has long been viewed as a requirement for the degree. The Graduate Division at the University of California, Berkeley, in its guidance on "Publishing your Dissertation," for example, states that:

> Your doctoral dissertation is a published work that announces the results of your research. The University of California holds to the tradition that you have an obligation to make your research available to other scholars. This obligation is met when the Graduate Division submits your dissertation to the University Library to be bound and shelved for public use.[9]

They add that "Legal opinion is divided on whether common law copyright is lost only upon actual printing of a manuscript or upon making it publicly available, e.g., by shelving it in a library. *The Attorney for the Regents has advised that shelving the dissertation or thesis voids the common law copyright* (emphasis added).[10] For Berkeley, at least, it would appear that including the dissertation in the library is publication.

Publication could occur as well via microfilm publication with UMI (now ProQuest). For 70 years, UMI/ProQuest has been "publishing" dissertations on microfilm as part of a program that was expressly intended to address the difficulties accompanying letterpress publication; it now uses digital delivery mechanisms (discussed below). In addition to publishing dissertations, UMI /ProQuest offers to register the author's copyright with the Copyright Office.[11] It is unclear, however, when UMI first began this practice. Dissertations that were submitted to UMI but did not have the proper copyright notices or were never registered or renewed may have entered the public domain.

On the other hand, many commentators suggest that dissertations remain unpublished, even when microfilmed or made available on library shelves. UCLA's library, for example, says "UCLA masters theses and doctoral dissertations are to be treated in the same manner as *unpublished, copyrighted works*" (emphasis added).[12]

The electronic theses and dissertations (ETD) movement has also had to address the issue of whether their electronic distribution might constitute publication—not because it would inject the dissertations into the public domain, but rather because "prior publication" might interfere with the ability of dissertation authors to formally publish their work. Surveys of authors and publishers reveal that few of them consider electronic distribution of a dissertation to constitute "prior publication."[13]

Given this uncertain legal arena, it is safest to assume that in the absence of formal publication, most dissertations are unpublished. Mere availability on a library shelf should not be seen as constituting publication (*Wright v. Warner Books*).

Special consideration should be given to dissertations submitted to UMI. Each dissertation found at UMI should be accompanied by a license that allows UMI to reproduce and distribute the dissertation, regardless of its copyright status. It may be also possible to consider dissertations submitted by the authors to UMI to be published for copyright purposes; UMI distribution would seem to comply with the definition of publication under both the 1909 and 1976 Copyright Acts. If the authors did not follow the requirements for notice, registration, or especially renewal, their work could have entered the public domain.

12.6 Is the work within the copyright term?

Whether a DTSP is still protected by copyright would depend in part on its publication status:

- If it is an *unpublished* (i.e., never subsequently published as a book or never submitted to UMI) work that was never registered with the Copyright Office, copyright endures for the life of the author plus 70 years.
- If it was *first published* through deposit with UMI or registered with the Copyright Office, copyright would endure as if for a published work. At a minimum, this would be for a period of 28 years, though renewal terms can allow copyright to endure for as long as 95 years after publication—or for life of the author plus 70 years (if published after 1977 (see Chapter 3).
- If it was *first published* prior to 1964 through deposit and distribution via UMI but there was no copyright notice or no renewal of the copyright, the work is in the public domain.
- If it was *first published* as a book or series of journal articles, copyright would endure for a period determined by the date of publication of the book or article (and not the date of the dissertation). Details of terms for works published at various historical dates are provided in Chapter 3.

12.7 Does the institution wish to perform one of the "exclusive acts" of the copyright owner?

For the purpose of this case study, we will concentrate on the digitization of DTSPs, as this appears to be a topical issue for cultural institutions.

The exclusive rights of the copyright owner include the reproduction and distribution of copyrighted works. This encompasses making a digital version of an item held in analog form and mounting it on a server where others can download. Digitization of copyrighted DTSPs, therefore, means that a cultural institution clearly risks infringing copyright unless it is the owner of copyright, has the permission of the copyright owner, or the digitization falls within an exemption in the Copyright Act.

12.8 Does digitization fall within any exemptions to infringement in the Copyright Act?

There are several scenarios in which a cultural institution might be able to digitize a DTSP using the exemptions available in the Copyright Act.

▶ If a library or archives owns an *unpublished* DTSP, that DTSP may be digitized for purposes of preservation. Access to a digital copy can be provided on the premises of the library or archives [17 U.S.C. § 108(b)].

▶ A library or archives may also digitize an *unpublished* DTSP in order to make an analog copy for deposit in another library or archives [17 U.S.C. § 108(b)].

▶ In response to a request from a user, a library or archives can provide that user with a copy (including a digital copy) of an entire *published or unpublished* DTSP if it has first determined, on the basis of a reasonable investigation, that a copy of the interview cannot be obtained at a fair price. The library or archives is not allowed to retain a copy of the digital file [17 U.S.C. § 108(e)].

▶ During their last 20 years of its copyright term, a library or archives may post on its Web site a digitized copy of a *published* DTSP, provided that certain requirements are met [17 U.S.C. § 108(h)].

This analysis suggests that DTSPs can be digitized without the consent of the copyright owners for some purposes, but that other uses will require consents from the owners of copyright.

12.9 Do laws designed to protect student privacy affect digitization?

The primary legislation protecting student privacy in the United States is the Family Educational Rights and Privacy Act of 1974, or FERPA.[16] FERPA, which applies to K–12 and postsecondary students, guarantees to students:

▶ Access to their education records
▶ An opportunity to seek to have the records amended
▶ Some control over the disclosure of information from their education records.

The concept of "education record" is key to FERPA.[17] An education record must be directly related to a student and maintained by an educational agency or institution. It can include personal information, enrollment records, grades, and schedules. It also covers student term papers that have been collected and maintained by teachers or other school officials. Except for a few narrow exemptions, the bulk of the student's education record is considered privileged. Personally identifiable information from the education record can only be released with the permission of the student.

In order to digitize and distribute papers from its students, therefore, the cultural heritage institution will need to secure the student's permission. If all identifying marks that could identify the student are removed from a paper, the demands of FERPA would be met—only permission of the copyright owner would be needed.

DID YOU KNOW?

Access to senior theses became an issue during the 2008 presidential campaign. The media sought to read both Hillary Clinton's senior thesis on Saul Alinsky housed in the Wellesley College archives and Michelle Obama's senior thesis on "Princeton-Educated Blacks and the Black Community," housed in the Princeton University archives.

The policy at both schools is that senior theses are routinely made available to interested researchers on site and via microfilm. Because the authors' explicit permissions had been secured, FERPA is not an issue. Digitizing and distributing the theses, however, requires the permission of the copyright owner. In Obama's

case, she (as the copyright owner) authorized the provision of a digital copy to the Web site http://www.politico.com.[14] Clinton did not authorize the digitization of her thesis, but that did not stop http://GOPublius.com from securing a copy and posting it—and thus risking a copyright-infringement lawsuit for their unauthorized reproduction and distribution.[15]

12.10 **Risk assessment**

The preceding analysis demonstrates that there is a considerable likelihood that digitizing an institution's historical collection of dissertations, theses, and/or student papers is often a technical violation of the law. The default position we have established is that DTSPs are unpublished, and hence protected by copyright until 70 years after the death of the author. It is the student, and not the institution, that in most cases owns the copyright in the work. In some cases, copyright in the thesis may have passed to a publisher (if the thesis is later published). Lastly, making a copy of student work available could violate the privacy requirements embedded in FERPA if the identity of the student author could be determined or inferred.

As discussed above, there are ways to eliminate some of the risks. The safest course would be to identify DTSPs that had been registered with the Copyright Office and whose copyright had not been renewed prior to 1964. These works would have entered the public domain. In addition, publication of DTSPs, most often through assignment to UMI, without proper notice or renewal would also have injected the manuscripts into the public domain. Lastly, institutional policies at certain times may have required students to grant authorization to the institution to reproduce and distribute the work; this prior permission would also reduce the risk.

For those works that are still protected by copyright, the safest course is to secure the permission of the authors of the DTSP. The permission of the copyright owner removes all legal liability. It also addresses any ethical issues (discussed in more detail below) that may arise. Peter Hirtle recently queried a number of library legal experts about digitization of theses; all concluded that the safest course would be to secure the permission of the copyright owner to digitize and distribute their works.

Nevertheless, it is likely that a DTSP digitization program will encounter works that are clearly still copyrighted or whose copyright owner either cannot be identified or located. Other programs may be reluctant to undertake the expense of trying to locate copyright owners. What can a program do at this point?

Here is where risk assessment must be taken into account. Each institution must weigh the possible risks and benefits associated with moving ahead with the digitization program in spite of the legal uncertainty and decide if it is comfortable with the answer.[18]

In some ways, the risk associated with a DTSP digitization project can be extreme:

- If there is a current valid copyright registration for the DTSP, theoretical statutory damages of up to $150,000 (for willful infringement), plus attorney's fees, court costs, and the impounding of the distribution servers are possible.
- If an unregistered DTSP has subsequently been published and all copyrights transferred to the publisher, the publisher could sue for up to $150,000.
- If releasing student papers was determined to be an uncorrected FERPA violation, the penalties against the institution can range up to the loss of all federal funds.
- If the digitized DTSPs are included as part of a commercial product, many copyright exemptions are not applicable.

On the other hand, there are factors that work to lessen the risk posed in digitizing DTSPs:

- If the DTSPs are truly unpublished and unregistered, then only actual monetary damages and legal fees are available as recourse to aggrieved copyright owners.
- In theory publishers can sue for statutory damages for reproducing and distributing copies of DTSPs, but we know of no such cases in practice.
- Graduate dissertations and theses and undergraduate honors theses traditionally include the written permission of the student allowing the release of the work.
- In some cases, a fair-use analysis could be used as a justification for digitization. We assume, for example, that GOPublius.com would defend its reproduction of Hillary Rodham's thesis (discussed in the box above) on the basis of its newsworthiness.
- FERPA violations can be avoided by securing the written permission of the student.
- An "opt-out" notification system as is used in at least one dissertation digital project may be enough to address any lingering concerns. (See the discussion of the ProQuest approach below.)

THE ETHICAL IMPERATIVE

More important than the legal issues in this case study are the ethical and moral issues. Each institution must determine its obligation to its former students and to scholarship at large. Will its students welcome the widespread and general availability of their work? Or will they feel that something important has been stolen from them and that the institution should have secured their permission in advance?

> ### ■ DID YOU KNOW?
> The University of Iowa discovered the sensitivities that can be associated with providing online access to student work. In March, 2008, former students of the famous Iowa Writers Workshop discovered the university's plans to require that master's theses be posted to an open-access Web server. The reaction was immediate and negative, and the University withdrew its plans later that spring.[19]

Almost all DTSPs are produced with the expectation that there would be some level of public access to the results. At a minimum, copies of the works are available in physical form in a library or archives. Limited copying—and sometimes copying of the entire work—is permitted. Some DTSPs are allowed to circulate via interlibrary loan or as microfilm copies. And most dissertations have been "published" by UMI—though there has been a widespread consensus that a microfilm or print copy of a dissertation secured from UMI is not the equivalent of a published volume sold through conventional channels.

Digital technologies have the ability to upset the public access assumptions of the past. Digital delivery of dissertations can suddenly seem less like the provision of microfilm and more like formal publishing—and hence less acceptable to authors. UMI found this out the hard way late in 2005 when it started selling its print-on-demand copies of dissertations through Amazon. Although the new practice was clearly permitted by the broad license that authors sign when depositing dissertations with UMI and arguably to the authors' benefit, it met with some disapproval. Out of respect for the wishes of authors, UMI quickly ended the program and removed all dissertations from Amazon.[20] However, dissertations can still be purchased in digital form through ProQuest, discussed below.

Each institution must decide whether the general distribution possible via the Internet is a natural extension of their previous access practices or an unacceptable intrusion on the rights of their students.

ANOTHER POINT OF VIEW

ProQuest Dissertation Digitization

Different organizations take different views of risk. A good example of this is ProQuest's "Digital Archiving and Access Program" (DAAP).

Since 1938, ProQuest has preserved and distributed doctoral and master's dissertations via microfilm. They could do this because they secured permission from the author of the dissertation or thesis at the time of submission.

DAAP is aimed not at authors but at libraries and archives holding dissertations and theses. Under contract to a library, DAAP will microfilm and digitize "your" dissertations (meaning the library's) and then make them available in print, microfilm, and online form (including through ProQuest's subscription database). "The Digital Archiving & Access Program," according to ProQuest, "makes your university's distinctive scholarly research available to anyone, anytime, anywhere on the Internet."[21]

The problem, of course, is that copyright in "your university's distinctive scholarly research" actually belongs to the authors who wrote it. A large number of the dissertations in any institution were likely submitted to UMI and hence ProQuest now has a license to distribute the works.[22] Dissertations that are not already part of the UMI collection, however, are likely never to have been registered for copyright nor published and would still be protected as unpublished works. Under Section 108, libraries or archives may preserve the material by microfilming it or digitizing it, but it is far from certain that those protections extend to the actions of contractors such as DAAP. And nothing in Section 108 would allow DAAP to keep a copy of digitized unpublished theses, nor allow DAAP or the University to make the material available online outside the library premises.

An institution that participates in DAAP might be able to argue that they were making a fair use of the material and hence avoid the worst penalties if the matter ever came to trial. ProQuest, however, because it is engaged in commercial conversion and delivery, would have a much harder time justifying its actions under fair use. In particular, it appears to be vulnerable to a potential lawsuit from a publisher who subsequently published a dissertation for which ProQuest does not have a distribution license.

For this reason, ProQuest works with universities to alert alumni about the existence of the program and advertise methods for opting out. They apparently recognize that the likelihood that they will be sued is small and that the damages associated with reproducing an unpublished work are limited. Although reproducing and distributing unpublished dissertations without the prior permission of the author may be a technical violation of copyright, the provision of "opt-out" mechanisms may be sufficient to allay author concerns. ProQuest very well could be right. Nevertheless, institutions that participate in the ProQuest program could be wise to insist on indemnification against any copyright actions brought forward because of ProQuest's use.

12.11 Practical suggestions arising from this chapter

☐ Investigate the institution's policy with regard to copyright ownership of student work:
  ☐ Look to see if there are different rules for students, undergraduates, and advanced degree students.
  ☐ Check whether individual schools or departments within an institution have their own policies.
  ☐ Determine whether these policies have changed over time.
☐ Look in the DTSP for evidence of outside support (such as research grants or fellowships) that may have their own requirements regarding reproduction and distribution of the DTSP.
☐ Look for evidence of a license from the students that could authorize the reproduction and general distribution of DTSPs.
☐ Investigate whether the DTSPs are unpublished, and hence still copyrighted, works, or if any of them have been registered with the Copyright Office.
☐ Consider whether you have ethical responsibilities to former students that may outweigh the purely legal concerns.
☐ If using an outside conversion and delivery service such as ProQuest's Digital Archiving & Access Program, consider securing indemnification against any us by the vendor of the material that is infringing.

FURTHER READINGS

THE FOLLOWING ITEMS address directly the issue of copyright in digitization projects:

American Association of Museums, Michael S. Shapiro, and Brett I. Miller. *A Museum Guide to Copyright and Trademark.* Washington, DC: The Association, 1999.

Besek, June M. *Copyright Issues Relevant to Digital Preservation and Dissemination of Pre-1972 Commercial Sound Recordings by Libraries and Archives.* CLIR Publication 135. Washington, DC: Council on Library and Information Resources and Library of Congress, 2005. http://www.clir.org/pubs/reports/pub135/contents.html.

Besek, June M. *Copyright Issues Relevant to the Creation of a Digital Archive: A Preliminary Assessment.* CLIR Publication 112. Washington, DC: Council on Library and Information Resources and Library of Congress, 2003. http://www.clir.org/pubs/abstract/pub112abst.html.

Cave, Mike, Marilyn Deegan, and Louise Heinink. "Copyright Clearance in the Refugee Studies Centre Digital Library Project." *RLG DigiNews* 4:5 (Oct. 15, 2000), http://worldcat.org/arcviewer/1/OCC/2007/08/08/0000070511/viewer/file915.html#feature1.

Covey, Denise Troll. *Acquiring Copyright Permission to Digitize and Provide Open Access to Books.* CLIR Publication 134. Washington, DC, Council on Library and Information Resources, 2005, http://www.clir.org/pubs/abstract/pub134abst.html.

Dames, K. Matthew. "Copyright clearances: fair use, action and apathy." *Online* 29:5 (2005): 32–4.

Hirtle, Peter B. "Copyright Renewal, Copyright Restoration, and the Difficulty of Determining Copyright Status." *D-Lib Magazine* 14:7/9 (2008). http://www.dlib.org/dlib/july08/hirtle/07hirtle.html.

Jones, Ruth Ann. "Empowerment for digitization: lessons learned from the Making of Modern Michigan." *Library Hi Tech* 23:2 (2005): 205–19. (Includes description of the project's copyright investigation workflow.)

King, Ed. "British Library Digitisation: access and copyright" (paper presented at the annual international meeting of the International Federation of Library Associations (IFLA), Quebec, Canada, August 10–14, 2008). http://www.ifla.org/IV/ifla74/papers/139-King-en.pdf.

Levine, Melissa Smith. "Overview of Copyright Issues." In *Handbook for Digital Projects: A Management Tool for Preservation & Access*, edited by Maxine K. Sitts. Andover, MA: Northeast Document Conservation Center, 2000.

Making of Modern Michigan. "Copyright Resources." Michigan State University. http://mmm.lib.msu.edu/html/copyright_resources.html. (Includes training video on identifying works in the public domain.)

Minow, Mary. "Library Digitization Projects and Copyright." *LLRX.com* (28 June 2002). http://www.llrx.com/features/digitization.htm.

Proffitt, Merrilee, Arnold Arcolio, and Constance Malpas. *RLG Copyright Investigation Summary Report* Mountain View, CA: OCLC Programs and Research, 2008. http://www.oclc.org/programs/publications/2008-01.pdf.

Pritcher, Lynn. "Ad*Access: Seeking Copyright Permissions for a Digital Age." *D-Lib Magazine* 6:2 (Feb. 2000), http://www.dlib.org/dlib/february00/pritcher/02pritcher.html.

Shincovich, Ann. "Copyright issues and the creation of a digital resource: artists' books collection at the Frick Fine Arts Library, University of Pittsburgh." *Art Documentation* 23:2 (2004): 8–13.

CASES CITED IN THE GUIDELINES

American Geophysical Union v. Texaco, Inc., 60 F.3d 913 (2d Cir. 1994)

Antiquesportfolio.com plc v. Rodney Fitch & Co [2001] FSR 345

Aymes v. Bonelli, 980 F.2d 857 (2d Cir. 1992)

B. Wilmsen, Inc. v. Consolidated Novelty Co. 251 F.Supp 874 (S.D.N.Y. 1965)

Bill Graham Archives v. Dorling Kindersley Limited 448 F 3d 605 (2nd Cir. 2006)

Brandir International, Inc. v. Cascade Pacific Lumber Co., 834 F.2d 1142 (2nd Cir. 1987)

Bridgeman Art Library, Ltd. v. Corel Corporation, 36 F. Supp. 2d 191 (S.D.N.Y. 1999)

Campbell v. Acuff-Rose Music, 510 U.S. 569 (1994)

Capitol Records, Inc. v. Naxos of America, Inc. 4 N.Y.3d 540 (2nd Cir. 2005)

Childress v. Taylor, 945 F.2d 500 (2d Cir. 1991)

Community for Creative Non-Violence v. Reid 490 U.S. 730 (1989)

Estate of Ernest Hemingway, et al. v. Random House, Inc. 23 N.Y.2d 341 (1968)

Estate of Martin Luther King, Jr., Inc. v. CBS, Inc., 194 F.3d 1211 (11th Cir. 1999)

Fantasy Inc. v. Fogerty, 94 F.3d 553 (9th Cir. 1996).

Feist Publications, Inc. v. Rural Telephone Service Co., 499 U.S. 340 (1991)

Frost Belt Intern. Recording Enterprises, Inc. v. Cold Chillin' Records, 758 F.Supp. 131 (S.D.N.Y. 1990)

Golan v. Gonzales, 501 F.3d 1179 (10th Cir. 2007)

Golan v. Holder, No. 01-cv-01854 (D. Colo. Apr. 3, 2009)

Grandma Moses Properties, Inc. v. This Week Magazine, 117 F. Supp. 348 (S.D.N.Y. Nov. 30, 1953)

Granse v. Brown Photo Co., 228 USPQ 635 (DC Minn 1985), aff'd 808 F.2d 841 (8th Cir. Dec 24, 1986)

Harper & Row, Publishers, Inc., et al. v. Nation Enterprises et al., 471 U.S. 539 (1985)

Hebrew Academy of San Francisco v. Goldman, 42 Cal.4th 883 (Cal. 2007)

Hoepker v. Kruger, 200 F.Supp.2d 340 (S.D.N.Y. 2002)

Hotaling v. Church of Jesus Christ of Latter-Day Saints, 118 F.3d 199 (4th Cir. 1997)

Internet Archive v. Suzanne Shell, Civ. No. 06-cv-01726-LTB-CBS (D. Colo., Feb. 13, 2007)

Innovative Concepts in Entertainment, Inc. v. Entertainment Enterprises Ltd., 576 F. Supp. 457 (E.D.N.Y. 1983)

Kelly v. Arriba Soft Corp., 280 F.3d 934 (2002) withdrawn, refiled at 336 F.3d 811 (9th Cir. 2003)

Kieselstein-Cord v. Accessories by Pearl, Inc., 632 F2d 989 (2nd Cir. 1980)

La Cienega Music Co. v. ZZ Top, 53 F.3d 950 (9th Cir. 1995)

Lumiere v. Robertson-Cole Distributors Corp., 280 F 550 (2nd Cir. 1922), cert. denied, 259 U.S. 583 (1922)

Marketing Information Masters Inc. v. The Board of Trustees of the California State University, 552 F.Supp.2d 1088 (S.D. Cal. 2008)

Matthew Bender & Co., Inc. v. West Publishing Co., 158 F.3d 674 (2nd Cir. 1998), *cert. denied*, 526 U.S. 1154 (1999).

Mattel Inc. v. Walking Mountain Productions, CV-99–08543 (CDCA Aug. 22, 2001), aff'd, 353 F.3d 792 (9th Cir. 2003)

Mazer v. Stein, 347 U.S. 201 (1954)

Metro-Goldwyn-Mayer Studios v. Grokster, Ltd., 545 U.S. 913 (2005)

Perfect 10, Inc. v. Google, Inc, 416 F.Supp.2d 828 (C.D. Cal. 2006), rev'd, *Perfect 10, Inc. v. Amazon.com, Inc.* 508 F.3d 1146 (9th Cir. 2007)

Pushman v. New York Graphic Society, Inc., 287 N.Y. 302 (2nd Cir. 1942)

Random House v. Rosetta Books, 150 F.Supp.2d 613 (S.D.N.Y., 2001)

Religious Technology Center v. Scott, 82 F.3d 423 (9th Cir. 1996)

Rogers v. Koons, 751 F. Supp. 474 (S.D.N.Y. 1990); amended on rehearing, 777 F. Supp. 1 (S.D.N.Y. 1991), aff'd, 960 F.2d 301 (2nd Cir. 1992), cert. denied, 506 U.S. 934 (1992)

Rushton v. Vitale, 218 F.2d 434 (2d Cir. 1955)

Shloss v. Sweeney, 515 F.Supp.2d 1083 (N.D. Cal. 2007)

Société Civile Succession Richard Guino v. Beseder Inc., 414 F.Supp.2d 944 (D. Ariz 2006)

Sony Corporation of America, et al. v. Universal City Studios, Inc., 464 U.S. 417 (1984)

Sundeman v. The Seajay Society, Inc., 142 F.3d 194 (4th Cir.1998)

Thomson v. Larson, 147 F.3d 195 (2d Cir. 1998)

Town of Clarkstown v. Reeder, 566 F Supp 137 (S.D.N.Y. 1983)

Twentieth Century Music Corp. v. Aiken, 422 U.S. 151 (1975)

Twin Books Corp. v. Walt Disney Co., 83 F.3d 1162

Wright v. Warner Books, Inc., 748 F.Supp. 105 (S.D.N.Y. 1990), aff'd, 953 F.2d 731 (2d Cir. 1991)

Yardley v. Houghton Mifflin Co., 108 F.2d 28 (2d Cir. 1939), cert. denied, 309 U.S. 686

NOTES

1 Introduction

1   *Mazer v. Stein*, 347 U.S. 201, 219 (1954).

2   *Harper & Row v. Nation*, 471 U.S. 539, 546 (1985).

3   *Twentieth Century Music Corp. v. Aiken*, 422 U.S. 151, 156 (1975) (citations omitted).

4   As is discussed in Part 3.4, at certain times and in certain states the sale of a material object could also transfer copyright with the object—or even inject the work into the public domain.

5   Compiled from Association of Research Libraries, "Copyright Timeline: A History of Copyright in the United States," http://www.arl.org/pp/ppcopyright/copyresources/copytimeline.shtml, and from Edward Samuels, *The Illustrated Story of Copyright* (New York: St. Martin's Press, 2000).

2 Copyright Fundamentals

1   U.S. Copyright Office, *Copyright Registration for Works of the Visual Arts: Circular 40* (Washington, DC: U.S. Copyright Office, 2008), http://www.copyright.gov/circs/circ40.pdf.

2   U.S. Congress. House. *Copyright law revision.* 94th Cong., 2nd sess., 1976. H. Rep. 94–1476.

3   June M. Besek, *Copyright Issues Relevant to Digital Preservation and Dissemination of Pre-1972 Commercial Sound Recordings by Libraries and Archives.* CLIR Publication 135 (Washington, DC: Council on Library and Information Resources and Library of Congress, 2005), http://www.clir.org/pubs/reports/pub135/contents.html.

4   *Estate of Ernest Hemingway et al. v. Random House, Inc.* 23 N.Y.2d 341 (1968).

5   Ralph R. Shaw, *Literary property in the United State* (Washington: Scarecrow Press, 1950).

6   See, for example, Scott Burnham, "Copyright in Library-Held Materials: A Decision Tree for Librarians," *Law Library Journal* 96 (2004): 425.

7   *Wright v. Warner Books, Inc.*, 748 F.Supp. 105 (S.D.N.Y. 1990), aff'd, 953 F.2d 731 (2d Cir. 1991).

8   *Feist Publications, Inc. v. Rural Telephone Service Co.*, 499 U.S. 340, 345 (1991).

9   *Matthew Bender & Co. v. West Publishing Co.*, 158 F.3d 674 (1998), *cert. denied*, 119 S.Ct. 2039 (1999).

10 *The Bridgeman Art Library, Ltd. v. Corel Corporation*, 36 F. Supp. 2d 191 (S.D.N.Y. 1999).

11 The UK case of *Antiquesportfolio.com v. Rodney Fitch & Co Co* [2001] FSR 23 held precisely this point: that photographs of three dimensional antiques were original works in which copyright subsists. The judge held that the selection of the item to be photographed, its positioning and lighting, the angle at which the photograph was taken and the focus that was used were matters of skill and judgment. Taken together, they could be sufficient to render the photograph an original work.

12 See, for example, Kevin Garnett, 'Copyright in Photographs' (2000) 22(5) *European Intellectual Property Review* 229; the 3 May 2007 seminar sponsored by the Metadata Image Library Exploitation (MILE) Project entitled "Bridgeman vs. Corel: Copyrighted Creativity or Commerce?", http://www.mileproject.eu/ixbin/indexplus?record=ART73, which concluded with a mock retrial of the cast; and Robert J. Allan, "After Bridgeman: Copyright, Museums, and Public Domain Works of Art," *University of Pennsylvania Law Review* 155 (2006): 961–989.

13 Susan Bielstein, *Permissions, A Survival Guide: Blunt talk about art as intellectual property* (Chicago: University of Chicago Press, 2006); Robert C. Matz, "Bridgeman Art Library, Ltd. v. Corel Corp.," *Berkeley Technology Law Journal*, 15 (2000): 3–23; Mary Campbell Wojcik, "The Antithesis of Originality: Bridgeman, Image Licensors, and the Public Domain," *Hastings Communications and Entertainment Law Journal (COMM/ENT)* 30 (2008): 257–286.

14 The Copyright Office identifies all of the relevant treaty obligations, including Berne members, in its circular *International Copyright Relations of the United States: Circular 38a* (Washington, DC: Library of Congress, Copyright Office, 2007), http://www.copyright.gov/circs/circ38a.pdf. Since publication of this compilation, Bhutan and Nepal have joined the Berne Convention. Treaty obligations can also be identified in *Treaties in Force* published by the Department of State and available at http://www.state.gov/s/1 /treaty/treaties/. The most up-to-date listing appears to be in Wikipedia at <http://en.wikipedia.org/wiki/Wikipedia:Non-U.S._copyrights#Dates_of_restoration_and_terms_of_protection>.

3 Duration and Ownership of Copyright

1 The latest version of "Copyright Term and the Public Domain in the United States" can always be found at http://www.copyright.cornell.edu/public_domain/.

2 Laura N. Gasaway, "When Works Pass Into the Public Domain," http://www.unc.edu/~unclng/public-d.htm.

3 Many wonder why works published before 1923 *must* be in the public domain. After all, copyright for published works can last for 95 years. Shouldn't the date before which copyrights must have expired be 1903, and not 1923?

The explanation lies in the Sonny Bono Copyright Term Extension Act of 1998. Prior to its passage, copyrights could only endure for a maximum of 75 years. That meant that works published in 1922 entered the public domain on 1 January 1998. The Act added 20 years to the term of works still protected by copyright, which meant that the term of copyright protection for a 1923 work was extended until 2019 [17 U.S.C. § 304(b)]. It did not restore copyright to works that had already entered the public domain.

4 Some of the challenges that foreign copyrights present for American copyright investigations are described in Peter Hirtle's article, "Copyright Renewal, Copyright Restoration, and the Difficulty of Determining Copyright Status," *D-Lib Magazine* 14:7/9 (2008), at http://www.dlib.org/dlib/july08/hirtle/07hirtle.html.

5 Emily Hudson and Andrew T Kenyon, *Copyright and Cultural Institutions: Guidelines for Digitisation* (Melbourne: University of Melbourne, 2005).

6 Melville B. Nimmer and David Nimmer, *Nimmer on Copyright* vol. 1, § 4.01[C][1] (Matthew Bender).

7   Library of Congress Copyright Office, *Highlights of Copyright Amendments Contained in the Uruguay Round Agreements Act (URAA): Circular 38b* (Washington, DC: Library of Congress, Copyright Office, 2004), http://www.copyright.gov/circs/circ38b.pdf.

8   The copyright notice that is used on media to protect the sound recording is different than that for written material. It consists of the symbol Ⓟ (the letter P in a circle), the year of first publication of the sound recording, and the name of the owner of copyright in the sound recording. See Library of Congress Copyright Office, *Copyright Notice: Circular 3* (Washington, DC: Library of Congress, Copyright Office, 2008), http://www.copyright.gov/circs/.

9   U.S. Congress. House. *Copyright law revision.* 94th Cong., 2nd sess., 1976. H. Rep. 94–1476.

10 Ibid.

11 Ibid.

12 Often the dividing line is the amount of support that the academic institution provides. If the institution provides support (in the form of research aid, equipment, laboratories, or technical support, for example) beyond the level that is normally afforded instructors, the likelihood that it will claim a copyright ownership in the resulting products increases. CopyOwn (http://www.nethics.umd.edu/copyown/), maintained the University of Maryland, is a good resource for information on academic ownership policies.

13 Authorship, as opposed to assignment of copyright, carries other benefits as well. For example, under U.S. law an assignment of copyright can be terminated so long as the work is not a work made for hire.

14 See, for example, *Frost Belt Intern. Recording Enterprises, Inc. v. Cold Chillin' Records*, which found that a contract requiring that future copyrights in master recordings be transferred to an employer was enforceable.

15 While the legislative history of the 1976 Act speaks of the Pushman presumption applying to manuscripts, we have found it only applied to works of art.

4 Exclusive Rights and Infringement

1   U.S. Congress. House. *Copyright law revision.* 94th Cong., 2nd sess., 1976. H. Rep. 94–1476.

2   Angelique Chrisafis, "Rejoyce . . . Irish MPs save festival," *The Guardian*, June 3, 2004, http://www.guardian.co.uk/uk/2004/jun/03/artsnews.booksnews.

3   Information on the rulemaking process is found at http://www.copyright.gov/1201/. On the 2003 exceptions, see Peter Hirtle, "The Impact of the Librarian of Congress's Rulemaking on the Digital Millennium Copyright Act," *RLG DigiNews* 7:6 (December 15, 2003), http://hdl.handle.net/1813/11310.

4   Peter Hirtle, "Digital Preservation and Copyright," Copyright and Fair Use: Stanford University Libraries Web site, http://fairuse.stanford.edu/commentary_and_analysis/2003_11_hirtle.html.

5   This may change. In 2007, Attorney General Antonio Gonzales posited the need for an Intellectual Property Protection Act that would, among other things, create a new federal crime of "attempted copyright infringement." See http://www.sourcewatch.org/index.php?title=Intellectual_Property_Protection_Act_of_2007.

5 Fair Use and Other Exemptions

1 Lawrence Lessig, *Free Culture* (New York: Penguin Press, 2004): Chapter 12.

2 For an interesting analysis of how courts weigh the various fair use factors, see David Nimmer, "'Fairest of them All' and Other Fairy Tales of Fair Use," 66 *Law and Contemporary Problems* (Winter/Spring, 2003): 263–287, http://law.duke.edu/journals/66LCPNimmer. Barton Beebe has also undertaken a comprehensive study of fair use opinions: "An Empirical Study of U.S. Copyright Fair Use Opinions, 1978–2005" 156 *Pennsylvania Law Review* (2008): 549–624, http://www.pennumbra.com/issues/pdfs/156-3/Beebe.pdf.

3 For an article considering transformative effect (and which was influential on the Supreme Court's decision in *Campbell v. Acuff-Rose Music*), see Pierre N. Leval, "Toward a Fair Use Standard" 103 *Harvard Law Review* 1105 (1990).

4 Fair Use and Unpublished Works: Joint Hearing on S. 2370 and H.R. 4263 Before the Subcomm. on Patents, Copyrights and Trademarks of the Senate Comm. on the Judiciary and the Subcomm. on Courts, Intellectual Property, and the Administration of Justice of the House Comm. on the Judiciary, 101st Cong. 107 (1990) (statement of Judge Pierre Leval), cited in Mary Minow, "Library Digitization Projects and Copyright," *LLRX.com* (28 June 2002), http://www.llrx.com/features/digitization.htm.

5 The briefs and other legal documents in the case can be accessed at http://news.justia.com/cases/featured/new-york/nysdce/1:2005cv08136/273913/.

6 The settlement agreement Web site, including a copy of the settlement document, is found at http://www.googlebooksettlement.com/.

7 *Bill Graham Archives v. Dorling Kindersley Limited* 448 F 3d 605, 614–5 (2nd circuit, 2006), quoting *Castle Rock* 150 F 3d at 146.

8 "Guidelines for Classroom Copying in Not-For-Profit Educational Institutions with Respect to Books and Periodicals," reprinted in Library of Congress Copyright Office, *Reproduction of Copyrighted Works by Educators and Librarians: Circular 21* (Washington, DC: Copyright Office, 1995): 7–8, http://www.copyright.gov/circs/circ21.pdf.

9 Ibid., 9.

10 Ibid., 22.

11 Conference on Fair Use, "Final Report to the Commissioner on the Conclusion of the Conference on Fair Use," (Washington, DC: Patent and Trademark Office, 1998), http://www.uspto.gov/web/offices/dcom/olia/confu/confurep.pdf.

12 http://ccumc.org/system/files/MMFUGuides.pdf.

13 For a full analysis and critique of copyright guidelines, see Kenneth D. Crews, *Copyright, fair use, and the challenge for universities: promoting the progress of higher education* (Chicago: University of Chicago Press, 1993); Kenneth D. Crews, "The Law of Fair Use and the Illusion of Fair Use Guidelines," *Ohio State Law Journal* 62 (2001): 599–702.

14 http://www.centerforsocialmedia.org/resources/publications/statement_of_best_practices_in_fair_use/.

15 http://www.centerforsocialmedia.org/resources/publications/fair_use_in_online_video/.

16 House Report on the new copyright law, H.R. Rep. No. 94–1476, quoted in Library of Congress Copyright Office, *Reproductions of Copyrighted Works by Educators and Librarians* (Washington, DC: Copyright Office, 1995): 10, http://www.copyright.gov/circs/circ21.pdf.

17 The TEACH Act Toolkit at http://www.provost.ncsu.edu/copyright/toolkit/ is an excellent guide to the implementation requirements of the TEACH Act.

18 Henry Lydiate, "Current Public Sculpture," in *Artlaw: Copyright Legislation*, http://www.artquest.org.uk/artlaw/copyright/32087.htm.

19 U.S. Congress. House. *Copyright law revision.* 94th Cong., 2nd sess., 1976. H. Rep. 94–1476.

6 The Libraries and Archives Exemptions

1 Section 108 Study Group. 2008. *The Section 108 Study Group report: an independent report sponsored by the United States Copyright Office and the National Digital Information Infrastructure and Preservation Program of the Library of Congress.* (Washington, DC: Section 108 Study Group). http://www.section108.gov.

2 Senate Committee on the Judiciary, *Digital Millennium Copyright Act of 1998*, 105th Cong., 2nd sess., 1998, S. Rep. 105–190, 62.

3 See *Copyright Act* (RS 1985, c C-42), ss 2, 30.1–30.4; *Copyright Act 1968* (Aust) ss 10(1), 10(4). For other international examples of library exemptions, see Kenneth D. Crews, *Study on copyright limitations and exceptions for libraries and archives.* (Geneva: World Intellectual Property Organization, 2008). http://www.wipo.int/meetings/en/doc_details.jsp?doc_id=109192.

4 For more on the 108(b) provisions, see Peter Hirtle, "Digital Access to Archival Works: Could 108(b) Be the Solution?" at http://fairuse.stanford.edu/commentary_and_analysis/2006_08_hirtle.html.

5 Memorandum by Mary Beth Peters to James Billington, "Recommendation of the Register of Copyrights in RM 2002–4; Rulemaking on Exemptions from Prohibition on Circumvention of Copyright Protection Systems for Access Control Technologies, 27 October 2003," p. 50, http://www.copyright.gov/1201/docs/registers-recommendation.pdf.

6 U.S. Congress. House. *Copyright law revision.* 94th Cong., 2nd sess., 1976. H. Rep. 94–1476.

7 Memorandum by Mary Beth Peters to James Billington, "Recommendation of the Register of Copyrights in RM 2002–4; Rulemaking on Exemptions from Prohibition on Circumvention of Copyright Protection Systems for Access Control Technologies, 27 October 2003," p. 52, http://www.copyright.gov/1201/docs/registers-recommendation.pdf.

8 *Code of Federal Regulations*, title 37, sec. 201.14, http://www.copyright.gov/title37/201/37cfr201–14.html.

9 Register of Copyrights, *Library Reproduction of Copyrighted Works (17 U.S.C. 108)*, January 1983, http://www.copyright.gov/reports/library-reproduction-1983.pdf.

10 See, for example, Linda Matthews, "Copyright and the Duplication of Personal Papers in Archival Repositories," *Library Trends* 32 (Fall 1983): 223–40.

11 "CONTU Guidelines on Photocopying and Interlibrary Arrangements," reprinted in Library of Congress Copyright Office, *Reproduction of Copyrighted Works by Educators and Librarians: Circular 21* (Washington, DC: Copyright Office, 1995): 18–19, http://www.copyright.gov/circs/circ21.pdf.

12 U.S. Congress. House. *Copyright law revision.* 94th Cong., 2nd sess., 1976. H. Rep. 94–1476.

13 *University of New South Wales v. Moorhouse* (1975) 133 CLR 1 (High Court of Australia).

14   See Mary Minow's digitization table at http://www.librarylaw.com/DigitizationTable.htm, part of "Library Digitization Projects and Copyright" (2002), http://www.llrx.com/features/digitization.htm.

15   Senate Committee on the Judiciary, *Digital Millennium Copyright Act of 1998*, 105th Cong., 2nd sess., 1998, S. Rep. 105

7 Copyright Permissions and Licenses

1   See, for example, Diane M. Zorich, *Introduction to Managing Digital Assets: Options for Cultural and Educational Organizations* (New York, Oxford University Press, 1999); Rina Elster Pantalony, *WIPO Guide on Managing Intellectual Property For Museums* (Geneva: World Intellectual Property Organization, 2007), http://www.wipo.int/copyright/en/museums_ip/; Lesley Ellen Harris, *Licensing Digital Content, A Practical Guide for Librarians* (Washington DC: American Library Association, 2002).

2   Black, Henry Campbell. *Black's Law Dictionary*. Abridged 8th ed. (St. Paul, MN: Thomson West, 2005): 765.

3   "A 'transfer of copyright ownership' is an assignment, mortgage, exclusive license, or any other conveyance, alienation, or hypothecation of a copyright or of any of the exclusive rights comprised in a copyright, whether or not it is limited in time or place of effect, but not including a nonexclusive license" [17 U.S.C. § 101]. "The owner of any particular exclusive right is entitled, to the extent of that right, to all of the protection and remedies accorded to the copyright owner by this title" [17 U.S.C. § 201(d)(2)].

4   There are provisions in the Copyright Act that allow authors to terminate transfers of copyright. This can only happen long after the initial transfer, however, and requires precise timing. It is seldom done. See 17 U.S.C. § 203 for termination of copyrights created after 1978, and 17 U.S.C § 304(c) and 304(d) for termination of transfers for works created prior to 1978.

5   See, for example, the "Draft Screenplay Option and Rewrite Agreement" at http://www.medialawyer.com/contract.htm.

6   Katie Dean, "Cash Rescues *Eyes on the Prize*," *Wired Magazine*, 30 Aug. 2005, http://www.wired.com/entertainment/music/news/2005/08/68664.

7   Lawrence Rosen, *Open Source Licensing: Software Freedom and Intellectual Property Law* (Prentice-Hall, 2004): 52, http://www.rosenlaw.com/oslbook.htm.

8   http://www.copyright.columbia.edu/model-permissions-letters.

9   http://www.copyright.iupui.edu/pgeneral.htm.

10 http://www.dspace.org/implement/policy-issues.html#distribution.

11 http://www.lib.virginia.edu/press/uvagoogle/pdf/Google_UVA.pdf. Because the University of Virginia does not own the copyright in most of the items that are to be digitized, the license is based on its rights as the physical owner of the material.

12 "Conditions for Use of this Site," found at http://rose.mse.jhu.edu/pages/terms.htm.

13 Ibid.

14 http://www.creativecommons.org.

15   Similarly, that institution would not be able to use a Creative Commons license to authorize use of the public domain materials once they were digitized.

16   "Public/Private Mass Digitization Agreements," http://www.oclc.org/programs/ourwork/ collectivecoll/harmonization/massdigresourcelist.htm; Lorne Manly, "Filmmakers and Others Petition Against Smithsonian's Showtime Deal," *New York Times*, 18 April 2006, http://www.nytimes.com/2006/04/18/arts/television/18smit.html; Brett Zongker, "Public Access Group Posts Smithsonian Images Online." AP article posted on Law.com, 21 May 2007, http://www.law.com/jsp/article.jsp?id=1179479096959.

17   See, for example, Jason Mazzone, "Copyfraud," *New York University Law Review* 81 (2006): 1026, http://papers.ssrn.com/s013/papers.cfm?abstract_id=787244; Carol Ebbinghouse, "'Copyfraud' and Public Domain Works," *Searcher* 16:1 (2008): 40–53.

18   Kenneth Hamma, "Public Domain Art in an Age of Easier Mechanical Reproducibility," *D-Lib Magazine* 11:11 (November 2005), http://www.dlib.org/dlib/november05/hamma/11hamma. html; Peter B. Hirtle, "Archives or Assets?" *American Archivist* 66 (Fall/Winter 2003): 235–247, http://www.archivists.org/governance/presidential/hirtle.asp or http://hdl.handle. net/1813/52.

19   Lisa Browar, Cathy Henderson, Michael North, and Tara Wenger, "Licensing the Use of Special Collections Materials," *RBM* 3:2 (Fall 2002), http://www.ala.org/ala/acrl/acrlpubs/rbm/ backissuesv013n02/rbmv013n02.cfm.

20   Peter B. Kaufman and Jeff Ubois, "Good Terms: Improving Commercial-Noncommercial Partnerships for Mass Digitization," *D-Lib Magazine* 13:11/12 (Nov./Dec. 2007), http://dlib. org/dlib/november07/kaufman/11kaufman.html; Max Planck Institute for the History of Science, "Best Practices for Access to Images: Recommendations for Scholarly Use and Publishing" 9 January 2009, http://www.mpiwg-berlin.mpg.de/en/news/features/feature4.

8   Locating Copyright Owners

1   Denise Troll Covey, *Acquiring Copyright Permission to Digitize and Provide Open Access to Books* (Washington, DC, Council on Library and Information Resources, 2005): 55, http:// www.clir.org/pubs/abstract/pub134abst.html.

2   Comment on the Orphan Works Notice of Inquiry: 70 Fed. Reg. 3739 (Jan. 26, 2005) by Steven Metalitz on behalf of the Motion Picture Association of America, to Jule Sigall, Associate Register for Policy and International Affairs, U.S. Copyright Office, 25 March 2005, OW0646- MPAA, http://www.copyright.gov/orphan/comments/OW0646-MPAA.pdf.

3   Library of Congress Copyright Office, *Renewal of Copyright: Circular 15* (Washington, D.C.: Copyright Office, 2006), http://www.copyright.gov/circs/.

4   Library of Congress Copyright Office, *Recordation of Transfers and Other Documents: Circular 12* (Washington, DC: Copyright Office, 2007), http://www.copyright.gov/circs/circ12.pdf.

5   Library of Congress Copyright Office, *Obtaining Access to and Copies of Copyright Office Records and Deposits: Circular 6* (Washington, DC: Copyright Office, 2008), http://www. copyright.gov/circs/circ6.pdf.

6   http://tyler.hrc.utexas.edu/us.cfm.

7   http://english.osu.edu/research/organizations/ijjf/copyrightfaqs.cfm.

8   See, for example, the University of Toronto's page that reprints John Gillespie Magee's poem, "High Flight," at http://rpo.library.utoronto.ca/poem/2736.html. It reports that "Magee's poem in effect entered the public domain shortly after his death because it was very widely printed during and after the war." While this does not appear to be legally accurate, it illustrates the dangers in relying on all such copyright statements.

9   http://www.authorsregistry.org/autcondir.html.

10 https://www.authorsguild.net/.

11 http://www.asja.org/.

12 http://dramatistsguild.com/.

13 The third project attempted to secure permission from a group of current publishers. They therefore were able to identify and locate 100% of the publishers. Covey, *Acquiring Copyright Permission*.

14 Ibid., pp. 35–36.

15 Ibid., p. 19.

16 Anderson, Chris. *The Long Tail Why the Future of Business Is Selling Less of More* (New York: Hyperion, 2006).

17 The Acquisitions and Appraisal Section of the Society of American Archivists has prepared a very useful compilation of state laws relating to abandoned physical property and how museums, libraries, and archives can assert ownership of those items. See http://www.archivists.org/saagroups/acq-app/abandoned.asp.

18 http://www.utsystem.edu/ogc/IntellectualProperty/permissn.htm; http://www.copyright.iupui.edu/permorg.htm. See also the International Federation of Reproduction Rights Organisations (IFRRO) at http://www.copyright.com/ccc/viewPage.do?pageCode=rh5 for information on overseas reproduction rights organizations.

19 "Copyright Clearance Center Announces Annual Copyright License for Academia," 22 June 2007, http://www.copyright.com/ccc/viewPage.do?pageCode=au143.

20 See, for example, Peter Hirtle, "Why you might want to avoid the CCC's Annual License," LibraryLaw.Com Blog, 5 July 2007, http://blog.librarylaw.com/librarylaw/2007/07/why-you-might-w.html; and James Boyle, "The inefficiencies of freedom," *Financial Times*, 1 July 2007, http://www.ft.com/cms/s/2/25cf260c-265c-11dc-8e18-000b5df10621.html.

21 "FAQ's—Annual Copyright License—Academic," http://www.copyright.com/ccc/viewPage.do?pageCode=h36.

22 Gretchen McCord Hoffmann, "Licensing Societies: What can the CCC, ASCAP/BMI/SESAC, and MLUSA/MPLC do for You?," *The Copyright & Media Law Newsletter* 11:1 (2007): 5–6, 9–10.

23 This example draws heavily from Linda Tadic's excellent presentation on "The Permissions Process," given in February, 2003 at the IMLS WebWise conference and available at http://digitalarchive.oclc.org/da/ViewObjectMain.jsp?fileid=0000016179:000000677070&reqid=6657.

24 http://www.copyright.gov/orphan/.

9 Other Types of Intellectual Property, Contracts, and Jurisdictional Issues

1   The U.S. Patent and Trademark Office provides useful introductory materials on trademarks at http://www.uspto.gov/main/trademarks.htm. The standard treatise on trademarks is J. Thomas McCarthy, *McCarthy on Trademarks and Unfair Competition*. (St. Paul, MN: West Group, 1996).

2   Federal trademark protection is governed by the Lanham Act, 15 U.S.C. §§ 1051—1127. State protection trademarks are usually governed by laws regulating unfair competition. The statutory provisions can differ, but most states have adopted a version of the Model Trademark Bill (MTB), http://www.inta.org/index.php?option=com_content&task=view&id=1393&It emid=154&getcontent=3, or the Uniform Deceptive Trade Practices Act (UDTPA), http://www.law.cornell.edu/uniform/vo17.html#dectr.

3   See Jon Carroll's column in the *San Francisco Chronicle*, Friday, 8 July 2005, on page E-18, consulted at http://www.sfgate.com/cgi-bin/article.cgi?file=/chronicle/archive/2005/07/08/DDGM7C8H401.DTL.

4   Peter Jaszi, "'Yes, you can!'—Where you don't even need 'fair use.'" (Washington, DC: Center for Social Media, American University, 2006), at http://www.centerforsocialmedia.org/files/pdf/free_use.pdf.

5   The standard treatise on publicity is Thomas McCarthy, *The Rights of Publicity and Privacy* (St. Paul, MN: West Group, 2000).

6   Mark Roesler, "Right Of Publicity," at http://www.markroesler.com/ipresources/rightof-publicity.htm.

7   http://www.cmgww.com/corporate/overview.htm.

8   Heather Briston, "The Right of Privacy and the Right of Publicity: It's not just about tabloids and fame" (paper presented at the Choices & Challenges: Hot Topics Facing Curators and Archivists conference, Henry Ford Museum, Dearborn, MI, 9 Oct. 2004; revised 1 Nov. 2004), http://hdl.handle.net/1794/2444.

9   Greg Levine, "The 'Greatest' Deal: Muhammad Ali Sells Name, Image," 12 April 2006, http://www.forbes.com/2006/04/12/muhammad-ali-elvis-cx_gl_0412autofacescano7.html.

10 "FAQs about the partnership of Elvis Presley Enterprises, Inc. and Robert F.X. Sillerman," Elvis Presley Web site, http://www.elvis.com/elvisology/faq/faq.asp?qid=31; "Top earning dead celebrities," Oct. 29, 2007, http://www.forbes.com/2007/10/29/dead-celebrity-earning-biz-media-deadcelebso7_cz_lg_1029celeb_land.html.

11 Briston reports that the Indiana law restricts the use of the publicity rights of individuals in fund-raising activities.

12 http://www.archives.gov/exhibits/nixon-met-elvis/.

13 http://www.nixonlibraryfoundation.org/index.php?src=directory&view=products&categor y=The%20Day%20Nixon%20Met%20Elvis.

14 http://www.archives.gov/exhibits/nixon-met-elvis/assets/doc_citations_transcript.html.

15 *Restatement of the Law, Second, Torts*, § 652, http://www.tomwbell.com/NetLaw/Ch05/R2ndTorts.html.

16 But jurisdictions outside the United States often take very different approaches to Internet defamation and limitation periods.

17   Clark Hoyt, "When Bad News Follows You," *New York Times*, 26 Aug. 2007, http://www.
     nytimes.com/2007/08/26/opinion/26pubed.html?ex=1346385600&en=6a108788302af4e
     1&ei=5124&partner=permalink&exprod=permalink.

18   For further discussion, see Marie C Malaro, *A Legal Primer on Managing Museum Collections*
     (2nd edition, 1998), chapter IV.

19   For some recent discussion and criticism of cultural heritage institutions that attempt to exert
     control over the use of public domain material, see the items cited in Chapter 7, notes 17
     and 18.

20   The legality of such agreements was challenged in a recent suit against the Berkeley Histori-
     cal Society. The case was settled out of court before any final judgment was reached, but
     see the discussion of the case on the LibraryLaw.com blog at http://blog.librarylaw.com/
     librarylaw/2007/04/minow_the_centr_1.html.

21   Michael Geist, "Music takedown strikes the wrong chord," *Toronto Star*, 29 October 2007,
     http://www.thestar.com/Business/article/271389.

22   See Emily Hudson, *Cultural Institutions, Law and Indigenous Knowledge: A Legal Primer
     on the Management of Australian Indigenous Collections* (June 2006), available for
     free from the Social Science Research Network at: http://papers.ssrn.com/so13/papers.
     cfm?abstract_id=955977.

23   "Resolutions adopted by ICOM's 22nd General Assembly, Vienna, Austria, 2007," http://icom.
     museum/resolutions/ereso7.html.

24   First Archivists Circle, "Protocols for Native American Archival Materials," 9 April 2007, http://
     www2.nau.edu/libnap-p/protocols.html.

10 Risk Management: How to Digitize Safely

1   One of the few examples of lawsuits involving reproduction services by libraries was settled
    over thirty-five years ago: *Williams & Wilkins Company v. The United States* 487 F.2d 1345
    (1973), affirmed by an equally divided Court, 420 U.S. 376 (1975) (libraries attached to the
    National Institutes of Health and the National Library of Medicine). One of the few lawsuits
    since then is currently under way: *Cambridge University Press v. Patton*, Case 1:2008cv01425,
    Georgia District Court (course pack and electronic reserve policies of Georgia State University
    Library).

2   National Coalition Against Censorship. "Significance: Hoepker v. Kruger—NCAC" (undated).
    http://www.ncac.org/art-law/sum-hoe.cfm.

3   The high cost of copyright litigation has led the Professional Photographers of America,
    among other organizations, to suggest that as part of the introduction of orphan works
    legislation, small-claims courts should be able to hear copyright infringement suits. See
    Mary Beth Peters, "Remedies for Small Copyright Claims," Statement of the United States
    Copyright Office before the Subcommittee on Courts, the Internet, and Intellectual Property,
    Committee on the Judiciary, United States House of Representatives, 109th Congress, 2nd
    Session, March 29, 2006, available at http://www.copyright.gov/docs/regstat032906.html.

4   Marjorie Heins and Tricia Beckles, *Will Fair Use Survive? Free Expression in the Age of Copy-
    right Control* (New York: Brennan Center for Justice at NYU School of Law, 2005), http://
    www.fepproject.org/policyreports/fairuseflyer.html.

5   For an academic analysis of this, see Justin Hughes, "Fair Use Across Time" *UCLA Law Review* 50:3 (2003): 775–800. http://ssrn.com/abstract=326980.

6   The California Digital Library has been a leader in establishing metadata standards for the recording of rights information as part of digitization projects. See http://www.cdlib.org/inside/projects/rights/record.html.

7   http://memory.loc.gov/ammem/coolhtml/ccres.html.

8   http://www.laborphotos.cornell.edu/copyright.php.

9   http://www.copyright.columbia.edu/copyright/?q=fair-use-checklist.

10 Michael Stratford, "Alum Sues *Cornell Chronicle*," *Cornell Daily Sun*, January 24, 2008, http://cornellsun.com/node/26579; Michael Stratford, "Alum Files $10 Mil. Lawsuit Against C.U.," *Cornell Daily Sun*, May 2, 2008, http://cornellsun.com/section/news/content/2008/05/02/alum-files-10-mil-lawsuit-against-cu.

11 Bill Steele, "Libel lawsuit over 1983 *Chronicle* news item is dismissed," *Cornell Chronicle Online* (June 9, 2008), http://www.news.cornell.edu/stories/June08/VanGsuit.ws.html.

12 Both suits are under appeal at the time of writing.

11 Case Study 1: Interviews and Oral Histories

1   An example might be Merle Miller's *Plain Speaking: An Oral Biography of Harry S. Truman* (New York: Berkley Pub. Co., 1974). While based on transcripts of oral history interviews with Harry S. Truman, the transcripts have been edited in such a way as to create a separate copyrightable work. (Critics have argued that the transcripts have not simply been edited, but were fabricated. See Robert H. Ferrell and Francis H. Heller, "Plain Faking?" *American Heritage Magazine* 46:3 (May/June 1995), http://www.americanheritage.com/articles/magazine/ah/1995/3/1995_3_14.shtml.)

2   John A. Neuenschwander, *Oral History and the Law* (Carlisle, PA: Oral History Association, 2002, 3rd edition.)

3   Lolly Gasaway notes that in those cases where there is no copyright release exists, "oral histories clearly belong to the interviewee, although the interviewer may hold copyright in the question he or she poses. The most important historical material, however, is the text or words spoken by the interviewee, and the interviewee owns the copyright in his or her words." Laura N. Gasaway, "Questions and Answers—Copyright Column," *Against the Grain* 19 (February, 2007): 57.

4   Kathryn Marie Dudley, "In the Archive, In the Field," in *Narrative and Genre*, ed. by Mary Chamberlain and Paul Richard Thompson (London: Routledge, 1998): 165.

5   Elinor A. Mazé, "The Uneasy Page: Transcribing and Editing Oral History," in *Handbook of Oral History*, ed. by Thomas Lee Charlton, Lois E. Myers, and Rebecca Sharpless (Lanham, MD: Altamira, 2006): 247.

6   *Childress v. Taylor*, 945 F.2d 500 (2d Cir. 1991): 508.

7   Ibid., 507.

8   *Thomson v. Larson*, 147 F.3d 195 (2d Cir. 1998) (on whether the contributions of the dramaturge for *Rent* constituted joint authorship)

9   17 U.S.C § 303(b), which was added to the law to overturn *La Cienega v. ZZ Top*, only applies to musical works. Distribution of a sound recording of a spoken work may still constitute publication of that work.

10 Oral History Association, "Principles and Standards," in *Oral History Evaluation Guidelines.* Pamphlet no. 3. Adopted 1989, Revised Sept. 2000 (Carlisle, PA: Oral History Association, 2001), http://alpha.dickinson.edu/oha/pub_eg.html.

11 Note, though, that many jurisdictions outside the United States take very different approaches to Internet defamation and limitation periods.

12 Case Study 2: Dissertations, Theses, and Student Papers

1   Special thanks go to Kenneth Crews, Lolly Gasaway, Georgia Harper, Austin McClean, Mary Minow, and Kevin L. Smith for their help in thinking about the issues in this case study.

2   http://scholar.lib.vt.edu/theses/.

3   http://www.ndltd.org/.

4   MIT Libraries, "Specifications for Thesis Preparation 2008–2009," http://libraries.mit.edu/archives/thesis-specs/.

5   For example, the University of California, San Francisco requires students to include in their dissertation a library release stating:

   Publishing Agreement
   It is the policy of the University to encourage the distribution of all theses and dissertations. Copies of all UCSF theses and dissertations will be routed to the library via the Graduate Division. The library will make all theses and dissertations accessible to the public and will preserve these to the best of their abilities, in perpetuity.

   See UCSF Graduate Division, "Guidelines for Preparing Theses and Dissertations" (undated), http://graduate.ucsf.edu/system/files/TDGuidelines.pdf.

6   University of California Office of the President, "Copyright Policy," 19 August 1992, found at http://www.ucop.edu/ucophome/coordrev/policy/8-19-92att.html.

7   *Code of Federal Regulations*, title 2, sec. 215.36, http://edocket.access.gpo.gov/cfr_2008/janqtr/pdf/2cfr215.36.pdf.

8   The idea that publication could possibly occur via cataloging is an extension of the ruling in the *Hotaling* decision. *Hotaling* found that listing items in a catalog was an offer to distribute those items. Publication is defined in the current Copyright Act as distribution to the general public by sale, lease, or lending. One could theoretically argue that authorized inclusion of a record in the catalog constitutes publication of the thesis.

9   Graduate Division, University Of California, Berkeley, "Publishing your Dissertation," available at http://www.grad.berkeley.edu/policies/dissertation_publish.shtml.

10 Graduate Division, University Of California, Berkeley, "Library Permission Form," available at http://www.grad.berkeley.edu/policies/pdf/LibrPermForm.pdf.

11 ProQuest, Publishing Your Graduate Work with *UMI® Dissertation Publishing* (undated), available at http://www.uab.edu/graduate/dissertation_publishing_agreement.pdf.

12 See http://www.library.ucla.edu/text/copyright/unpublis.html.

13 Gail McMillan, "Publishers," in *The UNESCO Guide for Electronic Theses and Dissertations*, available at http://www.etdguide.org/.

14 http://www.ed.gov/policy/gen/guid/fpco/ferpa.

15 20 U.S.C. § 1232(g).

16 Jeffrey Ressner, "Michelle Obama thesis was on racial divide," Politico Web site, posted Feb. 22, 2008, http://www.politico.com/news/stories/0208/8642.html.

17 See the blog posting "Hillary Clinton's Wellesley Thesis," posted Aug. 1, 2007, http://www.gopublius.com/?p=175.

18 This discussion about the importance of risk assessment when considering the digitization is mirrored in a study based on British law. Theo Andrew writes:

> If no contact can be made with a copyright owner, then depending on the library's assessment of the risk, it may wish to proceed without having gained the permission to host the material. If this action is taken then it is imperative to show that enough steps have been taken to show reasonable efforts towards locating the copyright holder, and that the material is for an educational, noncommercial, purpose. This option, taken at the risk of infringement, should not be considered lightly and is something that depends on individual institutional circumstances.

> Theo Andrew, "Intellectual Property and Electronic Theses," JISC Legal Information Service, Nov., 2004, available at http://www.jisclegal.ac.uk/publications/ethesesandrew.htm.

19 Andrea L. Foster, "U. of Iowa Writing Students Quash Planned Open Access," *Chronicle of Higher Education*, March 28, 2008.

20 Austin McLean, e-mail message to Peter Hirtle, May 23, 2008.

21 "The Digital Archiving & Access Program for your dissertations and master's theses," (undated), available at http://www.proquest.com/products_pq/literature/umi/daa_overview.pdf. More information on the program is available at http://www.umi.com/products_umi/dissertations/archivinggrad.shtml.

22 Whether that license would allow for digital delivery of the dissertations would depend on its exact language. In *Random House v. RosettaBooks*, the court found that the standard language in some author contracts with Random House ("print, publish and sell the work(s) in book form") did not include the right to distribute the works as ebooks. *Random House v. Rosetta Books*, 150 F.Supp.2d 613 (S.D.N.Y., 2001).

DATE DUE

DEMCO, INC. 38-2931

3951839

Made in the USA